ALDOUS HUXLEY

A STUDY OF HIS NOVELS

ALDOUS HUXLEY
A Study of His Novels

K. Bhaskara Ramamurty

ASIA PUBLISHING HOUSE
BOMBAY · CALCUTTA · NEW DELHI · MADRAS
LUCKNOW · BANGALORE · LONDON · NEW YORK

K. Bhaskara **Ramamurty** (1924)

ISBN: 0.210.22346.4

PRINTED IN INDIA

By G. G. Pathare at the Popular Press (Bombay) Pvt. Ltd., 35C Tardeo Road, Bombay 400 034 and published by P. S. Jayasinghe, Asia Publishing House, Bombay-400 038

PREFACE

Aldous Huxley is a brilliant product of the Two Cultures, the heir to both Julian Huxley and Arnold. In the nineteen-twenties, the gay twenties as they were called, the young Aldous, the Pyrrhonic aesthete he was at the time, launched out on his literary career. With the sense of humour of an amasseur and an ironist, with an aesthete's desire to take to living as a fine art, and with the firmness of conviction of an intellectual aristocrat, he looked at the world around him, and, with a pleasingly detached inquisitiveness, portrays what he calls 'the human comedy'.[1] But as the gay twenties moved into the serious thirties, his mood darkened, the jesting Pilate gradually transformed himself into a humanitarian agnostic. The amasseur and ironist became a seeker, and the jester a solemn salvationist. His quest was for peace and happiness, for a way to reconcile the dichotomies of the flesh and the spirit. And after a forty-year-old search, he came to the conclusion:

> Only in the knowledge of his own Essence
> Has any man ceased to be many monkeys.

His essays and monographs reveal to us the sincerity of the man and his attitudes and outlook in a fast changing world. His novels portray all the changing moods and temperament of contemporary Europe.

My aim in this study is to trace the progress of the Huxleyan attitudes towards life, his analysis of the ape and essence in man, and his recipe to help the ape realize its essence to achieve transcendence. I have traced by detailed analysis the shifting attitudes of the novelist at different stages of his career, and the development of his ideas about science, religion and society, his progress from cynical gaiety to mystical search. I have discussed in detail both the thematic and technical aspects of his novels.

---

[1] A portmanteau word. See Huxley, *Jesting Pilate*.

I am deeply indebted to my friends and teachers who have encouraged me in this work. I am grateful to Raja Saheb Shri P. V. G. Raju of Vizianagram, who has always shown enlightened interest in my work and goaded me on to meaningful effort. I pay my homage to my esteemed teacher, Prof. K. R. Srinivasa Iyengar, a profound humanist and a creative critic. My revered teacher and friend, Prof. K. Viswanatham of the Andhra University, gave me valuable guidance in this study. During my undergraduate days he moulded my tastes and temperament, and turned my attention from science to literature. I am ever grateful to him.

The British Council, I remember with gratitude. In answer to my request for a few books of Aldous Huxley, they obtained for me every available latest edition of Huxley's writings. I was amazed at the sudden arrival of a large parcel one morning. Their courtesy and consideration moved me deeply.

I express my gratitude to the Andhra University and my *alma mater,* the Maharajah's College, Vizianagram, for all the facilities they have extended to me. I owe much to Mr V. Venkata Rao, the former Principal, Mr C. Venkatachari, the librarian, and my friend and former colleague, Mr P. V. Ramanaiah of the Maharajah's College, for their most genuine help and encouragement. My former student and later a colleague, Mr Vishnu, has been of immense help in the preparation of the manuscript for the printers. I am specially obliged to Asia Publishing House for the active interest they have evinced in my work. As usual and as always, I cherish with deep love the affectionate interest my wife has shown, and the help she has given to me.

October 23, 1973   K.B.R.

ACKNOWLEDGEMENTS

The author and Publishers are grateful to the following for permission to quote copyright passages from the books named: Mrs. Laura Huxley, Chatto & Windus, London, and Harper & Row of New York, for passages from Aldous Huxley's books: *Crome Yellow, Antic Hay, Those Barren Leaves, Point Counter Point, Brave New World, Eyeless in Gaza, After Many a Summer, Time Must Have a Stop, Ape and Essence, Genius and the Goddess, Island, Ends and Means, Jesting Pilate, The Doors of Perception* and *Heaven and Hell, Do What You Will, Proper Studies, Brave New World Re-visited, Literature and Science, Collected Essays of Aldous Huxley* (A Bantam Classic), and *Stories, Essays and Poems of Aldous Huxley* (Everyman Series); Prof. Julian Huxley and Chatto & Windus, for extracts from *Aldous Huxley 1896-63: A Memorial Volume;* the author and Chatto & Windus for an excerpt from *The Living Novel* by V. S. Pritchett; the author and University Tutorial Press Ltd., London, for passages from *English Literature of the Twentieth Century* by A. S. Collins; the Society of Authors, London, on behalf of the Bernard Shaw Estate, for excerpts from *Back to Methuselah* by Bernard Shaw; the author and Martin Secker & Warburg Ltd., London, for excerpts from Prof. J. Isaacs' *An Assessment of Twentieth Century Literature;* the author and Curtis Brown Ltd., London, and F. A. Praeger, Inc., New York, for excerpts from *The Modern Writer and His World* by G. S. Fraser; the author and Holt, Rinehart and Winston, Inc., New York, for a passage from *Great Novelists and Their Novels* by W. Somerset Maugham; the author and Clarendon Press, Oxford, for excerpts from *Modern English Literature* by G. H. Mair and A. C. Ward, 3rd Edition (HUL 27) 1960; the author and Princeton University Press, and Routledge and Kegan Paul Ltd., London, for passages from *Philosophies of India* by H. Zimmer, edited by Joseph Campbell, Bollingen Series XXVI (copyright 1951 by Bollingen Foundation); the Executors of the John Middleton Murry Estate and Jonathan

Cape Ltd., London, for excerpts from *Reminiscences of D. H. Lawrence* by John Middleton Murry; Calder and Boyers Ltd., London, for excerpts from *Aldous Huxley* by John Atkins; the authors and Methuen & Company Ltd., London, for passages from *Twentieth Century Literature* by A. C. Ward, and *English Literature Between the Wars* by B. Ifor Evans; the author, Edward Arnold (Publishers) Ltd., London, and Harcourt Brace Jovanovich, Inc., New York, for passages from *Aspects of the Novel* by E. M. Forster; the author's Literary Estate and The Hogarth Press Ltd., London, for excerpt from *English Verse Satire* by Humbert Wolfe; Quentin Bell, Angelica Garnett, Hogarth Press Ltd., London, and Harcourt Brace Jovanovich, Inc., New York, for a passage from the essay "Leaning Tower" in *The Common Reader* by Virginia Woolfe; the author and Penguin Books Ltd., London, for excerpt from *A Short History of English Literature* by B. Ifor Evans; the author and Longmans Group Ltd., London, for an extract from *Fifty Years of English Literature* by R. A. Scott James; the author, Longmans Group Ltd., London, and Barnes and Noble, Inc., New York for passages from *Catastrophe and Imagination* by John McCormic; the author and Longmans Group Ltd., London, for the British Council, for passages from Walter Allen's article "Fiction" in *The Year's Work in Literature 1949;* the author and Longmans Group Ltd., London, for the British Council, for passages from Jocelyn Brooke's article "Aldous Huxley" in *The Writers and Their Work Series* No. 55, revised edition published in 1958; A. M. Heath & Company Ltd., London, agents for the Estate of the Late Jocelyn Brooke, for passages from Jocelyn Brooke's works; Laurence Pollinger Ltd., London, the Estate of the Late Mrs. Frieda Lawrence, and The Viking Press of New York, for passages from the following books of D. H. Lawrence: *Sons and Lovers,* copyright 1913 by Thomas Seltzer, Inc., all rights reserved, reprinted by permission of The Viking Press, Inc.; from *Phoenix;* the Posthumous Papers of D. H. Lawrence, edited by Edward D. McDonald, copyright 1936 by Frieda Lawrence, copyright renewed 1964 by the Estate of the Late Frieda Lawrence Ravagli, all rights reserved, reprinted by permission of The Viking Press, Inc.; from *The Letters of D. H. Lawrence* edited by Aldous Huxley, copyright 1932 by the Estate of D. H. Lawrence, copyright renewed 1960 by Angelo Ravagli and C. Montague Weekley, Executors of the Estate of Frieda Lawrence

Ravagli, reprinted by permission of The Viking Press, Inc.; from *Fantasia of the Unconscious,* copyright 1922 by Thomas Seltzer, Inc., renewed 1950 by Frieda Lawrence Ravagli, reprinted by permission of The Viking Press, Inc.; Laurence Pollinger Ltd., London, the Estate of the Late Mrs. Frieda Lawrence and Alfred A. Knopf, Inc., New York, for excerpts from *The Plumed Serpent* by D. H. Lawrence; the author, Cassell and Company Ltd., London, and Alfred A. Knopf, Inc., New York, for an extract from *The Counterfeiters* by Andre Gide (translated by D. Bussy); the author and George Allen & Unwin Ltd., London, and Macmillan Company, New York, for excerpts from *Mahayana Buddhism* by Beatrice Lane Suzuki; the editor and George Allen & Unwin Ltd., London, for a passage from Aldous Huxley's essay "Seven Meditations" in *Vedantha for the Western World* edited by Christopher Isherwood; the author, Faber and Faber Ltd., London, and Harcourt Brace Jovanovich, New York, for a few lines from *The Hollow Men* and *Choruses from the Rock* from *Collected Poems 1909-1962* by T. S. Eliot; the author, Faber and Faber Ltd., London, and Random House of New York, for a few lines from W. H. Auden's *The Age of Anxiety;* the author and Hutchinson Publishing Group Ltd., London, and Grove Press of New York, for a passage from *Introduction to Zen Buddhism* by Prof. D. T. Suzuki; the author and Phoenix House, J. M. Dent & Sons, London, for excerpts from *Tradition and Dream* by Walter Allen; the author and Asia Publishing House, Bombay, for excerpts from *Aldous Huxley—A Cynical Salvationist* by Dr Sisir Kumar Ghose; the author, Longmans Group Ltd., London, and A. D. Peters & Company, London, for excerpts from *British Authors* by Richard Church; the author, Methuen & Company Ltd., London, and A. D. Peters and Company, London, for excerpts from *The Growth of the English Novel* by Richard Church.

We have made every possible effort to contact the various Publishers for permission to use copyright material. We apologize for any inadvertent omission or improper form of acknowledgement, and we assure that necessary additions or corrections will be made in the second edition.

CONTENTS

CONTENTS

1

THE AGE OF ANXIETY

Estranged, aloof,
They brood over being till the bars close,
The malcontented who might have been
The creative odd ones the average need
To suggest new goals.   AUDEN

IN Elizabethan England, the University Wits formed a small exclusive group, a minority, who trumpeted in vain their own literary qualifications. But universities have since then grown in strength, and by the twentieth century they are seen to hold considerable influence on national life and thought, and the products of universities dominated the English literary scene between the two world wars and after.

The spirit of free enquiry engendered during the Renaissance by classical influences, nursed by the quarrels between science and religion during the eighteenth and nineteenth centuries, paved the way for the scepticism of the twentieth century, to an attitude that questioned the whole social and moral order. As an outcome of universal education, the age of good-mannered acceptance yielded place to the Age of Reason. Human attitudes and outlook have changed, even literature has put on a new look, and intellect has come to play a major role in both theme and technique of the literary art.

This worship of the intellect has led to terrific upheavals in the social, political and moral spheres. Cold, dissecting logic has replaced sympathy and understanding. The heart and emotions are rejected as untrustworthy guides. A ruthless weighing of pros and cons, cold calculation of profit and loss, advantage and disadvantage, have become admirable virtues. Individual salvation and the Ten Commandments have been relegated to the boudoirs, and social good, according to the fashion of the day, has become the chief aim in public life. This new philosophy has ushered in a Molochian era, an era of battles and bloodshed, wars and revolutions. By the end of the First World War, the pre-'14 optimism and romantic idealism lay buried on the battle-fields of Europe. Cynicism, disillusion and despair had taken root. A new generation had come up, a generation wriggling in an aimless drift, disillusioned with the past, uncertain of the future, and iconoclastic in the present.

A new generation of writers, the younger generation of the inter-war period, attempts to portray this collapse of the physical and moral world of man. The writers, no longer, sit in an ivory tower. They are participants in the general chaos. "They had nothing settled to look at; nothing peaceful to remember; nothing certain to come. During all the impressionable years of their lives they were stung into consciousness — into self-consciousness, into class-consciousness, into the consciousness of things changing, of things falling, of death perhaps about to come. There was no tranquillity in which they could recollect".[1] They sit on leaning towers. They find in the past little that is acceptable, and the idealism of the present is hypocritical. In anger and despair at the evil in man, and the society going to pieces, they attempt a ruthless portrayal of this chaotic world. Traditional patterns of literary art do not satisfy them. They take to new techniques. Freudian psycho-analysis has given them new insight into the human mind. They dissect the homo sapiens, they probe through the layers of their own consciousness, they yearn to revitalize the inner being, and find a solution to the ills of humanity.

Three major groups of these inter-war writers may be taken note of. The Slit Trench Group — Wilfred Owen, Siegfried Sassoon, Robert Nichols, Robert Graves, Edmund Blunden and others — who had fought in the 1914-18 war and experienced the horrors of trench warfare;[2] the Maida Vale Group[3] — Auden, Spender, Isherwood, Louis Macneice, Day Lewis and others — too young to participate in the war, but old enough by the nineteen

---

[1] Virginia Woolf, *Leaning Tower.*
[2] Roopert Brooke is an exception.
[3] Name given in jest by Virginia Woolf: Stephen Spender, *World Within World,* p. 152.

thirties to perceive the impending doom; the Bloomsbury Group[4] — E. M. Forster, T. S. Eliot, Edith Sitwell, Virginia Woolf, Aldous Huxley too — who did not participate in the war, but witnessed the catastrophe, the after-events and the drift towards the second war.

The Slit Trench Group write with bitter sarcasm of the brutalizing effect of war, the absence of all heroism in it, and of the soldier praying for a wound to be repatriated home. The Maida Vale Group, the Oxford Group of left-wingers wrote, as Virginia Woolf remarks, politician's poetry, not poet's poetry. It is the poetry of class-consciousness, expressing the poet's desire to fertilize the waste land. The Bloomsbury Group are writers with creative genius, more integrated than the former two groups in their outlook on life. They too express disgust with the crumbling world, but seek a cure for the spiritual sickness. Forster relies on a cultural awakening of the self, Eliot and Edith Sitwell lumber through the waste land to arrive at a reaffirmation of the Christian faith, Virginia Woolf finds solace in suicide, and Aldous Huxley in the Vedantic doctrine of non-attachment.

Aldous Huxley is, as Richard Church calls him, a congenital intellectual. His grandfather Thomas Henry Huxley was a celebrated naturalist. His father Leonard Huxley was a professor of Greek, and for some time editor of the Cornhill. He is related to Mathew Arnold on the mother's side, and to Mrs. Humphrey Ward too. His elder brother Prof. Julian Huxley is a renowned scientist. Huxley had a brilliant career at Eton and at Oxford. In 1911, at the age of seventeen, he left Eton because of partial blindness, the result of an accident, and this kept him out of the first war. During the early years of the war, he took his degree in English literature at Oxford. Later he taught school for some time before joining the Athenaeum run by Middleton Murry. He started writing from an early age, and published poems, essays, novels and short stories.

Huxley's first novel Crome Yellow, published in 1921, had a good reception. The next one Antic Hay (1923) was a better seller. Then followed Those Barren Leaves (1925), Point Counter Point (1928), Brave New World (1932) and Eyeless in Gaza (1936). In the forties he went to the States, and from California he published three novels, After Many a Summer (1940), Time

4 Ibid.

Must Have a Stop (1944) and *Ape and Essence* (1945). Then came *The Genius and the Goddess* (1955) and *Island* (1962).

They are brilliant pieces of writing. One may not agree with the mood and the tone, but there is no denying the fact that an artist is at work. In an age in which the novel is a very popular literary form, and many talented novelists, traditionals as well as innovators being in the field, to be considered one of the foremost is not an easy achievement. In a chaotic world skiing into disaster, and when every one, the professional and the quack, feverishly plans to skid the run, the literary artist finds in the novel an effective instrument for presentation of ideas. Prose, being more supple than verse, offers infinite scope for free-lancing and the novel, instead of indulging in dry abstractions, provides the human element and so appeals to the original 'virtue' in man—curiosity.

Huxley has chosen the novel for his instrument, and for his theme a layer of the post-war English society,[5] the intelligentsia particularly the younger generation, spiritually crippled and mentally perverted. Like Meredith he makes his characters betray themselves, the homo sapiens without the sapience, but unlike Meredith he only hovers in the background, some say with cynical amusement.

The pattern he has chosen for the novel is his own. Somerset Maugham, 'specifying' the qualities of a good novel, says: "it should have a widely interesting theme, by which I mean a theme interesting not only to a clique, whether of critics, professors, highbrows, truck-drivers or dish-washers, but so broadly human that it is interesting to men and women of all sorts. . . . The story should be coherent and persuasive; it should have a beginning, a middle and an end, and the end should be a natural consequence of the beginning".[6]

If one were to accept the views of Maugham, a new name would have to be invented for the types of fiction produced in England in the inter-war period and Huxley, not only Huxley but Virginia Woolf, James Joyce, Dorothy Richardson and many others would cease to be novelists. The twentieth century has been prolific in fictional writing. Many are the new innovations made. The doctrine of Art for Art's sake has gradually slunk into the

[5] *After Many a Summer, Time Must Have a Stop* and *Ape and Essence* deal with American life.

[6] Somerset Maugham, *Great Novelists and Their Novels*, p. 5.

background, and the literary art has become a powerful medium for propagation of new ideas, for social criticism, and for a searching analysis of the human mind. Poetry, drama and novel have all served these purposes. There is a breaking away from tradition, and the trend of the twentieth century novel has been towards a gradual fading away of the story element in it. The inside of man rather than the outside has become the novelist's main concern. The novel is aptly described by E. M. Forster thus:

> Yes — Oh dear yes — the novel tells a story. . . . It runs like a backbone—or may I say a tapeworm, for its beginning and end are arbitrary.[7]

Huxley's novels are of this tapeworm kind. The reader's interest is sustained by the presentation of ideas, by sparkling conversation rather than by the run of incident. In the novels of the twenties, the characters are a body of persons, irresponsible and self-centred, indulging in shallow verbiage, but conscious of a vacuum inside and the need for a spiritual prop. In the thirties, imitative of Wellsian scientific fiction in technique, Huxley presents in the *Brave New World* a human farm, a scientifically advanced society, soulless and devoid of human sympathies. In the Forties almost reminiscent of Swift is *Ape and Essence,* a fantastic tale of mankind degraded into devil-worship and savagery after a nuclear war. In 1936, between the automaton of the *Brave New World* and the savage of the *Ape and Essence,* is the introspective man sunk in sober thought in the *Eyeless in Gaza.* With the insight of a psychologist and a sociologist, with artistic skill and sensitive perception, Huxley presents in vivid prose the reactions of a class of individuals to the changing social and political conditions. The two novels, *Brave New World* and *Ape and Essence* are exceptions, and they are in the nature of a grim warning that humanity rushing headlong along the new tracks might ring in not the Biblical millennium but the Satan's era.

Critical opinion has been rather unfair to Huxley, expressed in varying tones of patronage. Many critics refer to his formidable 'literary ancestry' as if intellect is something that can be inherited like the family library. Richard Church says that Huxley, "hedged in by the stalwarts of the family", "has had good enough excuse

[7] E. M. Forster, *Aspects of the Novel,* pp. 27-28.

to suffer from an inferiority complex. If he has suffered thus, he has managed to sublimate his weakness" by choosing "to compete with his family on its own ground", applying "their scientific outlook and method to art and philosophy".[8]

Perhaps an inferiority feeling, rather than a complex, stimulated Huxley to creative writing. But it would be unfair to look at his writings as pieces of vain exhibitionism or schoolboyish attempts to assert his own superiority. Huxley is a man of firm convictions. He is an idealist and a lucid thinker. With courage and conviction he sets forth in vivid prose what he believes to be the malady pestering the contemporary society, more ruthlessly than his ancestor Mathew Arnold had done a century earlier, and like his ancestor he too faces carping criticism.

Admired for his versatile talents, scholarship and sparkling wit, he is condemned for the mood and the tone of his novels. Prof. A. S. Collins, tracing the development of Huxley as a novelist, writes:

His attitude was on the whole one of detached inquisitive amusement at the ridiculous, often rather pitiable human types, and the current ideas appropriate to each type. If he was born to live in the waste land, Huxley would at least enjoy it as far as his wit and curiosity could enable him, without taking up any moral or indeed positive intellectual position. . . . *Eyeless in Gaza*, however, was in the true line of his development, . . . the novel, crowded with ideas, rich in satire, seemed to promise that a combination of heart and intellect might make Huxley a great positive novelist. . . . The promise was, however, to be disappointed. . . . The mind behind it [*Ape and Essence*] seems one in which no pity mitigates the author's contempt for humanity, and which is unhappily apt in the imagination of what is vile. It was all warning, without hope or hint of escape. The negative, critical side of Huxley had at this stage triumphed, and reduced the artist to a labourer in hell.[9]

Huxley's novels are, of course, satirical in tone. But cynicism is not always the motive force behind satire. "The satirist holds a place half-way between the preacher and the wit. He has the

8 Richard Church, *British Authors*, p. 123.
9 A. S. Collins, *English Literature of the Twentieth Century*, pp. 232-42.

purpose of the first and uses the weapons of the second";[10] and
satire is perhaps a more effective instrument for social correction
than sermonization.   Huxley is no cynical portrayer of a strip-
tease age, nor is he a drain-inspector raking up the filth in social
life. His novels may not seem to offer any positive moral suggestion or panacea for the ills of the society, but he is not a negative
novelist. He deplores human folly, he does not ridicule it. Pity,
rather than contempt, is his reaction to it. His novels are not
showpieces of caustic wit, but wit is tempered with poignant
thought, and a yearning to transcend human frailty runs throughout as a subtle undertone.

Born at the close of the Victorian age, in an age of tradition
and discipline, brought up amidst an intellectual aristocracy,
Huxley has grown to live through the welter of the twentieth
century democracy, through the nightmare of two world wars and
a civilization fast crumbling. The past has nothing to offer, the
present is chaotic, and the future obscure. Huxley's novels present
a picture of this world around him. His non-fictional writings give
us a diagnosis of the disease afflicting the world, and its remedy.
The disease is spiritual and moral trauma, the remedy practice
of non-attachment. In *Ends and Means* he writes:

> The apparent pointlessness of modern life in time of peace
> and its lack of significance and purpose are due to the fact that,
> in the western world at least, the prevailing cosmology is what
> Gerald Heard has called the 'mechano-morphic' cosmology of
> modern science. The universe is regarded as a great machine
> pointlessly grinding its way towards ultimate stagnation and
> death; men are tiny offshoots of the universal machine, running
> down to their own private death; physical life is the only real
> life; mind is a mere product of the body; personal success and
> material well-being are the ultimate measures of value, the
> things for which a reasonable person should live. Influenced by
> this cosmology, the Europeans live through life hollow with
> pointlessness, trying to fill the void within them by external
> stimuli — newspaper reading, day-dreaming at the films, radio
> music and chatter, the playing and above all the watching of
> games, 'good times' of every sort. Meanwhile any doctrine that
> offers to restore point and purpose to life is eagerly welcomed.

[10] Humbert Wolfe, *English Verse Satire*, p. 7.

Hence the enormous success of the nationalistic and communistic idolatries. . . .[11]

The way out of this spiritual chaos is "through the practice of disinterested virtues and through direct insight into the real nature of ultimate reality"; Huxley says:

The ideal man is the non-attached man. Non-attached to his bodily emotions and lusts. Non-attached to his craving for power and possessions. Non-attached to the objectives of these various desires. Non-attached to his anger and hatred; non-attached to his exclusive loves. Non-attached to wealth, fame, social position. Non-attached even to science, art, speculation, philanthropy. Yes, non-attached even to these.[12]

But non-attachment is not self-liquidation as Richard Church mistakes it to be.[13] Huxley writes:

Non-attachment is negative only in name. The practice of non-attachment entails the practice of all the virtues. It entails the practice of charity, for example, for there are no more fatal impediments than anger (even righteous indignation) and cold-blooded malice to the identification of the self with the immanent and transcendent more-than-self. It entails the practice of courage; for fear is a painful and obsessive identification of the self with the body. (Fear is negative sensuality, just as sloth is negative malice). It entails the practice of generosity and disinterestedness, for avarice and the love of possessions constrain their victim to equate themselves with mere things.[14]

From spiritual trauma to non-attachment, from the inward death-bed to saintly disinterestedness, is a long journey, an ancient journey. Huxley's novels present a modern pilgrim's progress, some of his characters, characters with sense and sensibility, through self-education and self-exploration, seeking to achieve a fullness of the spirit. From Crome Yellow to Island is traced the progress of these mechano-morphic pilgrims, groping along the

11 Ends and Means, pp. 123-24.   12 Ibid., pp. 3-4.
13 Richard Church, British Authors, p. 124.
14 Ends and Means, p. 4.

way, now hanging on to a beaver, now seeking solace in a dope. Mescalin is, after all, a stage in this journey.

Reason, but not faith, is the guiding light in this journey. The mechano-morphic pilgrims swear by Reason, faith they have none. They question everything, they accept nothing. Changing sides on a spiritual death-bed or groping in blind alleys for spiritual props, they often indulge in an intellectual strip-tease, at times morbid and perverted. Huxley, himself a worshipper of Reason, presents these pilgrims dancing the antic hay to the erotic jazz of modern life.

Hence the cerebral emphasis in his novels. They are novels of ideas, rather than of action, of conversation rather than of incident. Even the conversation is not a sober exchange of ideas, but often talk running at cross-purposes, each participant blaring his or her own tune like the instruments in a mad orchestra, a bewildering medley, but with a strange rhythm of its own. Sometimes the conversation goes on in a sort of 'hashished' somnolence, several streams of thought flowing in a maze, criss-cross, not as tributaries to a common river.

Novel of ideas? "The chief defect of the novel of ideas is that you must write about people who have ideas to express — which excludes all but about .01 per cent of the human race. The great defect about the novel of ideas is that it's a made-up affair. Necessarily, for people who can reel off neatly formulated notions aren't quite real: they're slightly monstrous".[15]

This is, perhaps, Huxley's answer to critics talking of specimens and puppet stages. It's no puppet stage in his novels. There is not even a back-drop. The stage is the mother-earth sodden red. The duration is the inter-war and the post-war period, a period of anxiety, of revulsion and rebellion, of neo-thomism and communism, surrealism and existentialism. The characters are intelligent men and women, sane and sensible in their own way, each traversing a moral desert or groaning in a spiritual vacuum, suffering from some special obsession, teased by a self-consuming intellect. It is a portrayal of the contemporary world, the intelligentsia, the .01 per cent, wallowing in a strange darkness at noon, and turning to some stray obscure glimmer for enlightenment. With nothing solid from the past to stand on, and nothing lucid and benign to hope for, living like oysters though gregarious,

[15] *Point Counter Point*, pp. 409-10.

they are all like "parallel straight lines, only some more parallel
than others".

When and where can these lines converge and meet? How can
sympathy and understanding be brought about among men? Can
the ape and the essence be ever reconciled into a Leibnitzian
harmony to bring in the kingdom of god on earth? The mystery
of man! "What had been a blob of jelly within her body would
invent a god and worship: what had been a kind of fish would
create and, having created, would become the battle-ground of
disputing good and evil: what had blindly lived in her as a parasitic
worm would look at the stars, would listen to music, would read
poetry".[16] There is a schism at the root of our life: the split
between mind and body, love and lust, light and darkness, life
and death. Huxley is appalled by the strange phenomenon of
humanity — both gods and beasts, "moronic babies with giant
intellects" and "goddesses finding their way to Olympus by the
road of sensuality"[17] — the vulgar biological origins yet with a
touch of divinity, complex and mysterious creatures, the totality
of whose personality can be grasped only when looked at from
all sides, the physical and the biological, the psychological and
the sociological.

To present this multi-faceted picture, Huxley adopts, what he
calls, the technique of musicalization of fiction.

The musicalization of fiction. Not in the symbolist way, by
subordinating sense to sound. But on a large scale, in the construction. Meditate on Beethoven. The changes of moods, the
abrupt transitions. More interesting still, the modulations, not
merely from one key to another, but from mood to mood. A
theme is stated, then developed, pushed out of shape,
imperceptibly deformed, until, though still recognizably the
same, it has become quite different.... Put this into a novel.
How? The abrupt transitions are easy enough. All you need is
a sufficiency of characters and parallel, contrapuntal plots.
While Jones is murdering a wife, Smith is wheeling the perambulator in the park. You alternate the themes. More interesting,
the modulation and variations are also more difficult. A novelist
modulates by reduplicating situations and characters. He shows

16 Ibid., p. 2.
17 *The Genius and the Goddess*, pp. 8, 92.

several people falling in love, or dying, or praying in different ways — dissimilars solving the same problem. Or vice versa, similar people confronted with dissimilar problems. In this way you can modulate through all the aspects of your theme, you can write variations in any number of different moods. Another way: the novelist can assume the god-like creative privilege and simply elect to consider the events of the story in their various aspects — emotional, scientific, economic, religious, metaphysical, etc. He will modulate from one to the other — as from aesthetic to the physico-chemical aspect of things, from the religious to the physiological or financial. But perhaps, this is a too tyrannical imposition of the author's will.[18]

Typical of this Huxleyan technique is here a passage from his second novel *Antic Hay,* a reminiscence of one of the characters Coleman:

I remember, when I used to hang about the biological laboratories at school, eviscerating frogs — crucified with pins, they were, belly upwards, like little green Christs. — I remember once, when I was sitting there, quietly poring over the entrails, in came the laboratory boy and said to the stinks usher: 'Please, sir, may I have the key of the Absolute?' And, would you believe it, that usher calmly put his hand in his trouser pocket and fished out a small Yale key and gave it to him without a word. What a gesture! The key of the Absolute. But it was only the absolute alcohol the urchin wanted — to pickle some loathsome foetus in, I suppose. God rot his soul in peace![19]

Still another, Mark Staithes, a character in a much later novel *Eyeless in Gaza* says:

'Death', said Mark Staithes. 'It's the only thing we haven't succeeded in completely vulgarizing. Not from any lack of the desire to do so, of course. We're like dogs on an acropolis. Trotting round with inexhaustible bladders and only too anxious to lift a leg against every statue. And mostly we succeed. Art, religion, heroism, love — we've left our visiting card on all

[18] *Point Counter Point,* pp. 408-9.
[19] *Antic Hay,* p. 52.

of them. But death — death remains out of reach. We haven't been able to defile *that* statue. Not yet at any rate. But progress is still progressing.[20]

Such passages, 'brilliant' can be the word for them; 'filthy and disgusting', some have called them. Huxley, his strength and his weakness, is in such passages as these. A leap into religion and mysticism, a probing, almost surrealistic in manner, into the sub-conscious, at the same time a heavy and depressing consciousness of the foulness of the human body and its functions.

Huxley was far in advance of his generation. The reading public welcomed him with interest and amusement, but professional recognition came rather late. Critics called him smart, witty, schoolboyish, naughty, exhibitionistic, etc. Immediately after the publication of *Antic Hay,* Gerald Gould wrote: "I have no quarrel with Mr. Huxley for writing about the degenerate and the dyspeptic; they have immortal souls, and are just as important as anybody else; but he will have to rid himself of the illusions that people are interesting *because* they are degenerate and dyspeptic before he can hope to find scope for his really splendid talents".[21] This was written in 1924 when Victorian smugness and prudery were still alive. But even much later, critics found it hard to accept either his themes or his techniques. John McCormic, in his *Catastrophe and Imagination,* writes: "In re-reading Huxley the conclusion is inescapable that his vaunted brilliance is the pseudo-brilliance of the precocious schoolboy, the clever undergraduate, written for schoolboys and undergraduates".[22] Aesthetic dislike carried to the pitch of frenzy! When *Ape and Essence* was published, Walter Allen, himself a well-known novelist, wrote: "It appears to be Huxley's tragedy that having become a man of religion he has not become a man of the Christian religion; for charity, in the Christian sense, which must have mitigated his hostility to the frailties of human nature, plays no part in his faith".[23]

Richard Church puts Huxley on the rolls of the 'Gastric Ulcer School'. He says: "Swift, Shaw and Huxley — all three longed

20 *Eyeless in Gaza,* p. 409.
21 Gerald Gould, *The English Novel of Today,* pp. 90-91.
22 John McCormic, *Catastrophe and Imagination,* p. 286.
23 Walter Allen, *The Year's Work in Literature,* p. 31.

to scour the human race in an everlasting bath of carbolic, and to lower the temperature of the blood by means of some social mechanism yet to be invented. Such an aim is aristocratic: it denotes the aristocracy of intellect, turning with horror from the welter of democracy. It comes from too great a standard of perfectibility. The idealism had risen so high that the snows and airless inanition have settled round it. At that height, and in that solitude, ordinary men and women cannot move about for the authors to make their acquaintance and to learn to love them".[24]

Swift, Shaw and Huxley — all the three are brilliantly clear-headed. They can spin a superb tale, and they have a lucid prose style. But Swift is a misanthrope and a cynic, and his cynicism is closely allied with his personal disappointments in life. He lashes at humanity with a whip of scorpions. He has suffered throughout his life from a gnawing disquietude and despair, finally lapsing into insanity and death. His genius lay in negation.

Shaw is a social reformer with a sharp sense of humour. As Dr. Iyengar says: "he was truly the Peter Pan of the modern age. Like a Don Quixote doubled with a St. George, Shaw closed with the dragons of slum landlordism, prostitution, militarism, commercial medicine, democracy and persecution".[25] He seeks to infuse new life into the nation, clear it of cant and hypocrisy. He laughs at the foibles of men, but laughs without malice. He is essentially a social reformer who has laid the foundations of fabian socialism, and his plays are vehicles for propagation of his ideas, and media for discussion of problems in contemporary life and the solutions he has to offer.

Huxley is an institution by himself. He is deeper in content than Shaw. His canvas is a much bigger piece. The whole universe of man is his theme. In his presentation, he leaps into mysticism and religion, science and art, philosophy and psychology. He surveys the whole scene, probes into every corner. His problem is an ancient yet eternal problem awaiting solution — how not to be a Hamlet. He finds himself in a world that has the look of a mental and moral purgatory, an assembly area for heaven or hell, god knows which. He neither laughs at the world in puckish humour as Shaw does, nor does he spring at it like a she-cat in

[24] Richard Church, *The Growth of the English Novel*, p. 60.
[25] K. R. Srinivasa Iyengar, "George Bernard Shaw", in the *G.B.S. Commemoration Volume*.

the manner of Swift. He is ruthless in his portrayal, but not malicious. His instruments may be irony and sarcasm at times, but never ribaldry. There is a sadness, a profound sadness, running like an undercurrent through out. From *Crome Yellow* to *The Genius and the Goddess,* from the twenty-three-year old Denis Stone to the sixty-year-old John Rivers, it has been a search for a richer life and a fullness of the spirit, for the 'pre-established harmony', for a way to end the schism at the heart of our being.

2

THE SCHISM AND THE QUEST

Oh, wearisome condition of humanity,
Born under one law, to another bound,
Vainly begot and yet forbidden vanity,
Created sick, commanded to be sound,
What meaneth nature by these diverse laws,
Passion and reason, self-division's cause?

FULKE GREVILLE

THE schism at the heart of our being — the split between the
mind and the body, between Reason and instinct, the biological
origins and the spiritual cravings that tease the thinking individual,
"born under one law, to another bound" — the quest is for a
way to end the schism.

This schism is at once both the curse and the product of the
twentieth century. In spite of the advance of science and rational-
istic attitudes, in spite of Thomas Huxley and Darwin and intellectual approach to matters in preference to romantic flights, the
Victorian mind still inclined towards an intuitive philosophy and
a moral code nurtured on the Christian faith. The Victorians
unquestioningly accepted life's elemental things — joy, sorrow,
merit, sin, love, life and death — as revealed by the Christian
doctrines. But, for good or for worse, the World War I and
the communist revolution, Marxism and methodology, the advent
of Freud and the ever progressing progress of civilization induced
a basic dualism in our conceptions, a vivisection of the complex
oneness of things, a segregation of ends from means, technique
from theme, need from pleasure, politics from morals, and soul
from body. The modern man, at one extreme, is a first-rate animal,
divinely formless, amoebic in structure, shrinking or protruding
as the environment permits him. At the other extreme is the hyper-

sensitive being turned schizoid and hovering on the lunatic fringe seeking consolation from drugs and drink. In between is the normal thoughtful individual feeling forlorn in a world where a decayed past is still lingering and a future yet to take shape, unable to harmonize the real with the ideal, and tone down the basic discords that have arisen between religion, ethics, aesthetics, science, sociology and political thought. It is this layer of humanity out on the quest to discover the "route into hope and health".

Plato, in *The Symposium,* expounds the myth of the original divisioning of one being into two parts and the subsequent search for reunion. To Huxley, this divisioning of the being is not a myth but a reality. From *Crome Yellow* to *Island* is presented the struggle of the human being torn between divided allegiances, and the quest for integrity. The central character in all these novels except, of course, *Island,* appears to be the same individual.

Denis, in *Crome Yellow,* disgusted with his own bashfulness, yearns to be a bold he-man and a go-getter. Gumbril, in *Antic Hay,* hides his bashfulness behind a beaver, assumes the role of a lady-killer and money-spinner, and goes out on a world tour. Calamy, in *Those Barren Leaves,* returns from a world tour satiated with amour, and prefers the seclusion of a 'higher-lifer'. Philip, in *Point Counter Point,* concludes that 'higher-life' and 'search for truth' are just "refined substitutes for genuine living", and wonders whether he has the strength of mind to turn to the task of integral living. Anthony, in *Eyeless in Gaza,* starting where Philip leaves off, turns to humanism as a means for personal and general happiness. And all through is presented the conflict between the claims of the body and the refinements of the mind, and the need for a reconciliation between the two, the need to combine the theories of Rampion and Miller. *The Genius and the Goddess* attempts to prove that an Olympian temperament is a handicap to the human being, and, genius or goddess, one cannot transcend bodily desires. Thus the reader is led to the utopia of *Island* where sex and spirituality, passion and reason are harmonized, the individual and the society are re-habilitated in a benign symbiosis, and a psychological alchemy practised to achieve harmony of being as the basis for integral living.

Thus is presented a new pilgrim's progress from *Crome Yellow* to *Island,* and one wonders whether the central character in all these novels, except *Island,* is the same pilgrim though under

different names and set in different environments and circumstances. Leaving aside *Crome Yellow,* a casual look at the date
of publication and the age of the main character confirms this
view, as the interval between the publication of one novel and the
next one is approximately the same as the difference in age between
one main character and the other.

Date of Publication	Novel	Main Character	Age	Page
1923	*Antic Hay*	Gumbril	31-32	7
1926	*Those Barren Leaves*	Calamy	33-34	61
1928	*Point Counter Point*	Philip	36-37*	316, 436 & 538
1936	*Eyeless in Gaza*	Anthony Beavis	45**	9
1955	*The Genius and the Goddess*	John Rivers	61-62	14 & 94

*Calculated from circumstantial evidence.
**August 1933, he is said to be 42 years old.

Is Huxley himself this pilgrim on the quest? Denis, in 1921,
had just published a book of poems and was planning to write a
novel. Huxley too had, by then, published his book of poems
Leda, and was writing *Crome Yellow.* Gumbril renounces schoolmastering and drafts advertisements for his pneumatic trousers.
Huxley too was once a schoolmaster-turned-miniature-journalist.
Philip, undoubtedly the mouthpiece of Huxley, was presented
as a novelist who had just returned from India, and Huxley himself
was in India during 1925-26, immediately prior to the writing of
Point Counter Point. Philip escaped being drafted into the war
because of lameness, Huxley because of partial blindness. Anthony
Beavis reveals some facets of Huxley's own character, and Beavis's
feelings on the death of his mother during his schooldays were,
it is said, drawn from Huxley's own bitter experience. If Huxley
himself is the pilgrim, he very cleverly conceals his identity,
perhaps practising Calamy's advice to Miss Thriplow in *Those
Barren Leaves*:

One can get annoyed with imbeciles for failing to understand
what seems obvious to oneself; one's vanity may be hurt by

2

their interpretation of you — they make you out as vulgar as themselves. Or you may feel that you have failed as an artist, in so far as you haven't managed to make yourself transparently plain. But what are all these compared to the horrors of being understood — completely understood? You've given yourself away, you're known, you're at the mercy of the creatures into whose keeping you have committed your soul — why, the thought's terrifying. If I were you, I'd congratulate myself. You have a public which likes your books, but for the wrong reasons. And meanwhile you're safe, you're out of their reach, you possess yourself intact.[1]

Remaining teasingly out of reach, Huxley presents his themes, patronizingly pitied by some, ridiculed by others, grudgingly appreciated by a few, meanwhile selling his books like hot cakes.

I I

Huxley's first novel *Crome Yellow* (1921) presents Denis Stone, twenty-three-year old, a sensitive young poet who has just published a book of poems. Denis comes to Crome to join a house-party as a guest of the owners, a middle-aged couple, Mr. and Mrs. Henry Wimbush and their young niece Anne. There are other guests — Jenny Mullion, thirty years old, sitting apart in her secret tower of deafness; the twenty-three-year old Mary Bracegirdle, good-looking like a Chinese doll, ingenuous and stupid, the *femme supérieure;* the Byronic Gombauld, a 'black-haired young corsair of thirty', a painter of no mean talent; a spiritual journalist-humbug Barbecue Smith; and Scogan 'looking like an extinct saurian', Henry's school-fellow, a little over fifty, rude and prickly-pearish in talk. A little later, there joins them a rich and handsome young man Ivor, 'a butterfly in auricular wings', flitting from flower to flower, from Mary to Zenobia. The usual Peacockian setting.

The novel really begins with an almost Sartrean lamentation of

1 *Those Barren Leaves*, p. 52.

Denis in Anne's presence:

"One entered the world", says Denis, "having ready-made ideas about everything. One had a philosophy and tried to make life fit into it. One should have lived first and then made one's philosophy to fit life. . . . Life, facts, things were horribly complicated; ideas, even the most difficult of them, deceptively simple. In the world of ideas everything was clear; in life all was obscure, embroiled. Was it surprising that one was miserable, horribly unhappy?"

"My poor Denis!" Anne was touched. "But why can't you just take things for granted and as they come?" she asked. "It is so much simpler".

"Of course it is" said Denis, "but it's a lesson to be learnt gradually. There are the twenty tons of ratiocination to be got rid of first".

"I've always taken things as they come" said Anne. "It seems so obvious. One enjoys the pleasant things, avoids the nasty ones. There's nothing more to be said".

"Nothing — for you. But, then, you were born a pagan; I am trying laboriously to make myself one. I can take nothing for granted, I can enjoy nothing as it comes along. Beauty, pleasure, art, women — I have to invent an excuse, a justification for everything that's delightful. Otherwise I can't enjoy it with an easy conscience. I make up a little story about beauty and pretend that it has something to do with truth and goodness. I have to say that art is the process by which one reconstructs the divine reality out of chaos. Pleasure is one of the mystical roads to union with the infinite — the ecstasies of drinking, dancing, love-making. As for women, I am perpetually assuring myself that they're the broad highway to divinity. And to think that I'm only just beginning to see through the silliness of the whole thing! It's incredible to me that anyone should have escaped these horrors".

"It's still more incredible to me", said Anne, "that anyone should have been a victim to them. I should like to see myself believing that men are the highway to divinity. . . . What you need, Denis, is a nice plump young wife, a fixed income, and a little congenial but regular work".

"What I need is you!" mentally he shouted the words, but no sound issued from his lips.[2]

Perhaps Denis the dreamer needed Anne the pagan to keep him hooked on to the earth. But, "between the idea and reality, between the motion and the act, falls the shadow".

Crome Yellow presents two generations — an older one Victorian in smugness and faith and in acceptance of life and things as they come, the younger one born in another world, repelled by the past, unable to set their bearings in the present. Scogan is like an owl flitting between the two worlds, and Anne the pagan the link between the two. Henry is absorbed in a study of antiquity, his wife in the influence of stars on equine beings. The cosmos does not bewilder them. The stupid Mary who finds in Freud an excuse to succumb to amorous advances is tortured by no doubts. Ivor, young and opulent, racing from amour to amour, finds life quite absorbing. Scogan talks his way to death. Silent Jenny his female counterpart drawing caricatures in her stone tower, finds in biting sarcasm a means of escape from reality. But Denis has no peace of mind.

The novel ends with the stupid Mary releasing her repressions along with her philanderer-lover Ivor who flies to Zenobia, and pagan Anne locked up "in the beginnings of what promised to be an endlessly passionate embracement" of the vital Gombauld who believes in "pullulation and lots and lots of life". Driven to despair and tears, Denis, persuaded by Mary, decided to leave Crome. But when the moment of departure comes, he finds, to his surprise, Anne looking wretched, and even Scogan sad. "Never again", he said to himself with Sartrean nausea, "never again would he do anything decisive". "It sinks and I am ready to depart", aptly quoting Landor he gets into the 'hearse'. He departs, having failed in love, having found no answers to his anxious doubts.

2 *Crome Yellow,* pp. 22-23.

III

Huxley's next novel *Antic Hay* (1923) presents a greater variety
of character and incident. Quoting from Marlowe, Huxley
announces that his men "like satyrs grazing on the lawns, shall
with their goat-feet dance the antic hay".[3] *Crome Yellow* is just
a peripheral suburb, but *Antic Hay* draws us right into the
Huxleyan world. Huxley presents a multi-faceted picture of human
existence as conditioned not only by the biological and mental
functions, but also by all the organizations and institutions that
constitute the environment. With subtle touches he suggests in
the novel various conflicting circumstances of life. At the beginning
is a moving episode that brings into focus the conflict between
economic, legal and moral codes, the law for prevention of cruelty
to animals resulting in cruelty to man. In the boorish aristocrat
Bruno Opps's hatred for the poor — the canaille, he calls them
— and the tailor Bojanus's desire for a proletarian revolution,
Huxley hints at the class struggle immanent in the social set-up.
He presents in a graphic manner the clash within the individual,
and between the individual and the environment, and the grotesque
capers cut by each one in his or her quest for happiness.

The main character, Theodore Gumbril, about thirty-one years
old, fed up with schoolmastering, sends in his resignation to the
headmaster, and hopes to find in the outside world the secret of
becoming a complete man and a masterful mind. Like Denis,
"weighted down with ratiocination", he too complains:

> God as a sense of warmth of heart, God as exultation, God as
> tears in the eyes, God as a rush of power of thought — that
> was all right. But God as truth, God as 2+2=4 — that wasn't
> so clearly all right. Was there any chance of their being the
> same? Were there bridges to join the two worlds?[4]

As in *Crome Yellow*, in *Antic Hay* too are portrayed two
generations. Gumbril Senior, Theodore's father, is a charming old

---

[3] 'Hay' or more commonly spelt 'hey' is a winding country-dance. The
title 'Antic Hay' suggests that the characters go through a wild neurotic
dance on the dance-floors of life.

[4] *Antic Hay*, p. 7.

man. He is a talented architect, though not a very successful one, and his room is cluttered up with models which he tends with paternal affection. His old friend Porteous is an expert on late Latin poetry. Gumbril Senior working on his architectural models, bird-watching in the evenings, Porteous absorbed in his precious old editions, lead a serene life. They have, in themselves, strength of character, sobriety of thought and also a touching sense of humour to sustain them in life.

In sharp contrast to these two individuals, Huxley presents a motley crowd of the younger generation, each floundering in a personal cesspool — Theodore Gumbril and Mrs. Myra Viveash, Lypiatt a painter-poet, Mercaptan a shallow but popular literary journalist, Shearwater a scientist, and his wife Rosie in search of new sensations, Coleman a diabolic cynic, and his wife Zoe sullen and ferocious like a kilkenny cat, all of them friends moving in the same circle, and finally Emily, charming and innocent, who sways uncertainly on the verge but luckily escapes the swing of the antic hay.

Gumbril, renouncing pedagogy, decides to turn a money-spinner and cultivate a beaver. Money, he thinks, will give him the freedom and the confidence to face the insolent world. Wealth would teach him the art of being brutal. The beaver would help him in hiding his natural diffidence and shyness of manner. Like a bashful person peering at the world through tinted glasses, Gumbril hopes to face the world with the confidence stimulated by the beaver. Moreover, just as bad reputation in a woman is a sign of her approachability, the beaver is an open invitation to woman, an overt offer of readiness in man, thus making initial introductions easier.

Gumbril looks like an extension of Denis Stone, though much older, more mature. Anne's prescription for Denis's misery is "a nice plump young wife, a fixed income, and a little congenial but regular work". Gumbril starts his quest with a fixed income, three hundred pounds a year, a legacy from a deceased aunt. Schoolmastering he finds uncongenial, and to use Denis's own words "laboriously trying to make himself a pagan", he comes out to conquer the world of wealth and woman. Being rather bashful by nature, like Denis, Gumbril has spent tearful nights longing for Myra Viveash. Disgusted with his own diffidence, he now wants to don a beaver and pose as a he-man and a lady-killer.

Myra must have once been a happy-go-lucky pagan like Anne. The most delicious moments of her life were those spent with her lover Tony Lamb, who, one shining day in the summer of 1917, went to the war, and within a week died shot through the head. That wrecked Myra's life. Unable to fill the vacancy within, unable to find sympathy and response in the world outside, she hopes to get a kick out of life through drugs and night-clubs, boy-friends and drinks, but nothing vivifies her dead soul, and she lives in a "pre-Adamite empty world".

If life has mortified Myra's being, it has thrown Coleman into a frenzy of cynicism. Coleman and his wife Zoe are a fearful combination worshipping a strange dyad of Sade-Masoch. Zoe is sullen and ferocious; once she jabbed at him with a fork, another time she stuck a pen-knife in his fore-arm. Collapse of all ideals, frustration and disillusionment turned Coleman a cynic, a fearful and diabolic cynic. He is conscious only of the filthiness of man and of the filthiness of life. He glories in filth, and his religion is to make everyone feel the filth. His motives are purely ethical! He sounds like Shakespeare's Iago when he says:

Reproduction, reproduction. Delightful and horrifying to think they all come to that, even the most virginal, that they were all made for that, like she-dogs, in spite of their Chinablue eyes. What sort of a mandrake shall we produce, Zoe and I?[5]

He is a nihilist and a terrifying one at that:

"Does it occur to you", he asks, "that at this moment we are walking through the midst of seven million distinct and separate individuals, each with distinct and separate lives and all completely indifferent to our existence? Seven million people, each one of whom thinks himself quite as important as each of us does. Millions of them are now sleeping in an empested atmosphere. Hundreds of thousands of couples are at this moment engaged in mutually caressing one another in a manner too hideous to be thought of, but in no way different from the manner in which each of us performs, delightfully, passionately and beautifully, his similar work of love. Thousands of women are now in the throes of parturition, and of both sexes,

[5] Ibid., pp. 54-55.

thousands are dying of the most diverse and appalling diseases, or simply because they have lived too long. Thousands are drunk, thousands have over-eaten, thousands haven't had enough to eat. And they are all alive, all unique and separate and sensitive, like you and me. It's a horrible thought. Ah, if I could lead them all into that great hole of centipedes.... Oh all ye Beasts and Cattle, curse ye the Lord: curse him and vilify him forever."[6]

All Cattle and Beasts! Coleman's motives are purely ethical, seeking salvation cursing the lord, making mankind hate this world perhaps to turn their attention to some other world less filthy! Separatism in existence, fragmentation within one's own being turn Myra and Coleman into schizoid apes.

Myra and Coleman are sensitive and sensible individuals turned neurotic owing to spiritual imbalance, but Lypiatt and Shearwater are escapists. Lypiatt is a painter-poet, who, unlike Gombauld, is mediocre in skill, loud and bombastic in talk, living by self-delusion. "He was like a man who walks along a sinister road at night and sings to keep up his own spirits to emphasize and magnify his own existence".[7] He is desperately in love with Myra but she is bored with him as well as with his art. An exhibition of Lypiatt's paintings turns out to be a miserable failure drawing harsh comments from everyone including Myra. In misery and despair, he writes a long moving letter to her, and picks up his service revolver.

Shearwater is a masterful intellect in the laboratory but a moron at home. Ignorant of love and tender human relationships, his wife Rosie is to him a live item of the house-hold furniture designed to feed him and to keep silent company in bed. Rosie is sophisticated and refined, but because of a callous husband, is emotionally discontented, and so she falls a victim to the beaver Gumbril. At Gumbril's Friday party, Myra meets the scientist all-absorbed in a study of kidneys which, to him, are divine in organization and structure. Myra is tempted to test whether he is so much dedicated to science as not to be lured by feminine charms. She plays her trumps and the kidneys are forgotten. A day or two and she is bored with him, and when he calls on her, the maid is told to say she is out. Tormented by love and jealousy,

---

[6] Ibid., pp. 56-57.　　　　　[7] Ibid., p. 76.

he suddenly realizes he has all along been unkind to his wife Rosie. He now confesses to her his love for Myra and how he has salvaged himself from it. He offers to make amends for his past negligence, but Rosie who has just struck the antic hay with Gumbril pretends aversion to what she calls "the Joan-and-Derby business", and tells him in a fastidious lisp that it is highly 'civ-vilized' for the husband and wife to have their own pet avocations. Feeling helpless, ignorant of both life and love, the scientist escapes into his laboratory and pedals and pedals a stationary bicycle to experiment on the regulatory function of kidneys!

Gumbril is above all these people, superior in character, in attainments, attitudes and outlook. Passion and reason at conflict within, religion and God having not given the meaningful comfort he has hoped for, he turns to paganism, thinking that happiness lies in being the boss in affairs of the world and of the heart. Advised by Coleman, he wears a fan-shaped blond beard, and walking along Queen's Street, meets with Rosie. He does not know that she is Shearwater's wife. She is thrilled by her encounter with a beaver, and he by the conquest. The meeting culminates in love-making in her room. Later he cheats Rosie, giving her a wrong address to meet him, and "this clownish trick" in "the worst of deliriously bad taste" throws her into Coleman's arms.

One day, in the National Gallery, Gumbril meets with two sisters Molly and Emily. The beaver makes the introductions easy. Emily is charming and virginal. She disarms him with her innocence. When he meets her next, he casts aside the beaver and confesses his folly. They both spend a night in Gumbril's rooms locked up in each other's arms in a caress unravished by desire. Gumbril promises to spend a week-end with her in the countryside, but stupidly breaks the promise coaxed by Myra. Emily, thus deceived by him, realizes her folly, writes a moving letter, and vanishes leaving no address.

Having lost Emily, in sheer disgust, Gumbril plans to go out on a world tour spending the last night with Myra on a last ride, a night-long ride along the streets of London. On their way, they drop in at Gumbril Senior's for a late supper. Asked to show his models to Myra, the old man whispers that he has sold them to the Victoria and Alberts Museum to buy back for his friend Porteous some of the precious old editions sold by the latter to settle his drunkard son's debts. The library is Porteous's precious possession just as the models are Gumbril Senior's. Porteous has a passion for Notker's poems. "Notker was worth it", he used to say, "Notker was worth even the weariness and the pallor of a wife who worked beyond her strength, even the shabbiness of ill-dressed and none too well-fed children. . . . But there had been occasions when it needed more than the monocle and the careful distinguished clothes to keep up his morale." He keeps it up, right to the end. The library is lost, still he keeps it up.

Gumbril Senior refused to sell his models when the Victoria and Alberts Museum had asked for them. The models have been a part of himself. But, for his friend, without a pang, he now sells them away and sells them quietly: "I didn't want to blare it about in front of strangers", he told Gumbril, "as though it were a question of the house-maid's illegitimate baby or a repair to the water-closet".

Slowly, pensively, Gumbril follows his father wondering: "Beyond good and evil? Below good and evil? The name of earwig. The tubby pony trotted. The wild columbines suspended, among the shadows of the hazel copse, hooked spurs, helmets of aerial purple. The Twelfth Sonata of Mozart was insecticide; no earwigs could crawl through the music. Emily's breasts were firm and pointed and she had slept at last without a tremor. In that starlight good, true and beautiful became one". The proof for Denis's own belief that beauty, truth and goodness are one, Gumbril, though momentarily, perceives, but flippancy hasn't yet left him. He thinks: "write the discovery in books — in books quos, in the morning, *legimus cacantes*".

Thus with cloven feet the satyrs dance the antic hay. Only Gumbril Senior, Porteous and Emily have that inward strength of character to cushion themselves against the jolts of life. Serene and dignified, they carry on untainted in their attitudes. There is quiet in Emily's mind. She is native to that crystal world. But life is not so simple to thought-tormented Gumbril. Good and Evil, Beauty and Truth are at times felt in the quiet recesses of the soul, but one is not prepared to face the quietness nor explore it. Even among the sophisticated, most men are like Mercaptan who says:

What I glory in is the civilised, middle way between stink and asepsis. Give me a little musk, a little intoxicating feminine exhalation, the bouquet of old wine and straw-berries, a lavender bag under every pillow and pot pourri in the corners of the drawing-room. Readable books, amusing conversation, civilised women, graceful art and dry vintage music, with a quiet life and reasonable comfort — that's all I ask for.[8]

A little of stink and a little of dettol! Aesthetic animalism! But to the sensitive and perceptive individual responsive to the existential stimuli, striving for inner harmony, striving for sympathy and understanding with one's own fellow creatures, life seems to be a perplexing and, at times mortifying phenomenon. Collapse of all values, hypocrisy in everything human, variance between profession and practice, turn Coleman into a cynic. At war within himself, and at war with the outside world, he is like a wounded crocodile viciously lashing at everything within reach. He finds himself fearfully alone in the midst of "seven million distinct and separate individuals". Myra too harps on the same separatism in existence, and compares people to moving trains on parallel tracks having a rare glimpse of one another. The utter futility, cruelty, unfairness and purposelessness of war, and her lover's death leave her cold on a spiritual death-bed. Gumbril or Opps, Lypiatt or Mercaptan, none could pluck that chord of love in her heart as Tony Lamb could. She traverses a moral desert, needing male company for sheer physical exhaustion, a few hours' sleep, and then to wake up the next day, but "tomorrow will be as awful as today!" In her case, the sexual act is just a casual habit, nothing to do with love, yielding neither pleasure nor pain, nor even relieving her boredom. Rosie, neglected by an unthinking and unfeeling husband, needs a boy-friend to fill up an emotional vacuum, to experience a new sensation in life, to have an adventure, to exult in the thrill of conquest and tingling nerves. Gumbril, refined and tender, gives her delicious moments, but the affair with Coleman leaves her disgusted and ashamed. But, as if in a cruel comment on the human being, as if in justification of Coleman's cynicism, in all that humiliation of the spirit, "the flesh is overcome by a pleasure more piercing than anything she has ever felt before". Was Coleman after all right? Is it all that filthy? Are love and lust the same? Is the sexual act a necessary or inevitable consummation to love? To Myra, male company is to

[8] Ibid., p. 47.

lull her to sleep, to Rosie it is for a new sensation. To Mercaptan, living in a purgatory between stink and asepsis, woman is for delicious intoxication like a good cup of wine. To Lypiatt love is a spiritual need, and a harsh comment from the woman he has loved drives him to suicide. Gumbril, in Rosie's company, feels only the success of an experiment but no rich emotions. With Emily he sinks into a rare ecstasy .

How can this schism be ended? How can the body and the soul, lust and love, be reconciled? Can passion and reason be ever fused into a new union? Where and what is true happiness? The questions remain unanswered and the quest continues.

Myra is one classic victim of modern war-torn life. Coleman is another. Where life has driven Myra to suicidal inertia and boredom, it has driven Coleman to nihilistic cynicism. Myra and Coleman are schizoid extremes. Lypiatt and Shearwater are escapists. Lypiatt, a failure both in life and love, seeks solace in the world of art. He lives by self-delusion, boosting up his own morale, convincing himself with cracker-mottos of the greatness of his own art. A word about their real worth from the woman he loves — Myra says they look like Italian Vermouth advertisements— punctures his ego and drives him to suicide. Jilted by Myra, Shearwater runs to Rosie, but she, having found a lover, pretends aversion to Joan-and-Derby sentimentality. But, as the irony of life would have it, when, disrobed of all her fastidiousness by Coleman, she scampers home, she finds her husband cloistered in the laboratory, and at her own bidding! All the thrill of adventure and romance dead, she dumps herself in a domestic vacuum, bruised both physically and mentally. Unable to face reality, Lypiatt turns to suicide, Shearwater takes shelter in science. But escapism and sublimation bring no real happiness. Is there a psychological alchemy to turn men into Gods?[9]

Gumbril, in one of his conversations with Emily says:

There are quiet places also in the mind. But we build bandstands and factories on them. Deliberately — to put a stop to the quietness. We don't like the quietness. All the thoughts, all the preoccupations in my head — round and round, continually. And the jazz bands, the music hall songs, the boys shouting

[9] Huxley's novel *Island* refers to such a psychological alchemy.

the news. What's it for, what's it all for? To put an end to the quiet, to break it up and disperse it, to pretend at any cost it isn't there. Ah, but it is, it is there, in spite of everything, at the back of everything. Lying awake at night, sometimes — not restlessly, but serenely, waiting for sleep — the quiet re-establishes itself, piece by piece; all the broken bits, all the fragments of it we've been so busily dispersing all day long. It re-establishes itself, an inward quiet, like this outward quiet of grass and trees. It fills one, it grows—a crystal quiet, a growing expanding crystal. It grows, it becomes more perfect; it is beautiful and terrifying. Yes, terrifying, as well as beautiful. For one's alone in the crystal and there's no support from outside, there's nothing external and important, nothing external and trivial to pull oneself up by or to stand on, superiorly, contemptuously, so that one can look down. There's nothing to laugh at or feel enthusiastic about. But the quiet grows and grows. Beautifully and unbearably. And at last you are conscious of something approaching; it is almost a faint sound of footsteps. Something inexpressibly lovely and wonderful advances through the crystal, nearer and nearer. And, oh, inexpressibly terrifying. For if it were to touch you, if it were to seize and engulf you, you'd die. There would be an end of bandstands and whizzing factories, and one would have to begin living arduously in the quiet, arduously in some strange un-heard-of manner. Nearer, nearer come the steps; but one can't face the advancing thing. One daren't. It's too terrifying, it's too painful to die. Quickly, before it is too late, start the factory wheels, beat the drum, blow up the saxophone. Think of the women you'd like to sleep with, the schemes for making money, the gossip about your friends, the last outrage of the politicians. Anything for a diversion. Break the silence, smash the crystal to pieces. There, it lies in bits; it is easily broken, hard to build up and easy to break. And the steps? Ah, those have taken themselves off, double quick. Double quick, they were gone at the first flawing of the crystal. And by this time the lovely and terrifying thing is three infinities away, at least. And you lie tranquilly on your bed, thinking of what you'd do if you had ten thousand pounds and of all the fornications you'll never commit".[10]

[10] *Antic Hay,* pp. 146-47.

Gumbril, finding that neither religion nor its exponents could offer him 'the key of the Absolute', turns pagan, and believes that happiness consists in being the boss in life. He runs after wealth and amour, but neither gives him the sort of happiness he wants. Myra and Rosie, both leave him cold. Emily, he has lost because of his own doing. Having had a glimpse of heaven in Emily's company, having cherished, though for a moment, truth, goodness and beauty in his father's presence, still he suppresses the clamouring voice within, anodizes himself seeking shelter in flippancy, "starts the factory wheels, bangs the drum, blows up the saxophone" and goes out like Denis into the dark future on a world tour, to assert himself in the world of wealth and women, find the secret of happiness. The quest continues.

IV

From the dance halls of *Antic Hay, Those Barren Leaves* leads us to the wider arena of a Saxon enclave in a Latin atmosphere, to a rare mixture of bully beef and red wine. Another house-party as in *Crome Yellow,* another Peacockian setting.

The novel presents the main character Calamy standing under those barren leaves glittering beautifully on the withered trees in the winter twilight on the Apuan mountains, and reviewing those barren leaves in his own past personal history. Calamy is thirty-three, two years older than Gumbril. *Antic Hay* ends with Gumbril going out on a world tour in search of wealth and amour. *Those Barren Leaves* begins with Calamy, rich and handsome, returning from a world tour with the reputation of an accomplished amorist behind him. The scene is set in Italy, the Malaspina palace at Vezza owned by Mrs. Aldwinkle. Calamy arrives there to be received by another guest, Miss Mary Thriplow, thirty years old, handsome and intelligent, a popular sentimental-romantic novelist. Having heard of him as a charming Don Juan, she makes herself extremely smart to receive him, but, on his arrival, finds him a changed person bored with erotic hostesses and shallow social delights. She slyly deposits all the precious rings on her fingers in the crevices of her sofa, and assumes modest naivete. When she tells Calamy that she has heard of him as dazzlingly social, he says: "perhaps I was that sort of imbecile once. But now — well, I hope all that's over now".

Calamy is but Gumbril older and perhaps wiser. Wealth and woman having not given the happiness he has desired, he returns from the world tour sober and pensive. While he is engaged in a pleasant quiet talk with Miss Thriplow, Mrs. Aldwinkle with her guests bursts into the garden. Calamy remarks, almost echoing Gumbril's own words to Emily: "it's like heaving a great stone into a calm pool — all this noise I mean". Taking the words as a compliment to herself, Miss Thriplow pipes in the same tune: "what smashings of the crystal one has to put up with".

Mrs. Aldwinkle makes a dramatic entry, carrying her fifty years exceedingly well. When young, she was Venus and Diana rolled into one. Extremely fortunate, she has been endowed with beauty and brains, wealth and freedom. With aristocratic nonchalance, she has lived beyond good and evil, been a celebrated hostess presiding over a menagerie of artists and scientists, poets, novelists and musicians. Supremely unconventional, she has had a long queue of lovers — Cardan, succeeded by Elzevir the pianist to be followed by Lord Trunion or was it Lecoing? — or both? Even now, in her fifties, she loves to hold court like a princess among her courtiers, thirsting for male admiration to constantly fortify herself into thinking that decay and death are still far away.

Prominent among her guests is Tom Cardan, sixty-five years old, a self-acknowledged capripede, "at once gross and sensitively refined, serious and sly". A brilliant talker, subtle and sarcastic, benevolent yet malicious, he presents rather a sphingid front to the world. Once a lover of Mrs. Aldwinkle, he is now a semi-permanent guest, a small parasite, he calls himself, with all his life's accumulations amounting to only about twelve hundred pounds.

Living with Mrs. Aldwinkle is Irene, her niece and confidant, a charming and naive girl of eighteen. She genuinely loves her aunt, and looks up to her in warm heroine-worship. In love with her is another guest, Lord Hovenden, twenty-one years old, handsome and rich, simple and innocent, untainted by bohemian vulgarity. Admired by Lord Hovenden, with all the "snobbery of blood towards brains", is Falx, a labour leader, seventy-three years old, looking like a minor prophet, ready with his tirade against the idle rich, the vulgar and immoral parasites on the noble poor!

Then joins the group, saved from a drowning accident, Francis Chelifer, handsome and young, a sensitive poet condemned by poverty to be the editor of a Rabbit Fanciers' Gazette. A few days later, his mother, Mrs. Chelifer joins him as an Aldwinkle-guest. A noble and good lady who has taken all the blows of life without rancour, she finds happiness in gathering lame-ducks and looking after them.

Thus assembles an odd assortment of individuals, and a grotesque tragi-comedy unfolds itself. With the arrival of Chelifer, life in the Malaspina undergoes a sudden change. Mrs. Aldwinkle throws herself into love with Chelifer. The other guests are left to themselves. A fantastic mid-summer comedy of a "love of the parallels" begins—Mrs. Aldwinkle and Chelifer, Calamy and Miss Thriplow, Irene and Hovenden, then Cardan and an imbecile Miss Elver.

Life has treated Mrs. Aldwinkle with extreme kindliness, but time the tyrant is merciless, and her face is ravaged with pouches and crow's-feet and wrinkles. A lover to her is more a psychological than a physical need, if only to help her to convince herself that she is still young. She runs after Chelifer a score of years her junior. But Chelifer's is a strange case. Twice before he was entangled with women. Once he loved without being loved— Barbara, beautiful but vulgar—and she, in the end, preferred a fat and coarse Syrian. Then he, not loving, was loved—by his own secretary Miss Masson—he seduced her for fun, then quietly dropped her. Both affairs made him experience the utter boredom implicit in such love, and now perverse fortune has thrown him into the arms of an erotic dowager to learn more lessons. One night, Mrs. Aldwinkle invades him in his own room and offers herself. Rejected by him, she hides her face against his knees and begins to sob. He is repelled by her but feels helpless. Fortunately, the commotion caused by the death-agony of Miss Elver saves him. Mrs. Aldwinkle later retires to her chamber only to be told by Irene that she has agreed to marry Hovenden. That is the finale. The pagan queen realizes her fall. Desertion, decay, death! Everyone is leaving her. She weeps in open misery. Paganism, nursed in all its glory, free from all the crippling circumstances of life, has had to bow down before Time, Time that puts a stop to everything.

Cardan her one-time lover, is a hedonist. He has had all the amour he wanted in life, has been a successful parasite, but he too—he is sixty-five—sobered down by Time, pensively broods over "decay, decrepitude and death", "the soul at the mercy of the decaying body, the soul itself decaying". But, stronger in character than Mrs. Aldwinkle, he resigns himself to the inevitable, and thinks of providing himself for the future. Having heard of an antique Etruscan piece of sculpture with a grocer, he goes out to see it hoping to make money by re-sale. He discovers the piece to be worthless, but on his return loses his way and stays for the night as a guest of a young brother and sister, both English, Elver a sneak, a cad and a coward, and Miss Elver a congenital idiot. Elver is sore that life has given to the imbecile a legacy of twenty-five thousand pounds leaving him penniless. He has brought his sister to this remote Italian village, a marshy place, hoping that she will die of malaria. He fortifies himself with quinine leaving her unprotected. Cardan gets a brain-wave. Twenty-five thousand pounds! The interest alone will keep him in luxury. He decides to marry her, a marriage very paying to himself, and appearing altruistic and romantic to the outside world. He has had all the romance in life, what does it matter if the girl is a harmless imbecile? He abducts her and brings her to Malaspina. Then the whole party goes out on an excursion, and at a wayside inn, Miss Elver, against Cardan's advice, sulks and eats fish. Returning to Malaspina, she dies that night of food-poisoning. The sneak-brother who wants to murder his sister with malaria inherits the legacy, and Cardan who wants to save her pays the funeral bill! The irony of life!

Dethroned and discarded, Mrs. Aldwinkle decides to go to Monte Carlo, a migration perhaps from red wine to hashish and heroin. Cardan agrees to follow her, wryly remarking "one cannot reject free meals when they're offered".

Calamy and Miss Thriplow traverse a strangely different parallel. Miss Thriplow is attracted by the accomplished amorist. Calamy is drawn towards her by her looks, exasperated by "her unreal air of innocence". She is a novelist constantly on the search for sentiments and themes. Making a guinea-pig of herself, she deliberately "scratches her own heart to make it bleed and then write stories with the red fluid". Her affair with Calamy, in spite of all the thrill it gives, is just "an experiment in applied physiology with a few psychological impressions thrown in". Calamy is bored with her, but perversely drawn towards her. He wants to be free, free from bodily appetites, free from all enslaving desires and inhibitions that prevent the mind from knowing the Reality behind appearances. Finally he leaves her, goes up the Apuan mountains to get at the beauty and mystery of life through contemplation.

Irene and Hovenden, simple and naive, ignorant or erotic perversities, sentimental and romantic in their adolescent calf-love, are quite happy. Hovenden finds love more absorbing than socialism, Irene feels the full thrill of it. For such is perhaps the Kingdom of God! Huxley seems to suggest, as D. H. Lawrence does, that poets and psycho-analysts just destroy all the romance, sentiment and the simple pleasures in everyday life, especially sex-life. Innocents like Irene and Hovenden, ignorant of both poets and psycho-analysts, impelled by native human instincts and intuitions, seek and get the full thrill of the joy of living.

Thus ends the love of the parallels. Irene and Hovenden alone are happy. Almost childishly innocent, their love is neither romantically poetic and idealistic nor vulgarly physical. Theirs is a sweet and tender attachment. Chelifer started with too highly poetic notions of love, but even in the most thrilling moments with Barbara, he was conscious only of the essential transitoriness of all thrill, and he unltimately finds love a boring affair. To Mrs. Aldwinkle the pagan, love is a psychological need. To Miss Thriplow, it is an experiment in applied physiology. To Cardan the hedonist, love is for fun, pleasure and even profit. To Calamy, it is an enslavement from which he has to wriggle himself out. But what exactly love is remains a puzzle. Is it the life force that binds Irene and Hovenden together, or that which drives Mrs. Chelifer in search of disowned cats and congenital idiots? Is love a physiological or a spiritual need? Or both? If both, how can the demands of the spirit be harmonized with the cravings of the body? The answer is yet to be found.

Cardan, Calamy and Chelifer are a strange trio, the hedonist, the mystic and the realist. Their conceptions of life are singularly dissimilar. Cardan's view is:

Sooner or later every soul is stifled by the sick body; sooner or later there are no more thoughts, but only pain and vomiting and stupor. The tragedies of the spirit are mere struttings and posturings on the margin of life, and the spirit itself is only an accidental exhuberance, the product of spare vital energy, like the feathers on the head of a hoopoe or the innumerable populations of useless and foredoomed spermatozoa. The spirit has no significance; there is only the body. When it is young, the body is beautiful and strong. It grows old, its joints creak, it becomes dry and smelly; it breaks down, the life goes out of it and it rots away. However lovely the feathers on a bird's head, they perish with it; and the spirit, which is a lovelier ornament than any, perishes too. "The farce is hideous," thought Mr. Cardan, "and in the worst of bad taste".

Fools do not perceive that the farce is a farce. They are the more blessed. Wise men perceive it and take pains not to think about it. Therein lies their wisdom. They indulge themselves in all the pleasures, of the spirit as of the body—and especially in those of the spirit, since they are by far the more varied, charming and delightful—and when the time comes they resign themselves with the best grace they can muster to the decay of the body and the extinction of its spiritual part. Meanwhile, however, they do not think too much of death—it is an un-exhilarating theme; they do not insist too much upon the farcical nature of the drama in which they are playing, for fear that they should become too much disgusted with their parts to get any amusement out of the piece at all.[11]

But Calamy is of an entirely different view. He is not worried about death or the life to come. According to him, the kingdom of god is within everyone, and the conquest of that kingdom, now, in this life, is every salvationist's ambition. He thinks:

Up there, so near that it's only a question of reaching out a hand to draw back the curtaining darkness that conceals it, up there, just above me, floats the great secret, the beauty and the mystery. To look into the depths of that mystery, to fix the eyes of the spirit on that bright and enigmatic beauty, to pore over the secret until its symbols cease to be opaque and the light filters through from beyond—there is nothing else in life, for me at any rate, that matters; there is no rest or possibility

[11] *Those Barren Leaves*, pp. 281-82.

of satisfaction in doing anything else.

All this was obvious to him now. And it was obvious, too, that he could not do two things at once; he couldn't at the same time lean out into the silence beyond the futile noise and bustle —into the mental silence that lies beyond the body—he couldn't at the same time do this and himself partake in the tumult; and if he wanted to look into the depths of mind, he must not interpose a preoccupation with his bodily appetites.

Can there be a sort of "graceful Latin compromise?" he wonders:

An Epicurean cultivation of mind and body. Breakfast at nine. Serious reading from ten till one. Luncheon prepared by an excellent French cook. In the afternoon a walk and talk with intelligent friends. Tea with crumpets and the most graceful of female society. A frugal but exquisite supper. Three hours' meditation about the Absolute, and then bed, not unaccompanied.... It sounded charming, But somehow it wouldn't do. To the liver of this perfect Life of Reason, the secret, the mystery and the beauty, though they might be handled and examined, refused to give up their significance.... There could be no compromise.[12]

So he leaves Malaspina, hires a room in a shepherd's cottage in the Apuan ranges and decides to follow the path of the mystics, the path of meditation to get at the mystery and the beauty of life.

But, for Chelifer, it's cowardice to run away. "One has no right to ignore what for ninety-nine out of every hundred human beings is reality—even though it mayn't actually be the real thing". He says:

We are at the heart, here, of our human universe. Come, then, let us frankly admit that we are citizens of this mean city, make the worst of it resolutely and not try to escape.

To escape, whether in space or in time, you must run a great deal further now than there was any need to do a hundred years ago when Shelley boated on the Tyrrhenian and conjured up millennial visions....

An escape in space, even if one contrives successfully to make

12 *Those Barren Leaves*, pp. 226-27.

one, is no real escape at all. A man may live in Tibet or among the Andes; but he cannot therefore deny that London and Paris actually exist, he cannot forget that there are such places as New York and Berlin. . . .

An escape in time is no more satisfactory. You live in the radiant future, live for the future. You console yourself for the spectacle of things as they are by the thought of what they will be. . . . But a little reflection suffices to show how absurd these forward lookings, these labours for the sake of what is to be, really are. For, to begin with, we have no reason to suppose that there is going to be a future at all, at any rate for human beings. In the second place we do not know whether the ideal of happiness towards which we are striving may not turn out either to be totally unrealizable or, if realizable, utterly repellent to humanity. Do people want to be happy? If there were a real prospect of achieving a permanent and unvarying happiness, wouldn't they shrink in horror from the boring consummation? And finally, the contemplation of the future, the busy working for it, does not prevent the present from existing. It merely partially blinds us to the present.

The same objections apply with equal force to the escapes which do not launch out into space or time, but into Platonic eternity, into the ideal. An escape into mere fancy does not prevent facts from going on; it is disregarding of the facts.

Finally there are those people, more courageous than the escapers, who actually plunge into the real contemporary life around them, and are consoled by finding in the midst of its squalor, its repulsiveness and stupidity, evidences of a widespread kindliness, of charity, pity and the like. True, these qualities exist and the spectacle of them is decidedly cheering; in spite of civilization, men have not fallen below the brutes.[13]

Thus, Cardan, Calamy and Chelifer arrive at three entirely different points of view. All the three are highly intelligent individuals who have had a many-sided experience of life. Whether these three points of view represent three of, what Cardan calls, the eighty-four thousand paths to salvation, or only one of them is the true one, or the truth lies somewhere in between these three points of view as a sort of a circumcentre, is yet to be seen

13 Ibid., pp. 85-86.

as Huxley continues the quest. The novel ends with a trialogue, and Calamy has the final say. According to him, both in the physical and the moral world, the unknowable reality can be represented as the four-dimensional continuum. The axes of reference, in the moral world, vary from individual to individual depending on their mental make-up. But the axes chosen by the best observers, like Gautama, Jesus, Lao-tze for example, are startlingly like one another, and Calamy decides to trace the same axes, and pursue truth. Cardan leaves for Monte Carlo, Chelifer to Fetter Lane. Calamy, left alone under those barren leaves of the winter trees, looks up at the mountain peak gilded by the setting sun, and feels somehow reassured of the enlightenment to come.

The novel is a masterpiece in theme and technique. The various strands are picked up and superbly woven into delightfully intricate patterns. Denis's belief that woman is the broad highway to divinity is given the final go-by. Gumbril's hope that happiness consists in being the boss in life is discarded. Time and death mock at all bossism. Calamy yearns for enlightenment, and veers to the view that reality is behind the world of appearances, and unless one transcends all binding attachments, all cravings and desires, every type of enslavement, one cannot get at Reality. From *Crome Yellow* to *Those Barren Leaves,* the journey is traced from pagan worldliness to mysticism.

V

Point Counter Point (1928), the next novel, is a brilliant piece. Musical in conception and composition, with its notes and counternotes, the whole novel is like a mad orchestra with a central theme round which individual characters seem to play twisted shades of variations.

Crome Yellow, Antic Hay and *Those Barren Leaves,* in their own way, touch upon the various aspects of life, but their general trend seems to be towards self-assertion as a means to patch up self-division. *Point Counter Point* brings in a true sense of seriousness, and presents a massive picture with "parallel contrapuntal plots" modulating from "the aesthetic to the physico-chemical aspect of things, from the religious to the physiological or financial". Even D. H. Lawrence who confesses that he does not like Huxley's books, admits to the latter: "I do think that art has to reveal the palpitating moment or the state of man as it is. And I think you do that, terribly".[14]

Instinct or intellect, the Huxleyan hero seems to ponder. Lawrence-Rampion or Huxley-Quarles?

The title *Point Counter Point* signifies not merely the antipodal patterns of thought and action of individuals running at cross-purposes, but also the discords and the harmonies exciting the inner rhythm of personal existence. In *Do What You Will,* Huxley states: "My music, like that of every other living and conscious being, is a counterpoint, not a single melody, but a succession of harmonies and discords".[15] Strangely enough, the main character Philip Quarles is more a detached listener and spectator than a participant, while the orchestra swings round Mark Rampion. Philip, it is said, is Huxley's auto-biographical sketch, a self-portrait, whereas Mark and Mary Rampion take after D. H. Lawrence and his wife Frieda.

Philip is an extension of Calamy, and he takes up the cue where the latter has left. He is an introvert, a detached observer, undemonstrative and reticent by temperament. "All his life long he had walked in a solitude, in a private void, into which nobody, not his mother, not his friends, not his lovers had ever been permitted to enter". Mary Thriplow felt that Calamy, even when in her embrace, escaped her, he simply wasn't there. Philip's wife Elinor too feels almost the same way, that even when he held her pressed close to him "it was by wireless, across an Atlantic that he communicated with her". Calamy seeks refuge in the mountains away from the tumult of civilization to grasp the mysteries of life through contemplation. Philip has gone a step further. He has read books on *yoga,* practised breathing exercises, tried to persuade himself about the illusionistic nature of the physical universe. He has even gone to India and travelled about for ten months, a seeker after truth. Disappointed he returns home to London.

Calamy's running away from civilization is a precipitate renunciation by an uninitiated novice, and it fails. And so, with

14 Lawrence's letter to Huxley, dated 28th October, 1928.
15 *Do What You Will,* p. 234.

Philip, is shown a come-back to intellectual scepticism.

The novel begins in a dramatic manner, the first seven chapters serving as a sort of a conducted tour through a cubistic revel. The first chapter presents Walter Bidlake, twenty-four years old, a journalist, getting ready to go to a party, and Marjorie Carling begging him not to go. Marjorie, refined but stupid, coldly virtuous, was married to Carling, a drunken pervert and a brute. Pity for Marjorie has made young Walter a knight-errant. He persuades her to leave Carling and live with him. They have been living together for two years, but Carling has refused to divorce her. She is with child. Walter finds her now ugly, tired and boring. He has realized his mistake too late. He is infatuated with Lucy Tantamount, feels ashamed of himself, feels he is being a brute without at least the excuse of whisky that Carling has had. But flying away from conscience, drawn towards desire, he leaves for the party to meet Lucy.

The next four chapters present a kaleidoscopic scene with a crowd of characters paraded in the Tantamount House of Lord Edward Tantamount, an eminent biologist. Lady Edward, Lucy's mother, arranged the party, a musical evening. And there assemble a whole galaxy of individuals strangely crippled in mind and distorted in vision, comparable to the asymmetrical tadpoles in Lord Edward's laboratory. The sixth chapter introduces Philip and Elinor in India, the seventh takes the reader back to the Tantamount House and shows Lucy and Walter sneaking out of the party. And in the eighth chapter, Mark Rampion with Mary on his arm storms in and blows the tune; the theme takes on a new look, and the rhythm a new pattern.

The Rampions, Mark and Mary, are a delightful combination. They are made for each other, both high-strung and emotionally individualistic in a sort of a 'noble savagery'. Rampion says:

> Man's a creature on a tight-rope, walking delicately, equilibrated, with mind and consciousness and spirit at one end of the balancing pole, and body and instincts and all that's unconscious and earthy and mysterious at the other. Balanced. Which is damnably difficult. And the only absolute he can ever really know is the absolute of perfect balance.[16]

---

[16] *Point Counter Point*, p. 560.

The modern man, according to him, suffers from Jesus's, Newton's and Henry Ford's disease, religion, science and industrialization having stunted three-fourths of man's personality: "Christians and moralists and cultured aesthetes, and bright young scientists and Smilesian businessmen—all the poor little human frogs trying to blow themselves up into bulls of pure spirituality, pure idealism, pure efficiency, pure conscious intelligence, and just going pop, ceasing to be anything but the fragments of a little frog—decaying fragments at that". To discover truth, one must look for it with the whole being, not with a specialized part of it. To live completely, one must live fully, on all the facets of one's personality, including and harmonizing everything—reason, feeling, instinct, the life of the body. Religion has made us barbarians of the soul, and asceticism, he says, is but the fornicator's hatred of life in a new form. Politics, according to him, is only a silly fight "to decide whether we shall go to hell by communist express train or capitalist racing motorcar, by individualist bus or collectivist tram running on the rails of state control", the destination being the same in every case. Pure intellectualism leads us only to non-human truth. The relevant human truth is something we discover by living, living completely, with the whole man. The flesh, instinct and intuition are a much safer guide than the pure abstracted intellect, and he asserts that "if you treat your body in the way nature meant you to, as an equal, you attain to states of consciousness unknown to the vivisecting ascetics". Love, the natural contact and flow, the release from mental self-consciousness, the abandonment to instinct, leads us to a richer life and a true heaven. That phrase, he says, in the Christian marriage service, "with my body I thee worship", characterizes the genuine phallism which denotes the impassioned and religious quality of the old way of life as distinguished from the unimpassioned modern 'civilized' promiscuity.

But this is a philosophy comprehensible and practicable to a Mark and a Mary, but dangerous and even fatal to ordinary human beings. Rampion's abandonment to instincts is within the "bounds of accomplished matrimony in the company of an amiable spouse". He detests promiscuity. "That woman is worse. She gives me the creeps", he says of Lucy. On Shelley, he remarks: "think of his treatment of women—shocking, really shocking". With all his talk of noble passion, love and worship with the body, Rampion remains within the orbits of culture and tradition, and is neither immoral like Byron, nor amoral like Shelley, though his language sounds similar to theirs. Both the Rampions are extraordinarily sensitive individuals, passionate and by temperament puritanical though not in the Christian sense. Mark was brought up by a sternly religious mother, Mary is Nature's unspoilt child. To use Mark's own words, living comes to her easily. She lives by instinct, she knows what to do quite naturally, like an insect when it comes out of the pupa. Like the animals in Whitman's lines, as if untainted by the original sin, they "do not sweat and whine about their condition, do not lie awake in the dark and weep for their sins". To be a perfect animal and a perfect human is their ideal, and they live up to it. Life, luck, fate, fortune, chance, accident, all seem to have conspired to treat them with exceptional kindness. They are made for each other, and are brought together. Together they face life and the world, and together they consummate the marriage of heaven and hell, of mind and instincts, of reason and feeling, of conscience and desire, of even proletarianism and aristocracy. Theirs is a rare unity, Mark having brought proletary zeal, virility and vigour, Mary contributing aristocratic confidence and courage. Together they emerge as an Olympian dyad. What they feel, do or speak is beyond the pale, physical and spiritual, of ordinary mortals.

It has been said in the previous section that Huxley poses a trilemma on life through Cardan, Calamy and Chelifer who, in their diverse attitudes, stand as if in a triangle, while the truth about life might be said to be somewhere within as a sort of a circumcentre. Does Huxley present Rampion as that circumcentre? Rampion's philosophy is related to each of theirs but at the same time different.

Cardan believes life is a reality but a farce, and death an unpleasant but inevitable evil that puts a stop to everything. Rampion believes that life is not a farce but a solid reality, a human truth that should be lived and experienced fully. What man is concerned with is the relative little good and evil of individual casuistry, and everything else, god and the devil, death and eternity are all irrelevant non-human facts. Chelifer accepts life because ninety-nine out of every hundred human beings consider it real. "Come, then, let us frankly admit", he says, "that we are citizens of this mean city, make the worst of it resolutely and not try to escape".

Chelifer judges the world by his own intellectual, moral and aesthetic standards, and Rampion would perhaps call him an intellectual-aesthetic pervert. Rampion accepts life not because of majority or minority views but because he is born into it. He loves to live and experience it to the full with all the facets of his being. Metaphysical or metempiric conceits, sentiments and standards are just irrelevant non-human facts to him. Calamy accepts the illusionistic nature of the physical universe, and believes that reality is behind the world of appearances. Rampion would perhaps call Calamy a morality-philosophy pervert. Calamy thinks that truth can be realized only by freeing oneself from every type of enslavement, from all appetites and hungers of the body and mind. Rampion says that truth can be realized not by renunciation and resignation but through positive participation with the body and mind, with reason and instincts and intuitions.

Rampion has distilled his philosophy from a strange mixture of hedonism, realism and mysticism with a little of psychology and physiology thrown in. Huxley, at this stage, appears to have been almost enamoured of Rampion's doctrines, and it is Huxley's own voice we hear when Philip says of Rampion: "the chief difference between us, alas, is that his opinions are lived and mine, in the main, only thought". The Rampions alone can live up to their philosophy. Others are apt to misunderstand it, misinterpret it, and even use it as a convenient cloak for promiscuity. Spandrell, himself a degenerate pervert, calls it the gospel of animalism. The Rampions alone can live up to their philosophy, and the novel presents a host of other characters out on the rampage, playing diabolic variations on the Rampion theme.

Lady Hilda Edward is a charming and noble woman, fifty-five years old, with a delightful sense of humour and love of practical jokes. A Canadian who has married a British peer, aristocracy is, to her, a joke, but a joke worth living for. She has been married now for thirty years. Lord Edward is an eminent biologist with a giant intellect, but emotionally a fossil-child. A few years after her marriage, Hilda met John Bidlake, Elinor and Walter's father, a handsome satyr and a renowned painter. John Bidlake revealed to her new realms of pleasure, the potentialities of the human body. "It was a love without pretensions, but warm, natural, and, being natural, good so far as it went—a decent, good-humoured, happy sensuality. To Hilda, who has never known anything but a fossil-child's reticent apology for love, it was a revelation. Things which had been dead in her came alive. She discovered herself, rapturously. But not too rapturously. She never lost her head. If she had lost her head, she might have lost Tantamount House and the Tantamount millions and the Tantamount title as well. She had no intention of losing these things. So, she kept her head, coolly and deliberately; kept it high and secure above the tumultuous raptures, like a rock above the waves".

Hilda achieves the compromise between conscience and desire. Untroubled by religious or moral scruples, untainted in her outlook and feelings, living in contented domesticity, fond of Lord Edward and her daughter Lucy in her own way, she lives a sane and happy life. She and Bidlake had been good lovers for years, then their affair slowly faded away, they are now good friends— she fifty-five and he seventy-two—amusing themselves at the world's expense. She rope-walks with grace keeping perfect balance, with a lover for pleasure, a husband for sustenance, and genuinely fond of both. But will Rampion approve of the balancing pole? Can it be a safe tread to the end except by mere fluke?[17]

Lucy, her daughter, is an uninhibited sensualist, free from all scruples, ethical, religious, social, consciencious. She is twenty-nine, a leprechaun her mother calls her. Two years earlier, conveniently for her and fortunately for himself, her husband Reggie Tantamount—she had married her second cousin—died. She has had a series of lovers—Bentley and Jim Conklin, Reggie Tantamount and Maurice Spandrell and Tom Tivet and Poniatovsky and that young Frenchman who wrote plays, and various others; and now Walter and Illidge, and then a Tuscan in Paris. "For an intelligent young man, Maurice, you talk a lot of drivel", she once told Spandrell: "do you genuinely believe that some things are right and some wrong?" she asked him.

Walter, four years her junior, is desperately in love with her. But Lucy is ruthless. She is not for love, she is for fun. She wants to be herself, free, free to have him or drop him. She wants to enjoy herself consciously to the last limit, without surrendering herself, remaining free, emotionally, financially, legally. Walter's passion of tenderness moves her deeply, almost puts her to shame. But letting herself go only a little way towards surrender, suddenly

17 Huxley's *The Genius and the Goddess* gives a continuation of the Hilda-theme.

she used to draw back with her conscious will, and Walter "would be woken from his dream of love into what Lucy called 'fun', into the cold daylight of sharply conscious, laughingly deliberate sensuality". Forced by Walter either to admit or deny her love for him, she sums up her philosophy thus:

> Living modernly's living quickly. You can't cart a waggon-load of ideals and romanticisms about with you these days. When you travel by aeroplane, you must leave your heavy baggage behind. The good, old-fashioned soul was all right when people lived slowly. But it's too ponderous nowadays. There's no room for it in the aeroplane.
> "Not even for a heart?" asked Walter; "I don't so much care about the soul". . . .
> Lucy shook her head. "Perhaps it's a pity", she admitted. "But you can't get something for nothing. If you like speed, if you want to cover the ground, you can't have luggage. The thing is to know what you want and to be ready to pay for it. I know exactly what I want; so I sacrifice the luggage. If you choose to travel in a furniture van, you may. But don't expect me to come along with you, my sweet Walter. And don't expect me to take your grand piano in my two-seater mono-plane".[18]

Lucy too solves the problem of happiness in her own way. She has wealth and youth. Retaining her freedom, tasting the pleasures of the body with gay abandon, she too walks gracefully on the tight-rope. But is her balancing pole the right one? In her old age, can she hope to be serene like her mother, her sensuality trans-forming with age into tender sentiment, and her funsters becom-ing loyal friends? Or will she grow into a Mrs. Aldwinkle, into a lonely dowager whimpering over desertion and death? Or will she commit suicide in good time, as Spandrell has suggested to her? After all even a monoplane will have to land somewhere, and then will be felt the weight of the lumber and the luggage collected through a lifetime. Rumblings of a disquieting future she feels within herself, but she drowns them in the whirl of a fast life. Worship with the body can take as many grotesque forms as any other worship. Lucy's desire for fun and male company

[18] *Point Counter Point*, pp. 282-83.

is just to escape the terrors of an inner loneliness and boredom. But when the appetites fade away with age, when decay sets in and death draws nearer, then will one realize the terrors of a vacancy within, and the need for a spiritual prop that sustains and consoles.

John Bidlake is a Gargantuan, a brilliant painter, "handsome, huge, exuberant, careless; a great laugher, a great worker, a great eater, drinker and taker of virginities". Nobody can paint a nude, he says, "who hasn't learnt the human body by heart with his hands, and his lips and his own body". A healthy sensualist, he made his love "straightforwardly, naturally with the good animal gusto of a child of nature". Rampion disapproves of poetry, and calls Shelley "a fairy slug with the sexual appetites of a schoolboy". John Bidlake says: "don't expect me to talk about the stars and madonna lilies and the cosmos. They're not my line. I don't believe in them. I believe in. . . ." Body and mind, amour and art gave all the joy of life to John Bidlake. He too has worshipped with his body. But his dash and dare-devilry have all been founded on a deliberate, life-long ignorance, and when it is no longer possible to ignore, he is seventy-two years old now, he is caught in the grip of the sacred terror of death, and wails over what he calls god's practical jokes. Even if life happens to be a long sweet tale of good fortune with all the comforts recommended by Mercaptan, still there is one inescapable calamity which Cardan describes as "decay, decrepitude and death". John Bidlake faces it with "a slight obstruction at the pylorus". "Deplorable", writes Philip in his diary, "to see an Olympian reduced by a little tumour in the stomach to a state of sub-humanness". Gargantuan abandonment to instinct, and healthy worship with the body may be for youth but not for old age. Rampion's philosophy is not soulfully convincing to the old, and Huxley has said the same about Lawrence's: "Lawrence's, I should say, was not a very good philosophy for old age or failing powers".[19]

Hilda, Lucy and John are terrific go-aheaders with a lust for life, but though they are hale and healthy they are not whole. Hilda's happiness is built on a lie, Lucy's on a deliberate suppression of a cautioning inner voice. John is like the proverbial cat closing his eyes and lapping up the milk when the going is good.

[19] Huxley's Introduction to *Letters of D. H. Lawrence*.

They rope-walk in grace but on precarious supports. Of the three, Hilda alone is happy and sober, while Lucy has been having her anxious moments, and John has already started to totter.

Walter's is a sad case. He takes after his mother, religious, cultured, sentimental and sensitive. He is a romantic idealist, and he bungles in the face of reality. Mistaking pity for love, he has weaned Marjorie from her husband, and after living with her for two years, he falls in love with Lucy. Conscience prods him to be loyal to one, desire pulls him to the other. He is unable to put Lucy away from his thoughts. Marjorie is unable to go back to a husband whom she herself has deserted, and unable to sensibly retain a lover whom she has hastily followed. Under the tutelage of Mrs. Quarles, she ultimately finds solace in god and religion.

Lucy, at last, yields to Walter. In her arms, "filled with a drowsy tenderness", he "floats in warm serenity between being and annihilation". She gives him pleasure not love. He dreams that she is an angel, but finds she is a demon. He hates her, but is violently drawn towards her. The conflict goes on, between conscience and desire, between sentiments and appetites. He wriggles in agony unable to patch up a cloven heart. Finally, he gets nothing of love either from Marjorie or from Lucy. The one escapes into religion, the other into the arms of a sun-tanned Italian.

Hilda, Lucy and John have openly flouted the accepted moral codes. They are frank sensualists, decent and charitable. But Philip's father Sydney Quarles, and the journalist Burlap, are conscious hypocrites exemplifying putrefaction of sensuality. Sydney is a stupid old fumbler with pretensions to intellectual eminence. But behind this intellectual facade is a spiritual vacuum and filthy sensuality. In his fifties, he has been having escapades with the kitchen-maid and the game-keeper's daughter. On the pretext of going to the British Museum, he runs an affair with a typist girl in London, and gets her with child. One morning she invades the sanctity of his home in all her vulgarity, and exposes his meanness. Sydney, completely broken, confines himself to his own room, deliriously, perhaps hypocritically too, talking of impending death.

Burlap is forty, a spiritual journalist, editor of the Literary World. Rampion calls him a god-snob. Professing to be an ardent worshipper of St. Francis, he practises a diabolic technique for seducing innocent women. Pretending to be disconsolate on his wife's death, he entices her childhood friend Miss Cobbett, and gives her a job in his editorial office hoping to get into her bed in the end. But Miss Cobbett is genuinely virtuous, and so, thwarted in his attempts, he turns to another woman. Beatrice is thirty-five, a virgin terrified of male touch because of the advances of a brute uncle in her girlhood. She is drawn to Burlap by his talk of god and of the spirit. Burlap gains her confidence by slow stages with devilish patience and cunning, breaks down her defences, and finally draws her into his bed. Miss Cobbett turns on the gas and commits suicide. Beatrice is lured, an innocent but foolish woman, and drawn into greater and greater depravity. One cannot help feeling that she too may have to turn on the gas some day.

The Rampion theme is thus distorted into a carnal sport by individuals asynartetic by temperament, with a double-rhythm beating inside them. They all seem to play at see-saw with the hedonists Hilda, Lucy and John at one end, and the hypocrites Burlap and Sydney at the other, with Walter rolling this way and that along the plank as the ends move up and down. Two curiously pervert specimens—Molly and Mrs. Betterton—watch this sport with participant pleasure. They are both intelligent women, but also queer hypocrites and sadistic flirts, using the shapeliness of their breasts to compel men to admire their minds. Their game has always been to charm without being charmed, to draw around them a coterie of male admirers without the least intention of gratifying the desires they themselves have provoked. Talk was all that they had ever conceded. Even Philip falls a prey to Molly, and when she shrinks from his kiss in pained astonishment, he tells her in sheer disgust that if she is really civilized, as she pretends to be, she must make herself less desirable.

Hilda, Lucy, John and Walter, Sydney, Burlap, Molly and Mrs. Betterton, all play their variations and parodies of the Rampion theme. But a genuine commentary on that comes from Elinor. Elinor combines in herself Philip's intellectual scepticism, her mother's instinctive moral goodness, and her father's worldly wisdom, daring and love of pleasure. She is a refined and cultured woman. Philip's mother Rachel Quarles admirably sums up her character when she says that women like Marjorie think and feel rightly but invariably act wrongly, whereas Elinor thinks wrongly but acts in a manner entirely blameless.

Elinor is deeply in love with Philip, but loving Philip is like loving a book-case. He is a detached intellectual, shut up in a private void, in a solitary world of ideas. Once Elinor told him: "you're like a monkey on the superman side of humanity. Almost human, like those poor chimpanzees. The only difference is that they are trying to think up with their feelings and instincts, and you are trying to feel down with your intellect. Almost human. Trembling on the verge, my poor Phil". "A kind of Pyrrhonian indifference, tempered by a consistent gentleness and kindness, as well as by the more violent intermittences of physical passion— this was the state of being which nature and second nature had made normal for him". Elinor knows all this but still she is unhappy. She wants love, a soulful communion of ideas, feelings and emotions, but Philip gives her brilliant generalizations.

Everard Webley is in love with her. Leader of a fascist group, he is a dynamic figure, impetuous and domineering. He thrills her and she is drawn to him. But strangely enough, as her mind longs for him and his love, her body is repelled by his touch. "The spirit was a libertine but the flesh and its affections were chaste". Was Rampion, after all, right? Are the natural instincts a much safer guide than the conscious mind? But Elinor is exasperated with Philip. She has begged for love but he has given her a remote personal benevolence. Helping to draw him out of his shell, she has brought him and Molly together acting as a sort of a dragoman. But as if life has played a practical joke, when Philip, jilted by Molly, suddenly realizes, like Shearwater, his own callousness to Elinor and rushes home, she, in disgust, has withdrawn herself into a shell of angry reticence, and Philip slumps down in Shearwaterish helplessness.

Elinor fixes up an appointment to elope with Everard, but at the nick of the moment receives a message from her mother about little Phil's illness, and she rushes to Gattenden to witness death playing a cat-and-mouse game with the child. It has been a terrifying experience to her. Her scepticism melting away into superstition, she feels that Providence has saved her from the elopement, and that the little child's illness is a punishment for her sins. Neither her rational mind, nor her intuitive understanding consoles her in her sorrow. She was at the bed-side day and night. "She would have liked, if it had been humanly possible, never to eat or sleep at all. With Everard dead and the child in torture before her eyes, eating and sleeping seemed almost cynical". "But the very possession of a body is a cynical comment on the soul and all its ways. It is a piece of cynicism, however, which the soul must accept, whether it likes it or not".

Huxley and Elinor set us thinking. Has the body to be admired for shrinking from Everard's kiss, or has it to be condemned for insisting on breakfast, lunch and dinner even in the presence of death? Is the soul a fastidious excrement of the living body, as Cardan supposes it to be, or is the body a cynical coverlet for the soul? Can the soul and the body, the dream and the desire, the idea and the reality be ever fused into a harmony? What is it that can sustain one in the face of adversity, senility, bereavement and death? The Rampions have no worries. They are rare individuals, intellectuals both, who, while leading the life of the spirit, live the obvious with gusto. But the ordinary mortals need a spiritual prop to cling to. Some individuals like Lord Edward and his brother the marquis, instead of facing the music of life, seek solace in a life of the pure intellect. They are escapists—Lord Edward experimenting on asymmetric tadpoles, and his brother, the fifth marquis of Gattenden, a cripple confined to the bath-chair, evolving fatuous mathematical proofs for the existence of god. Philip, looking at the two brothers in deep conversation, remarks to Elinor:

Poor old creatures: What else have they got to talk about? Too old to want to talk about love—too old and much too good. Too rich to talk about money. Too highbrow to talk about people and too hermit-like to know any people to talk about. Too shy to talk about themselves, too blankly inexperienced to talk about life or even literature. What is there left for the poor old wretches to talk about? Nothing—only God.[20]

These are people whom Chelifer would call conscious cowards running away from life, and wealth enables them to indulge in the safe and easy luxury until some shocking reality of life pulls them out unceremoniously.

If Lord Edward and his brother are escapists, Illidge and Spandrell are both violent rebels and they fall out of the musical

20 *Point Counter Point*, p. 345.

theme like two broken fiddles. Both were basically sensitive and good individuals whom circumstances of life turned sour and rebellious. In a way, it can be said, it is filial love that has worked on them in such strangely different ways.

Illidge is Lord Edward's assistant in biological researches. In him can be seen the stultifying effects of poverty. Memories of an indigent boyhood, "the washing days and the pink crinkled skin of his mother's water-sodden hands" have turned him into a militant communist with a rabid hatred for the rich. A scientific materialist, he believes that God and religion, pure science and platonic love are all stupid idle products of wealth and leisure. He is for a revolution, and talks and talks of murder. His hatred is just pure envy and malice born of his own poverty and inferiority complex. It is the malicious sour-grapism of the have-not. By accident he had obtained a scholarship which enabled him to become a research scientist and fall amidst aristocracy. He hates bourgeois morality, and speaks of a communist organized society. But secretly he sends money to his mother, pays for his younger brother's education, and gives his sister sixty pounds when she has married, and blushes when Spandrell twits him about all these sentimentalities. Political ideologies cannot destroy natural affections. With all his proletarian hatred, inwardly he yearns to be an aristocrat, and sitting in Philip's club one day he wonders: "how extraordinary it was, how almost infinitely improbable that he should be sitting there, drinking claret, with the Prepetual Secretary of the British Academy two tables away and the second oldest judge of the High Court behind him". He goes to bed with Lucy, not for love, not for fun, not even for pleasure, but to proclaim proletarian victory over aristocracy, and she receives him fascinated with his bile and envy. Both asymmetric tadpoles, the one proletarian, the other aristocratic! Even his talk of political murder is just hollow ferocity, and when faced with Everard's corpse, he shrinks in terror, forgets his ideology, his hatred for the British Free-men, even the personal injury he has received at their hands, and begs Spandrell to let him go. Illidge's ideology only serves to feed his bile, and he bloats and bloats with malice till pop he goes like the frog in the fable. He is a consummate pervert, his whole substance twisted out of shape by malice.

Spandrell's is a tragic case similar to that of Beaudelaire. Like the latter, he too loved his mother deeply. At a critical moment

in his adolescence, he was fifteen then, his father suddenly died.
He was at a boarding-school. Unable to bear the poverty and
loneliness, his mother married a second time. Her marriage shocked Spandrell terribly, a shock from which, like Beaudelaire, he
never recovered. Love for his mother turned into hatred, vengeful
hatred and contempt for the whole womankind. He took a perverse pleasure in inflicting, like Coleman, the humiliation of crude
sensuality on the creatures he had enticed. "Inward personal revolution and consequent outward and social revolution", Rampion
sums up his case. Brandy and hired love give no lasting happiness,
and Spandrell sinks lower and lower in boredom and apathy, at
times feeling an inward putrefaction, a numbing of the soul. But
he could not and would not make the effort to save himself.

Disgusted with this world, disgusted with himself, he longs
for the eternal absolutes, for God and heaven. "He's like a silly
schoolboy", Rampion tells Mary; "can't you see that? He's a
permanent adolescent. Bothering his head about all the things that
preoccupy adolescents. Not being able to live, because he's too
busy thinking about death and God and truth and mysticism and
all the rest of it; too busy thinking about sins and trying to commit
them and being disappointed because he's not succeeding. It's
deplorable. The man's a sort of Peter Pan—much worse even
than Barrie's disgusting little abortion, because he's got stuck at
a sillier age. He's Peter Pan a la Dostoevsky-cum-de Musset-cum-
the-Nineties-cum-Bunyan-cum-Byron and the Marquis de Sade.
Really deplorable. The more so as he's potentially a very decent
human being".[21] Refined and sensitive by nature, with a genuine
love for music, he believes in a god and a heaven, in eternal
verities, in absolute good and evil. But unable to extricate himself
from the diabolic routine of a promiscuous life, he convinces himself that all things that happen are "a providential conspiracy".
He feels that everything that happens "is intrinsically like the
man it happens to".

He longs to know God, to realize him "as a felt experienced
quality of personal actions". He once tells Philip that he has
turned to God with love and devotion, but God has not come out
of his lair. God is a practical joker, and He must be drawn out
by violence. "One way of knowing god is to deny him", he tells
Lucy. One way of realizing absolute good is indulging in absolute

21 *Point Counter Point*, pp. 183-84.

evil! So he transgresses all the Ten Commandments. But God has not responded.

To accept Illidge's challenge, to fulfil the promise given to him, to invite him to a man-shooting party, to puncture the overbearing ego of Everard himself, to reach the finale in sin, and to draw God out of his lair by violence, he murders Everard Webley. Everard the Colossus lies huddled on the floor, Illidge the ferocious communist shrinks like a worm in terror. The strength of the British Freemen doubled overnight, Everard dead appears more powerful than Everard living, but Spandrell remains unchanged, dust-bin to dust-bin, dung to dung. He has not succeeded "in compelling God to pass from outsideness to insideness". He is sure that God exists. He wants a confirmation from Rampion, and he also wants to prove his manliness, and receive a final self-retribution for his actions. He writes an anonymous letter to the British Freemen to come armed at 5 p.m., to 37 Catskill Street one evening to meet the murderer of Everard. It is his own address. He arranges with the Rampions to be present at his lodging at that time to listen to Beethoven's music. The Rampions come. The records are played. Rampion is very deeply moved. Visibly disturbed, he exclaims: "it *is* heaven, it *is* the life of the soul. It's the most perfect spiritual abstraction from reality I've ever known. But why should he have wanted to make that abstraction? Why couldn't he be content to be a man and not an abstract soul? Why, why?" The disc is reversed, and the music begins again. Spandrell listens in ecstasy convinced of the existence of God and heaven. Five p.m., there is a knock at the door. "There they are," says Spandrell, and without answering Mary's 'who?' he walks out of the room. A deafening explosion, a shout, another, another. The Rampions rush out and find Spandrell on the floor, for once without a sardonic grin on his face. Three British Freemen stand there with pistols in their hands; "he fired first", they say.

Convinced of a happier life beyond, Spandrell leaves this world, and he leaves it with a bang not with a whimper. The novel comes to a close. The music fades away. There's only the scratching of the needle on the disc—the scratching of the needle—Burlap and Beatrice playing like little children in the bath-tub.

Spandrell departs in open defiance like a surrealistic nihilist. Rampion, visibly rattled, escapes from this Beethoven's "cancer of the soul". Of the various characters in the novel, only

Mrs. Quarles and Mrs. Bidlake display serenity and composure. Finding solace in God and religion, they have developed a technique of living and a courtesy of heart that sympathizes with and consoles everyone in distress. People might go wrong but theirs is not the business to judge, and so, without accusations, recriminations or feelings of revenge, with natural piety, affection and pity, they look after their erring husbands and children. They are in the same line as Mrs. Chelifer, a proof, as Chelifer remarks, that mankind has not completely fallen below the level of brutes, and make one wonder whether God is, after all, the ultimate source of comfort. Mrs. Quarles once tells Marjorie: "everybody strains after happiness, and the result is nobody's happy. It's because they're on the wrong road. . . . For it's not by pursuing happiness that you find it; it's by pursuing salvation. . . . Happiness is like coke—something you get as a by-product in the process of making something else".

By-product of what? That's the problem for Philip. He remains the detached observer and thinker and commentator throughout in spite of his involvements in the action. He lives in his secret tower of ideas, away from the tumult, and he is unaware even of the crisis in his own life, and the storm that has raged in Elinor's heart. His problem is to end the schism at the heart of our being, and find the basis for integral living. Rampion he has admired but could not entirely accept and appreciate. "The chief difference between us, alas", he says, "is that his opinions are lived and mine, in the main, only thought. Like him, I mistrust intellectualism, but intellectually, I disbelieve in the adequacy of any scientific or moral principle, but on scientific, philosophical and abstract-moral grounds. The problem for me is to transform a detached intellectual scepticism into a way of harmonious all-round living".[22]

From romantic sentimentalism to paganism, then to mysticism, from mysticism to intellectual scepticism, the pilgrim moves, and each proving to be a blind alley, he turns back to continue the quest.

This novel is undoubtedly the best of Huxley's. Vast in its range, intense in conception, and original in technique, the novel presents a human fugue in all its bewildering medley of notes. Rampion preaches a dangerous monism sanctifying the body and

<hr />

[22] *Point Counter Point,* 440.

its desires, refusing to accept anything else. He once tells Spandrell:

God's not apart, not above, not outside. At any rate, no relevant, humanly important aspect of God's above and outside. Neither is God inside, in the sense that Protestants use the phrase—safely stowed away in the imagination, in the feelings and intellect, in the soul. He's there, of course among other places. But he's also inside in the sense that a lump of bread's inside when you've eaten it. He's in the very body, in the blood and bowels, in the heart and skin and loins. God's the total result, spiritual and physical, of any thought or action that makes for life, of any vital relation with the world. God's a quality of actions and relations—a felt, experienced quality. At any rate, he's that for *our* purposes, for purposes of living.[23]

Rampion is not interested in the other aspects of God, or in any speculative truth for that matter. On the other hand, Spandrell believes in the existence of certain transcendental absolutes, and desires to "steer his life by those fixed eternal marks". He punctures Rampion's ego with Beethoven's music. Profoundly moved by the melody, Rampion exclaims: "why! why should he have created it?" Rampion, then sounds like an escapist, almost like John Bidlake, turning a blind eye to things spiritual. Beethoven's music and Spandrell's self-offering reduce him to a broken reed, and the musical theme comes to a close, the novel to a finis.

Spandrell is, like Coleman, disgusted with this world and with everything human. But Coleman is a nihilist who, swinishly cynical, exulted in stirring filth to make it more turbidly filthy. Spandrell desires to fly away from this hollow something into an other-worldly 'nothing', into a *nirvana,* if not Buddhistic, at least surrealistic. Philip watches the whole drama, and wonders:

Shall I ever have the strength of mind to break myself of these indolent habits of intellectualism and devote my energies to the more serious task of living integrally? And even if I did try to break these habits, shouldn't I find that heredity was at the bottom of them and that I was congenitally incapable of living wholly and harmoniously?[24]

[23] Ibid., p. 587.
[24] *Point Counter Point,* p. 444.

Huxley himself appears to pose these questions: Are human beings congenitally incapable of living harmoniously? Have they always to grind at the wheel of life, like the eyeless in Gaza, working and suffering like those slaves? Thus, he leads us on to the next novel in the series *Eyeless in Gaza*.

VI

"Huxley had now, at last, avowedly written a novel with a purpose", says Prof. Collins.[25] From Philip's barren intellectualism, Huxley leads us on to Dr. Miller's anthropological approach to happiness. Miller calls his technique "applied scientific religion" and it combines in itself an all-inclusive version of Rampion's love, Philip's intellectualism and Calamy's mysticism. Contrasting this doctrine with, what he calls, the entomological approach to life, that of considering one's fellow-beings as bugs, Miller says:

If you call a man a bug, it means that you propose to treat him as a bug. Whereas if you call him a man, it means that you propose to treat him as a man. My profession is to study men. Which means that I must always call men by their name; always think of them as men; yes, and always treat them as men. Because if you don't treat men as men, they don't behave as men.[26]

Separation and diversity are conditions of our existence. 'Unity' is the pre-requisite for happiness. That is the paradox of life, "born under one law, to another bound". After Calamy's precipitate renunciation and Philip's come-back, the Huxleyan hero seems to be on the look out for a *guru* for guidance. Philip turns to Rampion, is enamoured of him but not convinced by him. Anthony turns to Dr. Miller. It is then a long list of 'gurus' upto the last novel *Island*—Rampion, Dr. Miller, Propter, Bruno Rontini, and finally the super-*guru* Dr. Robert Macphail.

With a daringly original technique, taking the readers through

25 A. S. Collins, *English Literature of the Twentieth Century*, p. 239.
26 *Eyeless in Gaza*, pp. 576-77.

layers of time and layers of consciousness, Huxley presents a set of characters, men and women, blind slaves to their own egos, prejudices and perversions, each caught in his or her own spiritual kennel unable to find a means of escape. "I know what I ought to do, but continue to do what I know I oughtn't to do", laments Anthony Beavis quoting from Ovid. Looking at the hypodermic syringe in her own hand, Mary Amberley stammers: "do you think I *want* to do this? I hate it, absolutely hate it. But I can't help it". Her daughter Helen grieves that perhaps it was her fate "to worship cruelty and meanness, be adored by deficiency". Brian, torn between love and idealism, exclaims: "I wish to G-god, I know what to d-do", and when it has been too late to do anything he drops himself down a three-hundred foot precipice. Mark Staithes, crippled mentally with ego, physically with an amputated leg, wryly remarks: "what can *I* do now? Look on, that's all". Thus they suffer, unable to change themselves, unable to escape from themselves. They are in a living hell—"hell is the incapacity to be other than the creature one finds oneself ordinarily behaving as". Self-knowledge is an essential preliminary to self-change, and self-change should be the progress from fragmentation to unity of being.

The first chapter depicts Anthony Beavis in his Italian home on 30th August 1933, his forty-second birthday, going through, at random, an album of old photographs. That sets the key. It is as if a lunatic, somewhere in the mind, shuffled a pack of snapshots and dealt them out at random. Huxley, in a masterly fashion, shuffles different layers of time, evoking memories, anticipating events, with flash-backs and projections, and draws the life-story of a group of individuals, giving the impression of a continuous stream of individual life flowing into the present, and directed into, what appears to be, pre-destined channels of the future. Perhaps, one feels, Spandrell is quite right when he says that "everything that happens is intrinsically like the man it happens to".

Anthony stands as the central figure of the whole theme, making incursions into the lives of those around him. Anthony, Brian Foxe, Mark Staithes, Hugh Ledwidge have all been friends from school-days. Anthony's mother Maisie and Brian's mother Mrs. Foxe were friends. Mrs. Foxe is a very kind and religious lady. Widowed when Brian was still very young, she has brought him up with overwhelming love and religious fervour. But her influence has had a stunting effect on Brian. She has been, Anthony thinks, "like a vampire sucking the life-blood out of him". Brian grows up into a quiet, virtuous, idealistic, self-sacrificing individual. When at school, he has invited ridicule upon himself by trying to protect Hugh Ledwidge from ragging schoolfellows. When at the university, he withdraws from an election contest to enable Mark Staithes to win as Mark cannot take a defeat with ease. He is passionately in love with Joan. Once he kisses her in an ecstasy, but, all at once, draws back from the embrace, ashamed of himself—"the ordinary happy kind of love isn't morally right". He wants to prove himself worthy of her, but only succeeds in making her feel unworthy of him—a result of, what Rampion would call, non-human, abstract morality and religion divorced from normal and natural human instincts and emotions. Once, Brian, away at Manchester, writes to Anthony to look after Joan then in London. Hearing about her from Anthony, Mary, in puckish mischief, tells him that what Joan needs is a hug and a kiss, and challenges Anthony to prove his manliness by kissing her. Anthony, cornered with ridicule, accepts the challenge. Late one night, on their return from a theatre, he leaves Joan at her home, and when bidding good-night suddenly kisses her. She makes as if to withdraw, but all at once yields to him. Being emotionally discontented, the first real kiss sets her head reeling. She takes his kisses seriously, imagines he is in love with her, and, contrary to his advice, writes to Brian breaking off their engagement. Thus let down by both friend and fiancée, Brian the self-sacrificing idealist sacrifices himself jumping down a precipice. Pre-destination of temperaments and events?

Anthony first met Mary at his mother's funeral. He was then eleven, and she eight years older. A decade later he again meets with her at Oxford. She is twenty-nine, just divorced, and Anthony is charmed by her prettiness, sophistication and reckless nonchalance. She takes him on hand, initiates him into amour, and grooms him for about two years. Then, Brian's suicide drives them apart. Free, unattached, rich and reckless, she leads an extravagantly voluptuous life for fourteen years. By then she is forty-five, and Helen, her daughter, is nineteen, pretty and impetuous like her mother. In a moment of romantic passion, Helen gets herself engaged to a be-spectacled, sheep-faced scholar, Hugh Ledwidge, an amorous dreamer but an awkward and clumsy lover. Mary's latest find was Gerry Watchet, an aristocratic swindler with a sadistic streak. Running an affair with Mary, he seduces Helen, nineteen years old, still innocent and virginal. He carries on with both the mother and daughter, and finally he swindles Mary of her money, gets Helen with child, and runs off to Canada. Mary seeks shelter in morphia, and Helen in a Parisian abortionist's clinic. Non-humanly righteous, Brian seeks peace in suicide, non-humanly licentious, Mary sleeps in opiated stupor. Mrs. Foxe, selfishly possessive under a religious veneer, is dispossessed of her son. Unable to reconcile their romantic longings with the realities of life, both Joan and Helen bungle. Swindled by Jerry, advertised by an incompetent husband in a novel, insulted by Anthony's belated offer of love after everything has crumbled inside her, half-mad, Helen runs to Hugh, and meets with a German communist Ekki. Fascinated by him, she lives with him for a few delightful months in domestic bliss. But, one fine morning, Ekki has been bundled away to Germany and killed by his party-men. Miserable, Helen lives in ascetic mourning, but before a year is out, the same old appetites and cravings return to her. She returns to Anthony and wails: "they ought to have killed me. If you only know how I digust myself! I'm no good. Worse than no good. Just a lump of dirt". Blind slaves to their own passions and perversions, they all suffer alike.

Anthony and Mark Staithes stand in sharp contrast. Anthony is an introvert with a protective armour, living in a world of ideas. He wanted to be free, free from all enslavements, even love. Mark is an egoist and an extrovert. When a boy, he loved to be the school-bully. When Brian withdraws from an election to enable him to win, he takes it as a personal insult, and he too drops out. When his family obtains for him a decent job, he spurns the offer and instead goes to Mexico to work on coffee plantations. He remains an ascetic "for his own sake, that he might feel more separated, more intensely himself, in a better position to look down on humanity". He spurns even gratitude. The good samaritan he plays, but, Swift-like plays it in secret. He loves danger just to show off, and he goes to Mexico along with Anthony to help in an armed rebellion. On the way, while riding a mule uphill, the animal stumbles, he is badly injured in the knee. The wound turns gangrenous, and Dr. Miller, whom they meet by chance, amputates the leg. Mark, even in that pain and agony, receives

sympathy and kindness only with bad grace. A slave to his own
ego, crippled in mind, he is now crippled in body. When Dr. Miller
encourages him to turn a new leaf, he laments: "What can *I* do
now? Look on, that's all. We'd much better all look on. It won't
be for long anyhow. Just a few years; and then:

> Then old age and experience, hand in hand,
> Lead him to death, and make him understand,
> After a search so painful and so long,
> That all his life he had been in the wrong.
> Huddled in dirt the blustering engine lies,
> Who was so proud, so witty and so wise.

he recites.

Dr. Miller tells Anthony:

Really and by nature every man's a unity; but you've artificially
transformed the unity into a trinity. One clever man and two
idiots—that's what you've made yourself. An admirable
manipulator of ideas, linked with a person who, so far as self-
knowledge and feeling are concerned, is just a moron; and the
pair of you associated with a half-witted body. A body that's
hopelessly unaware of all it does and feels, that has no accom-
plishments, that doesn't know how to use itself or anything else.
Two imbeciles and one intellectual. But man is a democracy,
where the majority rules. You've got to do something about that
majority.[27]

Brian, Joan, Mary, Helen and Staithes have all been ruled by
the wrong majorities and they get crushed under the grind-stone
of life.

Anthony remains a disinterested spectator throughout, though
himself a participant. He is presented as a sociologist, a detached
intellectual, afraid of contacts, afraid of every kind of attachment,
even love. Though very fond of Helen, he shrinks from love, and
is prepared for fun but not matrimony. But when he offers his
love to her, too late it is, Helen spurns it with ridicule and chooses
Ekki. In jealousy and disgust, he goes off to Mexico with Mark

[27] *Eyeless in Gaza*, p. 14.

and meets with Dr. Miller. Miller has the courage of his own convictions, and practises what he preaches. Under his tutelage, Anthony transforms himself from a detached intellectual into a non-attached positive pacifist, working for peace, peace that results from unity of the inner individual self, and unity of all being.

Anthony's is an extended portrait of Calamy and Philip. Combining in himself the traits and opinions of both of them, Anthony wonders "how to combine the belief that the world is to a great extent illusory, with the belief that it is none the less essential to improve the illusion. How to be simultaneously dispassionate and not indifferent, serene like an old man and active like a young one?" Miller helps him to realize that awareness of being leads to self-knowledge. Self-knowledge is an essential preliminary to self-change. And self-change, in the right direction, will patch up the schism at the heart of our being, and promote unity.

Separation and diversity are the conditions of our existence; "conditions upon which we possess life and consciousness, know right and wrong and have the power to choose between them, recognize truth, have experience of beauty. But separation is evil. Evil, then, is the condition of life, the condition of being aware, of knowing what is good and beautiful". But peace lies in unity. Unity within ourselves and unity with all being. "Evil is the accentuation of division; good, whatever makes for unity with other lives and other beings". Pride, hatred, anger, lust and greed emphasize this separateness. Lust uses another as a means for one's own pleasure and thus intensified the awareness of separation. "That which is demanded, that which men come finally to demand of themselves, is the realization of union between beings who would be nothing if they were not separate; is the actualization of goodness by creatures who, if they were not evil, would not exist. Impossibility—but none the less demanded". An impossibility worth trying. Love, sympathy and kindness beget similar sentiments, at least some response even from the worst enemy. Hatred and malice breed only violence.

Under Miller's guidance, Anthony begins to preach positive pacifism. It is again a paradox that violence breeds out of opulence, sloth and pacifism out of poverty. But sloth is negative pacifism, the result of an emotional vacuum which a Hitler can any day fill in with violent revolutionism. Anthony wonders: "Have we time to fill the vacuum with positive pacifism? Or, having the time, have we the ability?" When about to go to address a pacifist meeting at Battersea, he receives an anonymous letter threatening him with dire consequences if he does not stop his "dirty pacifist speeches". Caught in two minds, to withdraw or to go ahead, suddenly he laughs aloud, all doubts vanishing in a flash of inner awakening. 'Unity' he whispers:

Frenzy of evil and separation. In peace there is unity. Unity with other lives. Unity with all being. For beneath all being, beneath the countless identical but separate patterns, beneath the attractions and repulsions, lies peace. The same peace as underlies the frenzy of the mind. Dark peace, immeasurably deep. Peace from pride and hatred and anger, peace from craving and aversions, peace from all the separating frenzies. Peace through liberation, for peace is achieved freedom. Freedom and at the same time truth. The truth of unity actually experienced. Peace in the depths, under the storm, far down below the leaping of the waves, the frantically flying spray. Peace in this profound subaqueous night, peace in this silence, this still emptiness where there is no more time, where there are no more words. Nothing but the experience of peace; peace as a dark void beyond all personal life, and yet itself a form of life more intense, for all its diffuseness, for all the absence of aim or desire, richer and of finer quality than ordinary life. Peace beyond peace, focussed at first, brought together, then opening out in a kind of boundless space. Peace at the tip, as it were, of a narrowing cone of concentration and elimination, a cone with its base in the distractions of the heaving surface of life and its point in the underlying darkness. And in the darkness the tip of one cone meets the tip of another; and, from a single, focal point, peace expands and expands towards a base immeasurably distant and so wide that its circle is the ground and source of all life, all being. Cone reversed from the broken and shifting light of the surface; cone reversed and descending to a point of concentrated darkness; thence, in another cone, expanding and expanding through the darkness towards, yes! some other light, steady, untroubled, as utterly calm as the darkness out of which it emerges. Cone reversed into cone upright. Passage from wide stormy light to the still focus of darkness; and thence, beyond the focus, through widening darkness into another light. From storm to calm and on through yet profounder and intenser peace to the final consummation, the ultimate light that is the source and substance of all things! source of the darkness, the void, the submarine night of living calm; source finally of the waves and the frenzy of the spray—forgotten now. For now there is only the darkness expanding and deepening, deepening into light; there is only this final peace, this consciousness of being no more separate, this illumination....[28]

The clock strikes seven. He gets ready to go to the meeting. Whatever may happen, he knows that all will be well now.

From *Crome Yellow* to *Eyeless in Gaza* is traced an inward development, a progress, from Denis's aimless perplexity through Gumbril's this-worldliness, Calamy's precipitate renunciation and Philip's intellectual scepticism to Anthony's positive pacifism. In Anthony himself is traced an inner progress from happy irresponsible sensuality and intellectual detachment to a responsible, constructive and disinterested endeavour for personal and general awakening. Miller's anthropological approach unites reason and faith, science and religion, commonsense and spirituality. Miller's conceptions of unity and peace carry traces of Buddhism and Taoism, Hinduism and Christianity. Does the novel suggest the beginnings of a perennial philosophy? The quest has attained a sense of direction and purpose, and the pilgrim an inner awakening. The progress has been from sterility to fruitfulness.

VII

In the next novel *The Genius and the Goddess* (1955), Huxley deals with the problem of sex. Unity is an essential pre-requisite for happiness. Unity at two levels—firstly, at the individual level, between the body with all its appetites and the mind in all its aspects both earthy and transcendental; secondly, at the social level, between individuals, sympathy, understanding and love, finally oneness of being with the whole universe. But love, a much-

[28] *Eyeless in Gaza*, pp. 618-20.

used word, as sexual attachment, instead of aiding this unity, intensifies the feeling of separateness. Within the individual, it evokes a strife between moral sentiments and bodily appetites, between idealism and actuality. At the social level, both literature and life tell us that at least half the ills of the world are due to this peculiarly human emotion. At its worst, decaying into lust, it produces petrefaction of feeling. At its best, it might result in joy born of togetherness, but never that transcendental oneness.

Huxley is almost obsessed with the sexual theme as an inescapable factor in life contributing to human happiness and misery. He deals with it at such length in his novels that he is accused by critics of indulging in "schoolboy smut" or suffering from "literary coprophilia", a critical evaluation which is, to say the least, unfair. In *Do What You Will* he states that the nineteenth century conception of love is a curious blend of two contradictory elements—the romantic worship of passion and the ascetic dread of passion—a conception which, in itself, is a source of inner conflict. Opposed to this, there is the twentieth-century realistic conception, a product of the idealistic collapse of the war years, which takes love for just a normal human activity like dancing or tennis, a sport, a recreation, a pastime. Disagreeing with both the religio-romantic and realistic conceptions of love, D. H. Lawrence propounds, what Huxley calls, a new mythology of nature, exemplified by Huxley through Rampion in *Point Counter Point*. But Lawrence's doctrine, as a philosophy of life, suffers from three drawbacks. Firstly, as Spandrell remarks, it sounds like a gospel of animalism. Secondly, rejection of all things spiritual as non-human irrelevant factors is palpably incorrect, as incorrect as the spiritualist's complete rejection of the body. Thirdly, Lawrence's philosophy is not, as Huxley himself states, soulfully convincing to the old.

In *Crome Yellow*, Huxley presents Denis Stone, a romantic sentimentalist who imagines that woman is the broad highway to divinity, but finds actuality far removed from his idealism. Anne laughs at him and says: "I should like to see myself believing that men are the highway to divinity". Then Gumbril, wavering between romantic idealism and paganism, even in the most blissful moments with Emily, is conscious only of the transitoriness of that thrill. Chelifer, again a romantic sentimentalist, feels the same way, in Barbara's embrace, experiencing "beneath the surface of every calm and silent trance" a profound uneasiness. On the other hand, Brian, a religious sentimentalist, kisses his fiancée in an ecstasy, but all at once breaks off suffering from a guilt-complex—"the ordinary happy kind of love isn't morally right". Then there is Burlap, a conscious hypocrite, preaching religion in public, and practising seduction and lechery in private. In a violent reaction to this hypocrisy, individuals like Spandrell or Coleman, turn neurotic, lose their bearings, and it is with hatred and contempt, not love, that they go to bed with a woman. There are others who, rejecting both poetry and religion, morality and tradition, indulge in irresponsible sensuality for pleasure, for fun and even for profit—Myra, Lucy, Mary Amberley, John Bidlake, Gerry Watchet. But the result of such indulgence might often be petrefaction of all feeling. Huxley quotes from Robert Burns:[29]

> I waive the quantum of the sin,
> The hazard of concealing;
> But oh! it hardens all within
> And petrifies the feeling.

Huxley finds that sexual love, like hatred, anger, greed, intensifies the feeling of separateness. But, at the same time, Huxley seems to imply, it is an essentially human emotion which neither intellectuals like Philip and Anthony, Shearwater and Lord Edward, nor mystics like Calamy, nor even satiated creatures like Myra and Mary Amberley can transcend. Even women like Emily and Beatrice, afraid of and disgusted with male touch because of masculine crudity, overcome their fear and feel the thrill when seduced by accomplished amorists. Only a freakish egoist like Mark Staithes, or some extraordinary saint might transcend the passion.

In *The Genius and the Goddess,* a short novel, Huxley shows that genius or goddess, intellectual giant or angelic woman, none can but be a slave to this peculiarly human emotion and a physical need. In *Point Counter Point,* he has left the Hilda-Bidlake theme as a loose-end, making the reader wonder whether he really approves of the compromise Lady Hilda has achieved between matrimony and amour. *The Genius and the Goddess* is an extension with a variation on the Hilda theme. The scene of action

[29] Huxley's essay "Fashions in Love" in *Do What You Will.*

5

is shifted from England to the New World, to Berkeley and St. Louis.

One Christmas eve, John Rivers, a fifty-eight year old physicist, receives a novelist-friend of his for a drink. Rivers has with him a biography of Dr. Maartens, a celebrated physicist, under whom, thirty years earlier, he worked as an assistant for about a year. While critically commenting on the biography, he calls it the soap-opera type, he falls into a reminiscent mood, and recounts his life with the Maartenses during those days. In the novel, Huxley makes the novelist-friend report verbatim what Rivers has told him, with all the amusing digressions, the chance interruptions, and generalizations incidental to such a reminiscence. The result is a moving story with individuals and events cleverly manipulated.

Dr. Henry Maartens was a celebrated physicist, then fifty-six years old, a genius but also a moron, a half-wit and a hungry lover. His wife Katy, thirty-six years old, was a charming woman, angelic by nature. They had two children, Ruth, a fourteen-year old poetess, and Timmy, a nine-year old boy. Rivers was then twenty-eight, had just taken his Ph.D., and he went to St. Louis to work as an assistant under Dr. Maartens. A Lutheran minister's son, he was taught by his mother that "the most wonderful wedding present a man could bring his wife was his virginity". And, at twenty-eight, Rivers still carried the precious gift with him. After a few days' stay with the Maartenses, he was accepted as a permanent guest in the family. At last free from his mother's possessive love, Rivers progressed from his religious priggishness into a Platonic worship of the pagan goddess Katy. Fourteen-year old Ruth, in her turn, worshipped him with all the passion of adolescent calf-love. The old maid Beulah treated him as her long-lost son. To Dr. Maartens, he had become an indispensable conscience-keeper. At that juncture, Katy had to leave for Chicago to attend on her dying mother. Separation from Katy turned Maartens neurotic. He worked himself up slowly into an insane jealousy, raved over imagined infidelities of Katy, and carried himself to death's door with pneumonia. Rivers was shocked at this transformation. Beulah told him that a similar thing had happened once earlier, and by falling ill, a neurotic mind conspiring with an obliging body, Maartens had forced Katy to come back. But Katy, says Beulah, with her miracle touch, she had that *virtue* in her, brought him back to life then. Katy now had to leave her dying mother and rush back home to save a dying husband. She looked a tired and distraught woman. Looking at her, Beulah exclaimed: "get some sleep. You can't help him now, not in the state you're in". But Katy rushed upstairs. She bent over the oxygen tent and whispered his name over and over again. The miracle miscarried. "Lazarus remained unraised".

That night Rivers was startled out of sleep by a groping touch of hand. Katy was in the room, she broke down telling him of her mother's death. The goddess was in grief, and Rivers, with all his virgin clumsiness, tried to console her. His attempts ended in his initiation into amour and loss of virginity. The next morning, Beulah was loudly praising the lord that the 'virtue' had come back to Katy. The miracle worked, Lazarus was raised. Maartens made a speedy recovery thereafter.

From a conscience-stricken prig, Rivers gradually changed into a hungry lover. Katy, proud of the miracle she had wrought, became overbearing, found fault with the children, exposed Ruth's make-up kit and, with cruel sarcasm, poured the perfumes down the drain. Ruth, provoked by suspicion, jealousy and vengeance, suspected the worst about the relations between her mother and Rivers. She wrote a poem depicting a disloyal wife and her lover, and the punishments awaiting them in hell. Rivers passed on the poem to Katy, they were both frightened, and Rivers decided to leave for home. On Friday, an alibi was prepared, and it was decided to have a farewell picnic at Maartens's country farm the next day so that Rivers might leave on Sunday. The next morning Katy started with the two children in advance in her roadster, and on the way, quarrelling with her daughter, she burst across a cross-road, in anger, and a truck hit them broad-side on. Both the mother and daughter were mangled to death.

Huxley presents his thesis through Rivers. Dr. Maartens, he says, is a genius, but "an absentee half-wit", "the psychological equivalent of a foetus" and a "hungry lover". His wife, to him, "wasn't a person; she was his food, she was a vital organ of his own body. When she was absent, he was like a cow deprived of grass, like a man with jaundice struggling to exist without a liver". Katy is a kind of "feminine Antaeus—invincible while her feet were on the ground, a goddess so long as she was in contact with the greater goddess within her, the universal Mother without". Her mother's illness, worry and misery broke her down. But an hour of love, a few hours of sleep, restore her to her natural grace, and the miracle works. Katy is a pagan. To conscience-stricken Rivers's priggish lamentations she replies:

> *You* can't bear it. *You're* too noble to be a party to a deception! Can't you ever think of anything but your own precious self? Think of *me,* for a change, think of Henry! A sick genius and the poor woman whose job it's been to keep the sick genius alive and tolerably sane. His huge, crazy intellect against my instincts, his inhuman denial of life against the flow of life in me. It wasn't easy, I've had to fight with every weapon that came to hand. And now here I have to listen to you—talking the most nauseous kind of Sunday School twaddle, daring to tell me—*me!*—you cannot live a lie—like George Washington and the cherry tree. You make me tired. I'm going to sleep.[30]

But the miracle she has worked has gone to her head. Normally tolerant and good-humoured, she now acts as an Olympian, but, after all, she is a woman, and an Olympian attitude is far beyond her, and there is disaster. Huxley reverts to his doctrine—the doctrine of pre-destination:

> The pre-destination of events, and at the same time the pre-destination of two temperaments, Ruth's and Katy's—the temperament of an outraged child, who was also a jealous woman; and the temperament of a goddess, cornered by circumstances and suddenly realising that, objectively, she was only a human being, for whom the Olympian temperament might actually be a handicap.[31]

Dr. Miller, in *Eyeless in Gaza,* speaks of the trinity in human personality. Rivers speaks of a trinity of 'Grace' for human happiness:

> At one end of the spectrum it's pure spirit, it's the Clear Light of the Void; and at the other end it's instinct, it's health, it's the perfect functioning of an organism that's infallible so long as we don't interfere with it; and somewhere between the

[30] *The Genius and the Goddess,* pp. 106-7.
[31] Ibid., p. 124.

two extremes is what St. Paul called 'Christ'—the divine made human. Spiritual grace, animal grace, human grace—three aspects of the same underlying mystery.[32]

The trinity of human personality must be blessed with the trinity of grace for unity to be achieved. But a life based on a lie, and a temperament incompatible with the environment lead but to a tragedy.

This is an unpleasantly moving tale. One wonders whether Huxley himself believes that "the possession of the body is itself a cynical comment on the soul", and that we are congenitally incapable of living harmoniously; or, is he just trying to give, with cynical pleasure, the Strachean version of a soap-opera biography?

But that does not seem to be so. This novel has a place in the general scheme of Huxley's fictional writings. John Rivers is a development from Philip and Anthony Beavis. Whereas Philip was only a seeker, and Anthony had at last chosen a path, Rivers has attained a certain stability of attitude and a balanced outlook. The bitter sarcasm and the pungent irony of the previous novels give place to sympathy and a wryness of remark in this book. The patience and love with which Rivers fondles his grandson Bimbo, the compassion he shows in his comments on his daughter and son-in-law, his remarks on life in general, the cosmic scheme of things, predestination of temperaments and events, reveal a sobriety and solidity of outlook and feeling, a balanced temperament. Rivers has gone a step further than Anthony, and seems to have achieved, to a certain level, inner unity. Combining in himself the traits of Calamy and Philip, he is a rational mystic, like Anthony he has developed a positive attitude towards life and things, and having achieved the trinity of grace, has transcended the fear of death too.

But as if in a tribute to the 'Cosmic Joker', and perhaps in sharp contrast to the Katy tale, in sharp contrast to the treatment of sex in general in the previous novels, here Huxley tells us that it is, after all, a woman who has helped Rivers to attain that grace. Huxley presents, in just about forty lines, the portrait of a superb woman, a real goddess, Helen her name, who has taught Rivers, by silent example, how to live and to die. One wishes that

32 Ibid., p. 99.

Huxley has confined the Katy episode to forty lines, and given the rest of the novel to Helen.

God isn't the son of Memory; He's the son of Immediate Experience. You can't worship a spirit in spirit, unless you do it now. Wallowing in the past may be good literature. As wisdom, it's hopeless. Time Regained is Paradise Lost, and Time Lost is Paradise Regained. Let the dead bury their dead. If you want to live at every moment as it presents itself, you've got to die to every other moment. That's the most important thing I learned from Helen.

The name evoked for me a pale young face framed in the square opening of a bell of dark, almost Egyptian hair—evoked, too, the great golden columns of Baalbek, with the blue sky and the snows of Lebanon behind them. I was an archaeologist in those days, and Helen's father was my boss. It was at Baalbek that I had proposed to her and been rejected.

"If she'd married me", I said, "would *I* have learned it?"

"Helen practised what she always refrained from preaching", Rivers answered. "It was difficult not to learn from her".

"And what about my writing, what about those daughters of Memory?"

"There would have been a way to make the best of both worlds".

"A compromise?"

"A synthesis, a third position subtending the other two. Actually, of course, you can never make the best of one world, unless in the process you've learned to make the best of the other. Helen even managed to make the best of life while she was dying".

In my mind's eye Baalbek gave place to the campus of Berkeley, and instead of the noiselessly swinging bell of dark hair there was a coil of grey, instead of a girl's face I saw the thin drawn features of an ageing woman. She must have been ill, I reflected, even then.

"I was in Athens when she died", I said aloud.

"I remember". And then, "I wish you'd been here", he added. "For her sake—she was very fond of you. And, of course, for *your* sake too. Dying's an art, and at our age we ought to be learning it. It helps to have seen someone who really knew how.

Helen knew how to die because she knew how to live—to live now and here and for the greater glory of God. And that necessarily entails dying too there and then and tomorrow and one's own miserable little self. In the process of living as one ought to live, Helen had been dying by daily instalments. When the final reckoning came, there was practically nothing to pay".[33]

Helen's 'here and now' theory of happiness takes us on to the next novel *Island*. Dr. Miller has led Anthony from sterility to fruitfulness, and Helen has paved the way to transcendence.

Reviewing *The Genius and the Goddess,* Angus Wilson calls Huxley "the naive emancipator", and the novel "a religious tract upon the vanity of human life".[34] Katy is, to him, a Lawrencian woman, and, in attacking Katy, he says, Huxley is aiming at paganism at its highest. Perhaps Wilson has gone far off the mark when he considers the novel a violently baroque lesson in human vanity. Lawrence would never have approved of Katy, just as Lawrence-Rampion had not approved of Lucy in *Point Counter Point*. Huxley has already dealt with the fall of paganism, in *Those Barren Leaves,* in Mrs. Aldwinkle's pitiable lamentation that everyone has been leaving her. Now, in this novel, Huxley shows that, genius or goddess, no human being can transcend the physiological cravings and desires. Harmony of being is possible only when the trinity of grace is achieved—animal grace, human grace, spiritual grace. The problem for Huxley is how to reconcile the satisfaction of these physiological desires with our religio-romantic conceptions of sexual love. Still on the quest, Huxley leads us from the tentative conclusions of this novel to his last novel *Island*.

[33] *The Genius and the Goddess,* pp. 9-11.
[34] *Encounter,* Vol. V, No. 1, July 1955, pp. 73-76.

3

THE ESSENTIAL HORROR

Though you forget the way to the Temple,
There is one who remembers the way to your door:
Life you may evade, but Death you shall not.
You shall not deny the stranger.

T. S. ELIOT

AFTER many a summer dies the swan. After many many
summers die the carp and the pike, the crocodile and the
tortoise. But to man is given the biblical span of three score and
ten—perhaps he may steal a decade or two more. Religion,
theology, science and superstition, all strive to allay the fear of
death with explanations and exhortations, threats and promises;
but theist or atheist, stoic or epicurean, rarely can one transcend
the fear of death or face it with equanimity. Maeterlink calls
it 'the great enigma', and Huxley 'the essential horror'.

Mark Staithes in *Eyeless in Gaza* wryly remarks: "We
are like dogs on an acropolis. Trotting round with inexhaustible
bladders and only too anxious to lift a leg at every statue. And
mostly we succeed. Art, religion, heroism, love—we've left our
visiting card on all of them. But death—death remains out of
reach. We haven't been able to defile *that* statue. Not yet at any
rate". John Bidlake (*Point Counter Point*) the Gargantuan laments
that God is a practical joker. "Deplorable", writes his son-in-law
Philip, "to see an Olympian rendered by a little tumour in the
stomach to a state of sub-humanness". Even the hedonist Cardan
(*Those Barren Leaves*) is worried over "decay, decrepitude and
death", and convinces himself with typical escapist logic that wise
men do not think too much of it. The fear of the unknown, the
doubt whether all one's sins are forgiven, the fear of hell, of
"falling into the hands of the living god", make the last days and

last moments of life miserable to a vast majority of human beings; death not merely at long last as a finis to the normal span of life, but what is horrifying is its sudden onset, the unexpected visitation, the cruel, inscrutable cat-and-mouse game it plays, at times, even with innocent children as in the case of little Phil (*Point Counter Point*).

Huxley feels that unless the fear of death is transcended there can be no happiness on earth. One might obtain all that Anne (*Crome Yellow*) had recommended for happiness—a fixed income, a plump young wife and congenial work—still there would be death and the unknown beyond to mar the joy of this life. From California, Huxley has published two novels on the life-and-death theme, *After Many a Summer* (1939) and *Time Must Have a Stop* (1945). The thematic value of both the novels can be aptly summed up in Huxley's own words on the latter novel, said to Isherwood. "It's a curiously *trivial* story, told in great detail, with a certain amount of *squalor*".[1] Ruthlessly sarcastic, *After Many a Summer* deals with certain experiments on longevity, but it does not read like scientific fiction; nor does *Time Must Have a Stop*, dealing with spirits and *séances*, read like metaphysical fiction. But both the novels, published at an interval of six years, read like complementary pieces.

There is the myth of the Cumaean Sybil to whom Apollo granted a life of as many years, as she had grains of dust in her hand. But she forgot to ask for eternal youth, and so she shrivelled to nothing. In *After Many a Summer*, Huxley appears to have taken the myth in reverse. An English aristocrat eats raw fish guts to aid rejuvenation and longevity. The experiment has been a success, the lord lives to be a bicentenarian, but he has grown into a strange creature, only the ape in him being alive, the essence having shrivelled away to nothing. *Time Must Have a Stop* depicts the travails of the spirit of a middle-aged epicurean, forced to leave a decrepit body and hover between earth and eternity unable to reconcile itself to either. Propter in the former and Bruno Rontini in the latter novel, both obviously extended portraits of Dr. Miller in *Eyeless in Gaza,* stand as commentators on this grotesque comi-tragedy of human existence.

---

[1] *Aldous Huxley—A Memorial Volume*, p. 160.

II

After Many a Summer presents Joe Stoyte, a sixty-year old oil baron. A financial wizard and a ruthless money-spinner, with the greed of a miser, the vanity of an aristocrat and a rich man's obsessive fear of robbers and hold-ups, he builds for himself an amazing monstrosity—a mediaeval castle with electronic burglar alarms and safety devices—and fills it with everything from jewellery to junk, from antique master-pieces to crude concrete and rubble. Deluding himself into sensations of youthfulness, he worships, with senile infatuation, a pretty twenty-two year old show-girl Virginia Maunciple, a rare specimen compounded of beauty and vulgarity, piety and lewdness. Superstitiously pious, yet ruthlessly in love with power and pelf, and then tormented by the guilty conscience of a greedy money-maker, he is scared of death and the punishments in hell, "of falling into the hands of the living god". So to keep himself tethered safe to the earth, he retains on his staff a research worker and a physician, Dr. Obispo, and provides him with an excellent lab and an efficient young assistant Peter Boone, to conduct experiments on rejuvenation and longevity. Obispo is a Mephistophilean, young, handsome and cynical, a scoffing virtuoso in sex. Every day, lulling Joe Stoyte to sleep under a strong dose of Nembutal, he indulges in an impish pleasure, taking Virginia in his arms and "reducing her unique personality into an epileptic body" gibbering in orgastic ecstasy. The Stoyte mansion is a veritable monkey-house, Joe, Virginia and Obispo bearing close resemblance to the three baboons—two males and a female—in a cage on the Stoyte farm. Using young Peter Boone as a decoy to draw Joe's suspicions, Virginia practises Nerciat under Obispo's guidance till, in a fit of mistaken fury, Joe once shoots Peter Boone dead.

Building upon the prevalent scientific theories, Obispo believes that senescence is due to certain degenerative processes caused by the accumulation of fatty alcohols in the body. In some long-living fish and animals, the fatty alcohols do not accumulate nor do they transform into the more poisonous sterols. The carp has achieved immunity from senescence because of its intestinal flora which prevents the formation of sterols. Obispo develops a technique to transfer the flora into the intestines of a mammal

and then protect it there from the digestive processes till it
establishes itself. His experiments have been a success first with
mice, then with dogs and baboons. Senescence is halted, the
animals are rejuvenated and look as if they are growing back in
age. Obispo hopes to apply his techniques to Joe Stoyte, and if
he succeeds, Joe will be an immortal and nothing but an accident
can cause his death.

At this time, in the Stoyte mansion, a fifty-year old English
scholar, Jeremy Pordage, has been editing the Hauberk papers,
twenty-seven box-loads of manuscripts said to be the diaries of an
English aristocrat, the fifth earl of Gonister. The papers reveal
that the earl has anticipated Obispo's discoveries. He has actually
eaten the raw guts of the carp along with his housekeeper-
paramour, and both have achieved rejuvenation and longevity.
Having had three bastards in his late eighties, he makes overtures
to a servant-girl, and these being exposed, to escape public fury
and prosecution, he retires with his housekeeper into an underground suite of cellars. He is then declared to have died and a
false funeral conducted. From all that the papers seem to suggest,
Obispo comes to believe that the lord may still be alive. While
helping to hush up Peter Boone's murder, Obispo blackmails
Joe and wangles a free trip to England. Virginia, Joe and Obispo
visit the Gonister castle, break into the cellars and witness a
disgusting spectacle:

On the edge of a low bed, at the centre of this world, a man
was sitting, staring as though fascinated, into the light. His
legs, thickly covered with coarse reddish hair, were bare. The
shirt, which was his only garment, was torn and filthy. Knotted
diagonally across the powerful chest was a broad silk ribbon
that had evidently once been blue. From a piece of string tied
round his neck was suspended a little image of St. George and
the Dragon in gold and enamel. He sat hunched up, his head
thrust forward and at the same time sunk between his shoulders.
With one of his huge and strangely clumsy hands he was
scratching a sore place that showed red between the hairs of
his left calf.
"A foetal ape that's had time to grow up", Dr. Obispo
managed at last to say, "It's too good!" Laughter overtook him
again. "Just look at the face!" he gasped, and pointed through

the bars. Above the matted hair that concealed the jaws and
cheeks, blue eyes stared out of carvernous sockets. There were
no eye-brows; but under the dirty, wrinkled skin of the fore-
head a great ridge of bone projected like a shelf.
Suddenly, out of the black darkness, another simian face
emerged into the beam of the lantern—a face only lightly
hairy, so that it was possible to see, not only the ridge above
the eyes, but also the curious distortions of the lower jaws, the
accretions of bone in front of the ears. Clothed in an old check
ulster and some glass beads, a body followed the face into the
light.
"It's a woman", said Virginia, almost sick with the horrified
disgust she felt at the sight of those pendulous and withered
dugs.

*   *   *

"The one with the Order of the Garter", said Dr. Obispo,
raising his voice against the tumult, "he's the fifth earl of
Gonister. The other's his house-keeper".

*   *   *

Dr. Obispo went on talking. "Slowing up of the development
rates . . . one of the mechanisms of evolution . . . the
older an anthropoid, the stupider . . . senility and sterol
poisoning . . . the intestinal flora of the carp . . . the Fifth
Earl had anticipated his own discovery . . . no sterol poisoning,
no senility . . . no death, perhaps, except through an accident
. . . but meanwhile the foetal anthropoid was able to come
to maturity. . . It was the finest joke he had ever known".[2]

But a finer joke, call it the irony of life or the pranks of the
Cosmic Joker or the inherent insipience of the homo sapiens, Joe
Stoyte asks Obispo:

"How long do you figure it would take before a person went
like that?" he said in a slow, hesitating voice. "I mean, it
wouldn't happen at once . . . there'd be a long time while
a person . . . well, you know; while he wouldn't change
any. And once you get over the first shock—well, they look
like they were having a pretty good time. I mean, in their own

2 *After Many a Summer*, pp. 242-44.

way, of course. Don't you think so, Obispo"?[3]

Faith and superstition, craving and fond hope, fear of the unknown and the consequent attachment to the known, coalesce into the basic earthy desire to live and go on living. Given all material comforts, still, does longevity, by dispelling the fear of death, bring happiness? If the duality of matter and spirit, body and soul, is accepted, where will physiological rejuvenation lead to without a corresponding psychological renovation? Or, if one agrees with Cardan, that the spirit is but an excrescence of the living body, and then goes on to believe that physiological rejuvenation is the path to immortality, still, is happiness possible, where the fear of death is replaced by the fear of an accident that may cause death? What are the implications, of the physiological, psychological and sociological impact that death-lessness may have on human life, life that is basically conditioned by time and craving? These are the questions which Huxley seems to pose to the reader for consideration.

In sharp contrast to Joe Stoyte and all that he stands for, Huxley presents William Propter, obviously his own spokesman, Joe's friend from school days, a practical sociologist and a profound thinker, and a voluble commentator on the Stoyte theme. Joe stands for big business, wealth and power, Propter for Jeffersonian democracy of peasants plus small machines and electricity. Joe is a terrestrial, Propter a transcendentalist. Propter says that happiness consists in liberation—"liberation from time, liberation from cravings and revulsions, liberation from personality". Longevity merely gives "another century or so of time and craving. A couple of extra life-times of potential evil". Viewed even from the strictly scientific angle, of physiological processes, of natural evolutionary forces, of glandular equilibria, mutations and development rates, one cannot say what happens when the life of an animal is artificially prolonged. From the psychological angle, Propter asks "what shall we all be doing at three hundred?"

"Do you suppose you'd still be a scholar and a gentleman?" Jeremy coughed and patted his bald head. "One will certainly have stopped being a gentleman", he answered. "One's begun

[3] *After Many a Summer,* p. 245.

to stop even now, thank heaven".

"But the scholar will stay the course?"

"There's a lot of books in the British Museum".

"And you, Pete?" said Mr. Propter, "do you suppose you'll still be doing scientific research?"

"Why not? What's to prevent you from going on with it for ever?" the young man answered emphatically.

"For ever?" Mr. Propter repeated. "You don't think you'd get a bit bored? One experiment after another. Or one book after another", he added in an aside to Jeremy. "In general, one damned thing after another. You don't think that would prey on your mind a bit?"[4]

Adam, in Bernard Shaw's *Back to Methuselah* speaks in the same tone:

What! Eve: do not play with me about this. If only there may be an end some day, and yet no end! If only I can be relieved of the horror of having to endure myself for ever! If only the care of this terrible garden may pass on to some other gardener! If only the sentinel set by the Voice can be relieved! If only the rest and sleep that enable me to bear it from day to day could grow after many days into an eternal rest, an eternal sleep, then I could face my days, however long they may last. Only there must be some end, some end: I am not strong enough to bear eternity".[5]

The views of Huxley and Shaw, on life and longevity, seem to run on curiously dissimilar tracks though their conclusions sound almost similar. Huxley, through Propter, states: "craving and time—two aspects of the same thing; and that thing is the raw material of evil. . . . Potential evil is in time; potential good isn't. The longer you live, the more evil you automatically come into contact with. Nobody comes automatically into contact with good. Men don't find more good by merely existing longer". Shaw thinks in a different way. He says:

. . . history and experience had convinced me that the

4 *After Many a Summer*, p. 85.
5 Bernard Shaw, *Back to Methuselah*, p. 12.

social problems raised by millionfold national populations are far beyond the political capacity attainable in three score and ten years of life by slow-growing mankind. . . . Though I am very far from being as clever and well informed as people think. I am not below the average in political capacity; yet in my 89th year I am no more fit to rule millions of men than a boy of 12. Physically I am failing: my senses, my locomotive powers, my memory, are decaying at a rate which threatens to make a Struldbrug of me if I persist in living; yet my mind still feels capable of growth; for my curiosity is keener than ever. My soul goes marching on; and if the Life Force would give me a body as durable as my mind, and I know better how to feed and lodge and dress and behave, I might begin a political career as a junior civil servant and evolve into a capable Cabinet minister in another hundred years or so.[6]

And so comes out his world classic *Back to Methuselah*. Shaw presents a utopian society in which, through creative evolution, mankind has become oviparous, development rates in the embryonic stage are quickened, longevity is achieved so that nothing but an accident can cause death to them. He-ancients and she-ancients run the society, ancients hundreds of years old, who, having lived through the gamut of human cravings and desires, have achieved the same liberation that Huxley speaks of. Shaw's He-ancient says:

Look at us. Look at me. This is my body, my blood, my brain; but it is not me. I am the eternal life, the perpetual resurrection; but (striking his body) this structure, this organism, this make-shift, can be made by a boy in a laboratory, and is held back from dissolution only by my use of it. Worse still, it can be broken by a slip of the foot, drowned by a cramp in the stomach, destroyed by a flash from the clouds. Sooner or later, its destruction is certain.[7]

He says that as long as thought is chained to this tyrannous body, human destiny cannot be achieved, the destiny to be immortal. The She-ancient prophesies "the day will come when

[6] Ibid., pp. 294-95.
[7] Bernard Shaw, *Back to Methuselah*, p. 269.

there will be no people, only thought".

The rationalist, soaring to the heights of pure reason, exults in the language of the mystic. Huxley hopes to achieve liberation in a single lifetime of three score and ten years. Shaw wants a few centuries, to go through the grind, experience everything, get bored with all and then transcend all passions and sensations only to become a vorticist and hope for release from the tyrannous body by living in the pure realm of thought. Shaw, the creative evolutionist, speaks of the Life Force, Huxley, the rational mystic, refers to it as God, Infinity or the Universal soul. Whereas Shaw's ancients speak of release from the tyrannous body, Huxley speaks of, of course meaning the same thing, transcendence, non-attachment, liberation through awareness and reflection. Huxley's 'forward to *nirvana*' makes more sense than Shaw's *Back to Methuselah*.

According to Huxley, man has his own place in the cosmic scheme. He can rise to divinity or fall down to apery to live in animal bliss. But at the human level, crippled by personal egos and enslaved by fears and prejudices, if we interfere with natural processes, and experiment on the physiological level ignoring the psychological forces, we will probably create only Frankinsteins and thalidomide babies. Material achievements, wealth, power and pleasure, even conquest of death, bring no real happiness. Longevity by itself is no boon. Huxley speaks through Propter:

> On the level below the human and on the level above. On the animal level and on the level . . . well, you can take your choice of names: the level of eternity; the level, if you don't object, of God; the level of the spirit—only that happens to be about the most ambiguous word in the language. On the lower level, good exists as the proper functioning of the organism in accordance with the laws of its own being. On the higher level, it exists in the form of a knowledge of the world without desire or aversion; it exists as the experience of eternity, as the transcendence of personality, the extension of consciousness beyond the limits imposed by the ego. Strictly human activities are activities that prevent the manifestation of good on the other two levels. . . . In a word, in so far as we're human beings, we prevent ourselves from realizing the spiritual and timeless good that we're capable of as potential inhabitants

of eternity, as potential enjoyers of the beatific vision. We worry and crave ourselves out of the very possibility of transcending personality and knowing intellectually at first and then by direct experience, the true nature of the world.[8]

III

Six years later, in 1948, Huxley published *Time Must Have a Stop* prefaced with a passage from Shakespeare, the dying Hotspur's summing up of the human situation:

> But thought's the slave of life, and life's time's fool,
> And time, that takes survey of all the world,
> Must have a stop.

Through Sebastian Barnack, a major character, Huxley explains the passage thus:

> Thought's the slave of life—undoubtedly. But if it weren't also something else, we couldn't make even this partially valid generalisation.
>
> .... Life's time's fool. By merely elapsing time makes nonsense of all life's conscious planning and scheming....

* * *

But Hotspur's summary has a final clause; time must have a stop. And not only *must,* as an ethical imperative and an eschatological hope, but also *does* have a stop, in the indicative sense, as a matter of brute experience. It is only by taking the fact of eternity into account that we can deliver thought from its slavery to life. And it is only by deliberately paying our attention and our primary allegiance to eternity that we can prevent time from turning our lives into a pointless and diabolic foolery. The Divine Ground is a timeless reality. Seek it first, and all the rest—everything from an adequate interpretation of life to a release from compulsory self-destruction—will be added. Or, transporting the theme out of the evangelical into

[8] *After Many a Summer,* pp. 98-99.

a Shakespearean key, you can say: "Cease being ignorant of what you are most assured, your glassy essence, and you will cease to be an angry ape, playing such fantastic tricks before high heaven as make the angels weep.[9]

The novel is a strange blend of fantasy and fact, and the theme contrapuntal to that in *After Many a Summer*. The central character is Eustace Barnack, a middle-aged gourmet, a connoisseur of art, woman and vintage. Joe Stoyte believes in hell and retribution. Eustace, like Cardan, believes in death as the final end. Joe clings to a medical man for survival. Eustace defies all medical advice and indulges in the pleasures of the table and the cellar. Joe, in superstitious terror, shrinks from the hands of the living God; Eustace, living in the sepulchre of his personal ego, brooks no nonsense about immortality. To him, the solid fleshy vertebrates are facts, God is just an empty nothing, a gaseous vertebrate.

The novel presents amusing contrasts. Eustace is a hedonist who believes in death as the final end: to use his cousin Bruno's words, "just one damned thing after another, until at last there's a final damned thing, after which there isn't anything". His mother-in-law Mrs. Gamble, a blind old crabbed lady, believes that nobody ever really dies, but just passes on to the other side leaving behind the body. But Mrs. Gamble's 'other side' is peculiarly her own, a strange squeak-and-gibber ghost-world where the spirits of the dead retain still their individualities and live as separate entities. So she lives through her blind old age in supreme confidence, holding *séances* and running after clairvoyant mediums. Eustace's step-daughter Mrs. Ockham, having lost her husband and only son, comes under a canon's religious influence, and runs after lame-ducks smothering them with her morbid sentimentality and compassion. But the canon's daughter, Mrs. Thwale, young and beautiful, in revenge against her father's moral blackmail, swings in abandon between secret sensuality and apparent decency, cocking snooks at everything in life. Tossed about as a billiard ball among the four is Eustace's nephew, Sebastian, a handsome young Adonis of seventeen. Exposed to all the filth and glory of life, yet fortunately remaining untainted, he is at last salvaged from the chaos by a distant cousin Bruno

[9] *Time Must Have a Stop*, pp. 296-98.

Rontini, a seller of second-hand books by profession, an anti-fascist in politics, a transcendentalist by religion. Bruno is a grey-haired, kindly, unpretentious, soft-spoken man practising genuine godliness in worldliness.

Eustace remains impervious to Bruno's entreaties. God, to him, is just a gaseous vertebrate. He ridicules the comedy of the good, of people like Bruno: "there's nothing I enjoy more than the spectacle of the Good trying to propagate their notions and producing results exactly contrary to what they intended. It's the highest form of comedy". Bruno twits him about the comedy of the clever, people like Eustace himself, "achieving self-destruction in the name of self-interest, and delusion in the name of realism". One night, after a deliciously sumptuous meal and three glasses of brandy, smoking a Romeo-and-Juliet, Eustace gets into the lavatory and dies there of heart failure. Now, with clever alternation, Huxley takes the reader chapter by chapter through two layers of existence, the fatuous bustle of the living on the earth, and the tragic agony of the spirit of Eustace in Infinity.

The spirit leaves the body, finds itself in a terrifying wilderness, free, ownerless, without possessions, an absence, a nothingness surrounded by a vaster absence, a vaster nothingness. It feels itself a stranger to the earth, it is terrified of the infinity around. Strange knowledge and enlightenment begin to dawn on it. The stupidity and folly of humanity fill its whole being with derision. It yearns for identification with infinity; at the same time, frightened, shuts itself off and moves "backwards and downwards" to the earth. Huxley describes it: "an unhappy dust of nothingness, a poor little harmless clot of mere privation, crushed from without, scattered from within, but still resisting, still refusing, in spite of the anguish, to give up its right to a separate existence". It has to choose one of the two alternatives, the *Fascinatio nugacitatis* of the earth, or total self-knowledge and self-abandonment, or total attention and exposure to the light.

Mrs. Gamble throws her net with a medium in a *séance*. The spirit is invited to the earth.

Suddenly and without warning there dawned a new, more blissful phase of his salvation. He was in possession of something infinitely precious, something of which, as he now realized, he had been deprived throughout the whole duration of these horrible eternities—a set of bodily sensations. There was an experience, thrillingly direct and immediate, of the warm, living darkness behind closed eyelids; of faint voices, not remembered, but actually heard out there in front; of a touch of lumbago in the small of the back; of a thousand obscure little aches and pressures and tensions from within and from without. And what an odd kind of heaviness in the lower inwards! What curiously unfamiliar sensations of weight and constriction out there in front of the chest.[10]

The spirit throbs with emotion. Yet, being bodiless, it is incapable of verbal expression and needs a medium, "the filter of an intermediate knowledge". But the medium bungles in translating the emotion into words, and in sheer disgust, the spirit gives up communication with the earth. Mrs. Thwale aptly comments on the *séance*: "perfectly genuine. Death cocking snooks at reverence and piety in exactly the same way as life does".

The farce goes on, on the earth and in Infinity. Sebastian goes through the grind for ten years, till one evening he meets with Bruno in a park, Bruno, an ex-prisoner now, a dying old man almost incapable of speech with advanced cancer of the throat. Sebastian takes him home and nurses him till he dies. Those fifteen weeks were a memorable period in his life. Bruno enlightens him and helps him along the path to liberation, scribbling his advice on little scraps of paper. Deploring Sebastian's remorse, self-reproach, and desire to expiate, Bruno scribbles "you're not Joan of Arc, you know. Not even Florence Nightingale". "There's only one effectively redemptive sacrifice, the sacrifice of self-will to make room for the knowledge of God". A little later, on another scrap of paper: "Don't try to act somebody else's part. Find out how to become your inner not-self in God while remaining your outer self in the world".

Fifteen weeks he suffers, but never with a complaint. At last one day, listening in delight with closed eyes to Mrs. Louise's song coming from the kitchen, he opens his eyes, shakes hands with Sebastian, whispers with a smile "finished, finished?" and then makes his exit. Bruno dies in peace with a smile and a swan-song. Eustace's swan-song is an unspoken wail: "Sebastian! Don't let me die. Don't let me".... The Earl of Gonister's swan-

10 *Time Must Have a Stop,* p. 175.

song is a farewell to sane living, "a simian memory of the serenade in Don Giovanni".

Huxley, in the post-script, through Sebastian, puts forward his creed:

> That there is a Godhead or Ground, which is the unmanifest-ed principle of all manifestation.
> That the Ground is transcendent and immanent.
> That it is possible for human beings to love, know and from virtually, to become actually identified with the Ground.
> That to achieve this unitive knowledge, to realize this supreme identity, is the final end and purpose of human existence.
> That there is a Law or Dharma, which must be obeyed, a Tao or Way, which must be followed, if men are to achieve their final end.
> That the more there is of I, me, mine, the less there is of the Ground, and that consequently the Tao is a Way of humility and compassion, the Dharma a Law of mortification and self-transcending awareness.[11]

*   *   *

> True religion concerns itself with the givenness of the time-less. An idolatrous religion is one in which time is substituted for eternity—either past time, in the form of a rigid tradition, or future time, in the form of Progress towards Utopia....
> What have been the consequences of our recent shift of attention from Past to Future? An intellectual progress from the Garden of Eden to Utopia; a moral and political advance from compulsory orthodoxy and the divine right of kings to conscription for everybody, the infallibility of the local boss and the apotheosis of the state. Before or behind, time can never be worshipped with impunity.[12]

There can be no escape from life, no escape from death. Happiness consists in transcendence, in learning to live 'here and now' with awareness, and learning to die with no regrets. Sticking on to life like Joe Stoyte, or blinding oneself to future in self-delusion like Eustace, leads only to misery and despair.

[11] Ibid., pp. 294-95.
[12] Ibid., p. 297.

Life is to be a preparation for death, and death the gateway to unitive knowledge. This is Huxley's thesis.

IV

From *Crome Yellow* to *Eyeless in Gaza,* Huxley has presented Good-timers like Gombauld, Gumbril and Cardan, Truth-searchers like Shearwater and Lord Edward, Higher-lifers like Calamy, Philip, Anthony Beavis. But good-timers, truth-searchers and higher-lifers, he tells us, are all escapists, avoiding the responsibilities of living, seeking shelter in their own egotistic burrows. They will have to face, some day, the jarring music of life, and then they will be kicked into wakefulness. Peace and serenity are possible only when the individual, through awareness, achieves unitive knowledge and liberation from all cravings and desires. Miller, in *Eyeless in Gaza,* suggests physical control as a preliminary stage in the training for awareness. He calls it a non-theological praxis of meditation beginning with physical control, and through it control of impulses and feelings:

> To learn proper use one must first inhibit all improper uses of the self. Refuse to be hurried into gaining ends by the equivalent (in personal, psycho-physiological terms) of violent revolution; inhibit this tendency, concentrate on the means whereby the end is to be achieved; then act. This process entails knowing good and bad use—knowing them apart. By the 'feel'. Increased awareness and increased power of control result. Awareness and control: trivialities take on new significance. Indeed, nothing is trivial any more or negligible. Cleaning teeth, putting on shoes—such processes are reduced by habits of bad use to a kind of tiresome non-existence. Become conscious, inhibit, cease to be a greedy end-gainer, concentrate on means: tiresome non-existence turns into absorbingly interesting reality.[13]

Touching upon this theme of awareness, of living here and now, in conscious disinterested experience, feeling our own feelings,

13 *Eyeless in Gaza*, p. 327.

Huxley goes a step further portraying Helen in *The Genius and the Goddess*. In the novel, Helen's husband Rivers says:

> Dying's an art, and at our age we ought to be learning it. It helps to have seen someone who really knew how. Helen knew how to die because she knew how to live—to live now and here and for the greater glory of God. And that necessarily entails dying too there and then and tomorrow and one's own miserable little self. In the process of living as one ought to live, Helen had been dying by daily instalments. When the final reckoning came, there was practically nothing to pay.

Seeing, feeling, experiencing and knowing, the individual progresses to liberation. Trying to conquer death like Joe Stoyte, or turning a deliberate blind eye to it like Cardan and Eustace, leads us nowhere. Death is inevitable. But when it is realized that death too is an experience and a lesson the soul has to experience, the pain and the panic will disappear. Huxley presents in *Island* a death-scene in which Robert Macphail, the typical Huxleyan healer, and his daughter-in-law Sushila, guide old Lakshmi, the former's wife, through her dying moments. Sushila explains to Will Farnaby, an invited by-stander, their process of helping the dying:

> "What do you say to people who are dying?" he asked. "Do you tell them not to bother their heads about immortality and get on with the job?"
> "If you like to put it that way—yes, that's precisely what we do. Going on being aware—it's the whole art of dying".
> "And you teach the art?"
> "I'd put it another way. We help them to go on practising the art of living even while they're dying. Knowing who in fact one is, being conscious of the universal and impersonal life that lives itself through each of us—that's the art of living, and that's what one can help the dying to go on practising. To the very end. Maybe beyond the end".
> "Beyond?" he questioned. "But you said that was something that the dying aren't supposed to think about".
> "They're not being asked to think about it. They're being helped, if there is such a thing, to experience it. If there is

such a thing", she repeated, "if the universal life goes on, when the separate me-life is over".

"Do you personally think it does go on?"

Sushila smiled. "What I personally think is beside the point. All that matters is what I may impersonally experience— while I'm living, when I'm dying, maybe when I'm dead".[14]

Then Sushila sits by the dying Lakshmi, caressing her hand, preventing her from passing on into a coma, directing her consciousness to recollections of the bright and happy events of the past, urging her to be aware of the dying present, to experience everything here and now. Then Robert Macphail enters, sits on the bed and holds her up in his arms:

"My little love", he kept whispering. "My little love"... Her eyelids fluttered open for a moment. "Brighter", came the barely audible whisper, "brighter". And a smile of happiness intense almost to the point of elation transfigured her face.

Through his tears Dr. Robert smiled back at her. "So now you can let go, my darling". He stroked her grey hair. "Now you can let go. Let go", he insisted. "Let go of this poor old body. You don't need it any more. Let it fall away from you. Leave it lying here like a pile of worn-out clothes".

In the fleshless face the mouth had fallen open and suddenly the breathing became stertorous.

"My love, my little love...." Dr. Robert held her more closely. "Let go now, let go. Leave it here, your old worn-out body, and go on. Go on, my darling, go on into the Light, into the peace, into the living peace of the Clear Light...."

Sushila picked up one of the limp hands and kissed it, then turned to little Radha.

"Time to go", she whispered, touching the girl's shoulder".[15]

Maeterlink's remarkable essay *Death,* presenting his views on the life beyond and the need to overcome the fear of death, makes an interesting study, his views running collateral with those of Huxley. Huxley's own progress, from his amusing 'Squeak and Gibber' and 'Harp and Scream' theories of his early manhood,

[14] *Island,* p. 239.
[15] Ibid., p. 260.

presented in his *Music at Night,* to the Buddhistic notions of awareness and enlightenment, is itself a progress from irresponsible sensuousness to responsive sensitiveness. In the essay *Shakespeare and Religion,* written just before his death, Huxley explains the Hotspur passage in a new light. The two explanations, this and the one in *Time Must Have a Stop,* collated, reveal Huxley's own journey from nonchalant irony to sobriety and seriousness, from a total rejection to a selective acceptance:

> We think we know who we are and what we ought to do about it, and yet our thought is conditioned and determined by the nature of our immediate experience as psycho-physical organisms on this particular planet. Thought, in other words, is Life's fool. Thought is the slave of life, and Life obviously is Time's fool in as much as it is changing from instant to instant, changing the outside and the inner world so that we never remain the same two instants together.
>
> Thought is determined by life, and life is determined by passing time. But the dominion of time is not absolute, for time must have a stop in two senses, from the Christian point of view in which Shakespeare was writing. It must have a stop in the last judgement, and in the winding up of the universe. But on the way to this general consummation, it must have a stop in the individual mind, which must learn the regular cultivation of a mood of timelessness, of the sense of eternity.[16]

[16] *Aldous Huxley—A Memorial Volume,* pp. 174-75.

4
REASON AND RHYTHM

Papio's procurer, bursar to baboons,
Reason comes running, eager to ratify;
Comes, a catch-fart with Philosophy, truckling to tyrants;
Comes, a pimp for Prussia, with Hegel's patent History;

      *   *   *

Comes with the Calculus to aim his rockets
Accurately at the orphanage across the ocean;
Comes, having aimed, with incense to impetrate
Our Lady devoutly for a direct hit.

ALDOUS HUXLEY

THE human being is a manifold fugue. The true rhythm of life consists in organizing and modulating all the polyphonic and contrapuntal strains in individual nature. But, whereas Rhythm depends on variety and discipline, Reason insists on uniformity. A genuine liberal tries to bring about unity into diversity, a despot aims at uniformity. Uniformity demands identity of views, a pre-requisite for social stability. To achieve identity and stability, a dictator may indulge in liquidation. But liquidation having now almost gone out of fashion, a modern dictator, armed with applied psychology, may resort to brain-washing. But the very idea of brain-washing implies the possibility of a re-washing, so a purely scientific dictator may resort to an irreversible process of genetic conditioning. If reason is not tempered with humanism, science is sure to run riot. Applied Physics and Chemistry have brought humanity close to disaster, and misapplied biology may hasten the end.

Huxley has written two novels, *Brave New World* (1932) and *Ape and Essence* (1949), both intended as warnings of the possible consequences of misapplied science on human lives.

Brave New World is written, in light-hearted humour, by a Pyrrhonic aesthete, as Huxley claims himself to have been at that time. He calls the novel a fictional essay in utopianism. The fable is built around contemporary research trends in molecular biology and prophecies which might conceivably come true.

Recently, Prof. James Bonner of the California Institute of Technology, told a seminar of science writers that it would be possible, in not too distant a future, to produce a master-race of super-babies—'Clones' he calls them—by growing them in the laboratories. He further said that the world could benefit from production of Mozart, Einstein and Edison Clones who could be reproduced indefinitely and in any number required to solve the problem of mankind. The super-babies would all be identical twins. Huxley says that in the Brave New World, scientists have perfected a process of growing in their laboratories not only super-babies but also morons, with several gradations in between, the "Alpha-plus" at the intellectual top and "Epsilon-minus", semi-morons, at the bottom. At the time the novel was written, Huxley, the intellectual sceptic he was, believed that human beings were left with the unpleasant choice between the insanity of extreme Reason and the lunacy of superstitious primitivism. It was only in 1946, in his foreword to a fresh edition of the novel, Huxley admitted that, between the utopian and primitive horns of his dilemma, man could still traverse the path of sanity, a path exemplified later in *Island*. A passage of Nicolas Berdiaeff prefacing the novel says that life progresses towards utopias, but the 'anguishing question' facing the world today is how to evolve a society 'not utopian, less perfect but more free'. The reason is, utopias, being highly over-organized societies, tend to stamp out individual differences, insist on identity, curb personal taste and eccentricity. The individual will decay into an automaton, the richness and variety of human feeling, perception and achievement will vanish, and the paradox of civilization blossoming into a neo-primitivism will be a utopian truth. In *Brave New World*, Huxley sounds a warning about the mirage of utopian happiness and the insanity of a rational state.

Suggestions of the outlines of this novel could be found in *Crome Yellow* written over a decade earlier. One of the characters, Scogan, an amusing caricaturist, says that the goddess of applied science has presented the world with the means of dissociating love from propagation. "So an impersonal generation will take the place of Nature's hideous system. In vast state incubators, rows upon rows of gravid bottles will supply the world with the population it requires. The family system will disappear; society, sapped at its very base, will have to find new foundations; and Eros, beautifully and irresponsibly free, will flit like a gay butterfly from flower to flower through a sunlit world".[1] Later on, Scogan describes a Rational State in which examining psychologists will sort out all children into separate species according to their talents, and then the children, labelled and docketed, receive education suitable to them. The three main species he has named are the Directing Intelligences, the Men of Faith and the Herd.

Brave New World presents the West European division of a World State founded not on liberty, equality and fraternity, but on community, identity and stability. Its capital is London, the chief administrator of the division is the Controller, Mustapha Mond by name, an alpha-plus who maintains law and order not with tear-gas and truncheon but with 'soma' vapour and hypnopaedic persuasion. Huxley describes it as an ultra-modern, sophisticated society of the year 600 A.F. (After Ford), about 2500 A.D., with *eau-de-cologne* baths, helicopter taxis and theatres presenting not merely movies but 'feelies'. It is a scientifically 'civilized' world in which motherhood and child-bearing have become social disgraces, mother and father are obscene words, matrimony is unknown, and sticking to one partner in amorous dealings quite out of form and officially discouraged. Being a 'Welfare State', the government makes free monthly supplies of contraceptives and weekly ration of 'soma' tablets to all its citizens. Women contribute their ovaries to the State Hatcheries as a national service, of course with a bonus of six months' salary into the bargain. Individuals are hatched in laboratories in just the required numbers and categories. The intellectuals needed for the state, the alphas and the betas are hatched one individual out of each egg, and are given the best pre-natal treatment. The gammas, deltas and epsilons, individuals almost sub-human, are produced through a systematic process of dysgenics by the Bokanovsky process, large numbers of identical twins hatched at the rate of ninety-six per each egg by budding. A batch of identical twins, with identical mental make-

[1] *Crome Yellow*, p. 28.

up, produced out of the same egg and conditioned in a similar way, working in the same office or factory, will entirely revolutionize social and professional relations, and form the very foundation of their national ideals—community, identity, stability. The problem is only with the alphas, that one-ninth of the population, left with the capacity to think for themselves. But even they are conditioned in the nursery stages to toe the general line and be happy with the environment. If still they find life unpleasant, they have the miracle panacea 'soma', an analeptic and soporific drug, supplied free to everybody by the state, to relieve mental tension, to subdue anxiety, to transport them into a chemically induced bliss, or, with an over-dose, to lull them to sleep. If still non-conformists exist, they are exiled to some islands, punishment-reservations for such individuals.

"The optimum population", says the Controller, "is modelled on the iceberg—eight-ninths below the water line, one-ninth above". And they are happy below the water line, the betas, deltas, gammas and epsilons. Their life is childishly simple. "No strain on the mind or the muscles. Seven and a half hours of mild, unexhausting labour, and then the 'soma' ration and games and unrestricted copulation and the 'feelies'. What more can they ask for?" A truly welfare state! And thus the Scientist-dictator rules, the almighty boss, directing the destiny control, supervising the genetic conditioning, and determining which germ shall be an alpha and which a gamma or an epsilon. Through effective mind-manipulation by means of brain-washing, sleep-teaching and chemical persuasion, people are made to love their servitude. For this happiness, art, science, religion, everything is sacrificed. Shakespeare and the Bible are replaced by 'soma' and the contraceptive girdle.

By way of contrast, Huxley shows that in this World State there still remain some pockets of primitivism, Savage Reservations they are called, in which mother and father, matrimony and childbearing, religion and monogamy still exist. From one such reservation comes John Savage brought on a visit to London. John is the son of a beta-minus female Linda, brought to be with child by a tragic contraceptual error, and treacherously left stranded by her lover in the reservation. John was born there. Educated by his mother, he grew up into a half-primitive, half-romantic idealist, believing in god and penitente-ism side by side with Shakespeare and the romantic world of Romeo-Juliet. John looks like a strange primitive specimen from a zoo, to the 'Londoners'. They appear to him as horrid beings on the way to perdition. He looks at these nice, tame, sexually promiscuous animals in horror. Left alone as an outcast by the natives in the reservation, he yearned for friendship and company there. In the complete absence of all privacy in the Brave New World, he craves for solitude. He feels he has desecrated himself by his contact with the 'Londoners', and in a fury of penitente-ism he whips himself. To civilization, his penance appears to be a whipping-stunt, and crowds after crowds come and beg him to put on the show again. Finally, in disgust, he hangs himself. An early morning crowd of visitors find only a dangling body with the toes swinging round—south, south-east, east. . . .

This is the Rational State. Huxley presents with masterly skill the consequences of Reason stretched to extremes, and going awry. The state is evolved for the people, but the people are not created for the state. But, to the dictator, the state is paramount, the rigid framework of some cock-eyed ideals supreme. The individual is degraded into a cart-horse. Science, accepting as truth only that which can be learnt by experiment, observation and inference, believes that happiness consists in catering to the physical and physiological needs, and the only psychological need it recognizes is the need to fill up leisure and avoid boredom. This is fulfilled through games, the 'feelies', and the 'soma' ration. For this utopian happiness, everything is sacrificed, art, science, even religion. God has no place in this scientist's heaven, the stars do not govern our conditions, the Director of Hatcheries does it. Even nobility and heroism are discarded as unnecessary because they are only the products of an anarchist society. It is, perhaps, one of life's little ironies, that even a scientific utopia thrives on muzzling up science and taking a holiday from facts. Through secrecy, half-truths, brain-washing, chemical persuasion and sleep-teaching, what Huxley calls a 'psychological slave-trade' is carried on in the name of happiness. The final picture that emerges is of a society that has achieved stability and contentment by descending to a sub-human level nearer the ape, rather than by transcending the human level to realize the essence.

When the novel was published, many readers felt that it was a grotesquely amusing tale similar to Book IV of *Gulliver's*

Travels. Huxley himself, in a half-serious tone, calls it an essay in utopianism. But recent world trends show that Huxley's prophecies may become true much sooner than the year 600 After Ford. In *Brave New World Revisited,* Huxley says that increasing populations, technological advances and emergence of Big Business have led to centralization of power. This is a totalitarian trend. Mass communication and subliminal advertising, now carried on even in democratic countries, atrophy personal taste and degrade the human being. Huxley says that, with an effective system of mind-manipulation, and efficient supply of "enough bread, circuses, miracles and mysteries, there seems to be no reason why a thoroughly scientific dictator should ever be overthrown".

It is an irony of life that human beings have first evolved the 'State' for their own good, and now, for the good of the State, human beings are systematically dehumanized, a reversal of nature's evolutionary processes. True happiness consists in becoming fully human, and realizing the utmost possibilities of human achievement. To give right direction to human endeavour, Huxley says that the modern trends in every field—political, economic, sociological and technological—should be reversed. Decentralization of power and finance, smaller village communities with co-operative enterprise instead of the huge modern industrial metropolises, may lead to genuine democratization. A new set of values has to be evolved.

> The value, first of all, of individual freedom, based upon the facts of human diversity and genetic uniqueness; the value of charity and compassion, based upon the old familiar fact, lately rediscovered by modern psychiatry—the fact that, whatever their mental and physical diversity, love is as necessary to human beings as food and shelter; and finally the value of intelligence, without which love is impotent and freedom unattainable.[2]

It is precisely such a society that Huxley attempts to present in his last novel *Island.*

[2] *Brave New World Revisited,* p. 149.

II

If *Brave New World* shows what misapplied biology can do to mankind, *Ape and Essence* gives a horrifying picture of the possible consequences of misapplied Physics and Chemistry. The novel is in the form of a film script with a prologue stuck on. The atom-bombing of Hiroshima and Nagasaki in 1945, and the destruction which just two bombs could work in a moment's mushroom blast, and the subsequent slow festering death of thousands, horrified all sensitive individuals, while the militarist clapped in glee. Eminent intellectuals, all sensitive and sensible individuals, stared helpless in shock and disgust at the callousness of the ruling groups which ordered the bombing, spurning the appeals of the men that really mattered including Prof. Einstein himself, not to drop the bomb on populous areas. The consequent disillusionment of scientists led to the leaking of atom secrets to the Russians by men like Klaus Fuchs. Then has started a nuclear race and piling up of atomic warheads, and with it spread the fear of global destruction either by an accident owing to human error, or a false alarm of an enemy attack, or even, possibly, a general running amuck. Obsessed with such fears, driven to near disgust at the cruelty, greed and lust for power of every 'ism' and 'ist', Huxley has written this 'cautionary tale', a utopia in reverse.

It presents a North American State in Southern California as existing in 2108 A.D., a century after a nuclear war, the Third World War Huxley calls it, which has resulted in the total collapse of the twentieth century civilization. The wheel of life has by then come full circle, and mankind has gone back to primitivism. Superstition and fear grip the minds of the people still festering with radiation poisoning. Priests and primates wield the whip. The people think that it is safer to propitiate the vengeful devil than to worship a benign God. Belial is their deity, the sign of the horns their sacred symbol, and eunuch-priests hold supreme sway. Woman is the weaker vessel, the slave and the toiler, the scapegoat for all sins. Man is the carefree drone. Radiation sickness is attributed to the anger of Belial. Deformed children are sacrificed to the 'God', and the mothers shaven and whipped as a punishment for such begetting. Women wear huge aprons flaunting the word 'No', and sexual relations are prohibited except during the two weeks following the Belial Day. This is a punishment for having been punished, and the law-breakers, if caught, are buried alive. The Arch-priest of Belial is the boss, and the 'Unholy of Unholies' is their place of worship.

To this state, comes on a visit an expedition from New Zealand which happened to remain unaffected by the nuclear war. The expedition consisting of scientists and sociologists, comes to Los Angeles to rediscover America from the West. A member of the group, Dr. Alfred Poole, an agricultural biologist, is caught prisoner by the Americans and taken to the Arch-vicar. The remaining members, after a futile search, sail away. Dr. Poole lives with the tribe for some time, watches their life with horror, and faced with the danger of being enrolled into the eunuch-priesthood, escapes to safety with a woman he has fallen in love with.

Huxley administers a frightening shock-therapy to show that Reason without charity and humaneness will take mankind back to primitive brutishness. The novel has elicited scathing commentaries from critical reviewers. A. S. Collins says that it is "a warning without hope or hint of escape. The negative, critical side of Huxley had at this stage triumphed and reduced the artist to a labourer in hell".[3] Walter Allen regrets that "charity, in the Christian sense, which must have mitigated his (Huxley's) hostility to the frailties of human nature, plays no part in his faith".[4] Prof. Scott James says "it is difficult to see what purpose is served by this fantasy of unrelieved ugliness".[5] Prof. Srinivasa Iyengar terms it "a wild scream of protest"[6]

It is, of course, a grotesque tale, a vehement protest of a sensitive individual against the way to perdition mankind has chosen but Huxley tones down the horror of the tale by various means. He, first of all, presents it as a rejected film-script written by a rejected misanthrope who ultimately commits suicide. Even the lorry carrying the script to the incinerator rejects it, and thus it falls into the hands of a journalist and his friend, a shallow

[3] A. S. Collins, *English Literature of the Twentieth Century*, p. 242.
[4] Walter Allen's essay "Fiction" in *The Year's Work in Literature*.
[5] R. A. Scott James, *Fifty Years of English Literature*, p. 174.
[6] K. R. Srinivasa Iyengar's review of S. K. Ghosh's book, *Aldous Huxley—A Cynical Salvationist*.

7

Hollywood scribe. Then the novel ends in a typical Huxleyan way, with even the central characters, Dr. Poole and his lady-love Loola, rejecting the misanthrope, cracking eggs on the headstone and scattering the fragments over the grave, thus lust for life rejecting the cynic's longing for death. Dr. Poole's escape might also mean the hope of return to civilization, and New Zealand perhaps carrying the white man's burden anew to civilize the world once again.

Both *Brave New World* and *Ape and Essence* are cautionary tales on the wrong direction that applied sciences are taking. At one extreme is fatuous liberalism leading to anarchy, the life-source of totalitarianism. At the other is the brave new world of scientific efficiency in which there will only be "a non-violent totalitarianism" or "democracy and freedom in a Pickwickian sense". Both ways mankind seems to be heading for disaster. The cure that Huxley suggests is that Reason should be tempered with humanism, charity and compassion should be the moving impulses behind all activity. There should be a reversal from the vast impersonal metropolises to small village communities co-operating in meaningful enterprise. In such a society, human beings will grow fully human. Life, effort, achievement and happiness will assume a new meaning. Prof. Collins rightly says: "Huxley seemed to declare—humanise and vitalise the intelligence".[7] Huxley says:

> Cruelty and compassion come with the chromosomes;
> All men are merciful and all are murderers.
> Doting on dogs, they build their Dachaus;
> Fire whole cities and fondle the orphans;
> Are loud against lynching, but all for Oakridge;
> Full of future philanthropy, but today the NKVD.
> Whom shall we persecute, for whom feel pity?
> It is all a matter of the moment's mores,
> Of words on wood-pulp, of radios roaring,
> Of communist kindergartens or first communions.
> Only in the knowledge of his own Essence
> Has any man ceased to be many monkeys.[8]

[7] A. S. Collins, *English Literature of the Twentieth Century*, p. 237.
[8] *Ape and Essence*, pp. 54-55.

5

THE SUMMING UP

'I' am a crowd, obeying as many laws
As it has members. Chemically impure
Are all 'my' beings. There's no single cure
For what can never have a single cause.

ALDOUS HUXLEY in *Island*

ISLAND (1962) is a utopian fantasy, a final summing up of the Huxleyan theme, Wellsian in technique. Wells, one of Huxley's women characters remarks, reminds one of rice paddies, acres and acres of shiny water but never more than two inches deep, all veneer and little depth. But Huxley's novel makes a heavier reading, deep in content, comprehensive in conception, aiming to span the gulfs between science and mysticism, sex and spirituality, politics and religion. In his foreword to the 1946 edition of *Brave New World*, Huxley describes, what he believes to be, a community of sane individuals:

> In this community economics would be decentralist and Henry Georgian, politics Kropotkinesque and co-operative. Science and technology would be used as though, like the Sabbath, they had been made for man, not (as at present and still more so in the Brave New World) as though man were to be adapted and enslaved to them. Religion would be the conscious and intelligent pursuit of man's Final End, the unitive knowledge of the immanent Tao or Logos, the transcendent Godhead or Brahman. And the prevailing philosophy of life would be a kind of Higher Utilitarianism, in which the Greatest Happiness principle would be secondary to the Final End principle—the first question to be asked and answered in every contingency of life being: 'How will this thought or action contribute to,

or interfere with, the achievement, by me and the greatest possible number of other individuals, of man's Final End?[1]

It is such a community that Huxley presents in his last novel *Island*.

But, curiously enough, Huxley, who has earlier denounced Pavlovian conditioning, here advocates a strange psycho-physical conditioning on the plea that his conditioning is for the good of the individual and the society but not for the benefit of an armed dictator. From the anxious queries of his early days, whether the soul is an excrescence of the living body or the body a cynical comment on the soul, Huxley has progressed to accept in *Eyeless in Gaza* the trinary nature of the human being, and the need to induce harmony into the trinity to achieve unity which is a pre-requisite for peace and happiness. Rachel Quarles, in *Point Counter Point* says: "Happiness is like coke—something you get as a by-product in the process of making something else". Sebastian Barnak, in *Time Must Have a Stop,* says: "Peace doesn't come to those who merely work for peace—only as the by-product of something else". Through Miller, Propter and Bruno Rontini, Huxley states that both peace and happiness are by-products of unitive knowledge that liberates the spirit from all cravings and desires. Human grace, animal grace, spiritual grace—all the three are essential and they need to be dovetailed. And so, Huxley's *Island* is ruled not by scientist-dictators as in *Brave New World,* nor by theocrats as in *Ape and Essence,* nor by Nazi or Fascist neurotics, but by a Privy Council learned in such strange branches of knowledge as pure and applied autology, neuro-theology, meta-chemistry, myco-mysticism and the ultimate science thanatology.

'Pala' is the island, an imaginary one, thrown somewhere among the East Indies. The island is the meeting place of the East and the West, of science and mysticism, drugs and divinity, the land of Tom Krishnas and Mary Sarojinis. Its capital is Shivapuram, its deity is the 'Tathagata', and its temple is in the vicinity of its High Altitude Station. The people are taught to develop in themselves *karuna* the Great Compassion of the Buddhists. They seek enlightenment through meditation, and use a '*moksha-*medicine' to aid uninhibited meditation. Politically they have a

1 Foreword to *Brave New World,* pp. viii-ix.

consitutional monarchy, but the then Rajah being a minor, a
Privy Council headed by Dr. Robert Macphail rules the country.
Economically rich in natural resources, especially oil, but aware
of the attendant evils of capitalistic competition and Big Business,
they believe in what Propter calls the Jeffersonian democracy of
peasants plus small machines and electricity. But surrounded by
greedy capitalistic governments, and a military dictator Col.
Dipa as the closest neighbour, Pala lives in conscious imminent
danger of being ravaged by alien cultures.

From the irresponsible good-timers and the escapist truth-
searchers of his early novels, Huxley has later turned to positive
and constructive thinkers like Miller, Propter and Bruno Rontini.
And now, in this novel, Miller's anthropological approach,
Propter's Thoreau-Gandhi metaphysical sociology, and Bruno's
transcendental mysticism are harmonized to evolve the new way
of life in 'Pala'.

Discarding Manichaeanism, Huxley has by now accepted the
trinity of being and the need to induce unity. Huxley has come
to believe that "God is immanent and man is potentially self-
transcendent". Transcending our egos, passions and prejudices,
rejecting the Manichee in us, keeping aside what we think we
are, and knowing who in fact we are, results in Good Being.
Good Being results in the right kind of Good Doing. The ending
of sorrow lies in, as the Buddha says, "self-knowledge, total
acceptance, the blessed experience of Not-Two". The basic
principles of Palanese life, Huxley states thus:

> Good Being is knowing who in fact we are; and in order to
> know who in fact we are, we must first know, moment by
> moment, who we think we are and what this bad
> habit of thought compels us to feel and do. A moment of clear
> and complete knowledge of what we think we are, but in fact
> are not, puts a stop, for a moment to the Manichaean charade.
> If we renew, until they become a continuity, these moments
> of the knowledge of what we are not, we may find ourselves
> all of a sudden, knowing who in fact we are.
> Concentration, abstract thinking, spiritual exercises—syste-
> matic exclusions in the realm of thought. Asceticism and
> hedonism—systematic exclusions in the realms of sensation,
> feeling and action. But Good Being is in the knowledge of

who in fact one is in relation to all experiences; so be aware
—aware in every context, at all times and whatever, creditable
or discreditable, pleasant or unpleasant, you may be doing or
suffering. This is the only genuine 'yoga', the only spiritual
exercise worth practising.[2]

Training in this awareness is given in Pala right from childhood. Anthony Beavis, in *Eyeless in Gaza,* laments that such
training is not possible as the right kind of teachers are not
there. But, in Pala, they have first started with the teaching of
teachers over a century earlier.

The minor Rajah's great-great-great-grandfather, Murugan the
Reformer and his court physician Dr. Andrew Macphail, Robert's
great-grandfather, initiated this way of life. Dr. Andrew, with
his scientific training and anti-dogmatic humanism, has come to
accept the virtue of pure and applied *Mahayana.* The Rajah, a
Tantrik Buddhist, has realized the value of pure and applied
science. Together they have evolved a new way of life, making
the best of both worlds, the western world of knowledge, power
and progress, and the eastern world of Buddhism and applied
metaphysics. This best-of-both-worlds programme set the tenor
in every field of activity in Pala.

Huxley's theory is that the human being is a complex creature.
To evolve a harmonious individual, an all-inclusive psycho-
physical conditioning is necessary. To develop an individual
'holy, healthy and whole' we have to work simultaneously on all
the fronts "from diet to auto-suggestion, from negative ions to
meditation". If this is done, the world will be rid of neurotics,
erotics, escapists, fanatics and paranoids. Life will neither be a
tale told by an idiot nor one told by a fanatic. Between the two
horns of idiocy and lunacy, there can be a path of sanity on
which Spandrells and Colemans, Mary Amberleys and
Mrs. Aldingtons need no longer stew in their own juice.

For instance, in Pala, their family and social relationships are
free, genuine and voluntary. A family, in the modern sense,
consists of "a single set of parents with their children, foisted
by hereditary pre-destination". One can't get out of the group,
nor go "for a change of moral or psychological air". Sushila,

[2] *Island,* p. 39.

Dr. Macphail's daughter-in-law, compares the European and
Palanese families thus:

> Take one sexually inept wage-slave, one dissatisfied female,
> two or (if preferred) three small television-addicts; marinate
> in a mixture of Freudism and dilute Christianity; then bottle
> up tightly in a four-room flat and stew for fifteen years in
> their own juice.[3]

The product is the European family. The Palanese family is
evolved thus:

> Take twenty sexually satisfied couples and their offspring; add
> science, intuition and humour in equal quantities; steep in
> Tantrik Buddhism and simmer indefinitely in an open pan in
> the open air over a brisk flame of affection.[4]

The result is an inclusive, un-predestined and voluntary
family. They have, what are called, Mutual Adoption Clubs.
"Every MAC consists of anything from fifteen to twenty-five
assorted couples. Newly elected brides and bridegrooms, old-
timers with growing children, grandparents and great-grand-
parents—everybody in the club adopts everyone else". So, whenever children find their parental home unbearable, they migrate
to one of the other homes. Grown up children go out and adopt
another set of elders, a different group of peers and juniors.
The MAC's consist of responsible groups, with genuine and
voluntary attachments, sharing the chores, fulfilling their
responsibilities. The MAC is a free voluntary society. It is not
militaristic. It teaches no dogmas, manufactures no party
members. It has no official baby-tamers. Its aim is to create
better human beings, more balanced individuals. And hence, it
helps to produce healthier relationships, wider sympathies, and,
what Huxley calls, hybridization of micro-cultures. Feelings of
separation in existence, loneliness and boredom, feelings like those
of Myra Viveash, are eliminated by the MAC's.

In all family and social relationships, there is an important
factor which contributes a lot both to human misery and happiness,

---

[3] Ibid., p. 90.

[4] Ibid.

and that is Sex. In *Do What You Will,* Huxley deals with the different conceptions of sexual love, and how, these conceptions, conflicting in nature, lead to disharmony. Huxley says that religion considers sexual love as vulgarly mundane, and deifies the ascetic dread of passion. Romanticism has elevated it to divinity while realism has brought it down to the level of a sport or pastime. In all his novels up to *Island,* Huxley has dealt with a variety of sexual experiences in such detail that critics have accused him of being obsessed with sex and of indulging in schoolboy smut. Huxley's novels depict in detail the reactions of a large variety of individuals to sexual love, how these reactions emanate from an interplay of emotion and environment, how mistaken notions lead to misery, and how ignorance and imbalance lead to perversions and, at times, even to death. In *Island,* Huxley sums up his ideas on sexual love and lays down the cures. He attempts to reconcile sex with spirituality, socio-economics with mysticism, physiological craving with transcendental knowledge.

The Palanese, Huxley says, originally Shaivites, have been influenced by Mahayana Buddhism with *Tantrik* trimmings. The *Tantrik* does not renounce the world, but makes use of everything he does, everything that happens to him, everything that he sees, touches and tastes, as so many means to his liberation from enslavement to Self. Awareness leads to enlightenment, "awareness of one's own sensations and awareness of the not-sensation in every sensation". Coition is also an experience. So, except when they want children, the Tantrik practises what is known as male continence or *coitus reservatus.* The Palanese call it *Maithuna* or the *yoga* of love. This technique of love-making makes possible awareness of one's own sensations of this psycho-physical experience. It makes possible paying attention to, as one of the characters Nurse Radha says:

> To myself and at the same time to my not-self. And to Ranga's not-self, and to Ranga's self, and to Ranga's body, and to my body and everything it is feeling. And to all the love and the friendship. And to the mystery of the other person—the perfect stranger, who's the other half of your own self, and the same as your not-self. And all the while one's paying attention to all the things that, if one were sentimental, or worse, if one were spiritual like the poor old Rani, one would find so

unromantic and gross and sordid even. But they aren't sordid, because one's also paying attention to the fact that, when *one's* fully aware of them, those things are just as beautiful as all the rest, just as wonderful.[5]

This *yoga* of love combines in itself social, economic and metaphysical principles. For a *Tantrik* Buddhist, birth-control is an almost sacred duty, as "begetting is merely postponed assassination". To a small village community, birth-control is a social and economic need.

Sexual relations in Pala are free, voluntary and untainted by jealousy, guilt complex and mutual recrimination. Sex education and training in this *yoga* of love are given at school from the age of fifteen and a half, about the same time as they start teaching biology and trigonometry. Sade-Masochs like Coleman and Spandrell, hypocrites like Burlap and Sydney Quarles, irresponsible sensualists like Lucy Tantamount and Mary Amberley, never exist in a Palanese society. One may see a Katy here, but she need never die here in an accident resulting from accusations and frayed tempers. People here are happy, sane and contented, with their religious sentiments, physiological needs and material welfare attended to.

These principles of applied mysticism and psycho-somatic conditioning are employed in all fields of activity. Both medicine and education, in Pala, are preventive rather than curative in principle. Their doctors are paid to keep the people well, not to drug them or chop them up after they fall ill. They not only use anti-biotics and synthetic vitamins, but also employ hypnosis and auto-suggestion to aid the mind rejuvenate the body. Hypnotic suggestion is used to condition the minds of infant children. Physical contact and soft repeated suggestion are expected to create in infant minds the required favourable impressions. Like Dr. Miller, they believe that friendliness evokes friendliness. If one is friendly, even the serpent does not use its poison on him. A king cobra lives quietly in a niche in Shanta's home, and she hopes her baby will make friends and play with it. This psycho-therapy is built into their educational system to mould the character of children.

Their elementary education is based on a bridge-building

[5] Ibid., p. 79.

system, correlating the training of the mind-body with formal instruction. They educate their children on the conceptual level without killing their natural ability for intense non-verbal experience, that is, a reconciliation of analysis with vision. In the biology class, a formal analytical study of a flower is followed by a session in meditation, a pure unconceptualized experience of the flower as a whole, a 'Mahakasyapa' view of things, as Buddhists call it. Biology and self-knowledge are thus bridged together. In the same way, children are taught to relate everything they have learnt, art, language, religion, self-knowledge. Dance, drama, music and auto-suggestion are combined to condition the body-mind. The emphasis is on the sciences of life rather than on physics and chemistry. The MAC's and the bridge-building system of education evolve the children into fair, friendly and sympathetic individuals. Schizoid and paranoiac tendencies are curbed at an early age. Personal eccentricities and vanities are rounded off. Self-pride and tendency to bully others to show oneself off, are sublimated and canalized. Intense physical exercise combined with mind-body training keeps the child healthy and whole. First lessons given in ecology at an early age, make the children realize that all living is relationship. Then there is the ethics of relationship, the fair principle of balance, of give and take, and no excesses. This elementary ecology of give-and-take at two levels, on the emotional plane in our relations with fellow-beings, on the economic plane in the 'conservation-morality' in our relations with nature—leads us to elementary Buddhism and higher education. The Palanese Secretary for Education says:

> What we give the children is simultaneously a training in perceiving and imagining, a training in applied physiology and psychology, a training in practical ethics and practical religion, a training in the proper use of language, and a training in self-knowledge. In a word, a training of the whole mind-body in all its aspects.[6]

Then Huxley switches over to higher education. The grown-ups are a mixture of mind and physiology, and so, purely intellectual work might turn a person into "a bad-tempered sitting-addict". So, in Pala, even intellectuals put in an hour or two of physical

[6] Ibid., p. 208.

work as a form of therapy. Moreover, paranoiac tendencies in individuals can be canalized into a desire to achieve difficult and dangerous things. For instance, in the case of certain individuals, the muscle-men, rock-climbing is prescribed as a course of instruction. Hanging down a precipitous rock, one is strangely aware of himself, of the world around, aware of the nearness of death.[7] From a mystical point of view, rock-climbing leads to a threefold *yoga*—the *yoga* of danger, the *yoga* of the jungle and the *yoga* of the summit. Beauty, horror, beauty; "beauty made one with the horror in the *yoga* of the jungle. Life reconciled with the perpetual imminence of death in the *yoga* of danger. Emptiness identified with selfhood in the Sabbath *yoga* of the summit". This is a strange symbiosis of psychology and mysticism—desire to show off sublimated into a desire for doing things which others cannot; doing difficult and dangerous things transformed into a mystical exercise, a *yoga* leading to enlightenment.

Huxley does not stop here. He goes a step further. He says that, normally, we look at the world through a lattice of preconceived notions after censorship by the subconscious mind. For a true understanding of things, the doors of perception must be cleansed, and the mind liberated from passion and prejudice. Awareness leads to enlightenment, awareness of everything in life, awareness of the nearness of death, of even death itself. "Start by being fully aware of what you think you are. It'll help you to become aware of what you are in fact". This awareness leads to unitive knowledge, of one in All and all in One. "Thou art That, and so am I, That is me. And That's also him". This is the blessed experience of Not-Two, the oneness of all being, the Shaivite Advaita, the Buddhist *Nirvana,* a *nirvana* not apart from life but coeval with life.

So, to cleanse the doors of perception, instead of the chalice with holy water, Huxley brings in a beaker with a *moksha*-medicine, and the world of critical reviewers burst into peals of ridicule. To help them pass into a genuinely mystical state of mind, the Palanese, Huxley says, use a psychodelic drug, a 'reality-revealer'. After a difficult session in rock-climbing, the climbers sit in the Nataraja temple, and in a religious service they offer their achievement to the God, and then each of them receives a dose of the drug. The *moksha*-medicine is said to be different

[7] Wordsworth speaks of a similar experience in *Prelude,* Book I.

from the 'soma' in *Brave New World*. It is a mind-releasing substance which pulls down the barriers between the conscious and the sub-conscious. It vivifies the silent areas of the brain and "opens some kind of neurological sluice and so allows a larger volume of Mind with a large 'M' to flow into your mind with a small 'm' ". The response to the drug is full-blown mystical experience, the basic experience of One in all and All in one, with its corollaries, boundless compassion, fathomless mystery and meaning. Showing the image of Shiva and Parvathi, Dr. Roberts explains the symbolism:

> How beautiful! And in their tenderness what depths of meaning! What wisdom beyond all spoken wisdom in that sensual experience of spiritual fusion and atonement! Eternity in love with time. The One joined in marriage to the many, the relative made absolute by its union with the One. Nirvana identified with samsara, the manifestation in time and flesh and feeling of the Buddha Nature.[8]

Godliness in worldliness is Huxley's theme. Awareness, pure, constant and uninhibited, from infancy to eternity, is his path to salvation. One of his characters Vijaya says:

> Breathe deeply, and as you breathe, pay attention to this smell of incense. Pay your whole attention to it; know it for what it is—an ineffable fact beyond words, beyond reason and explanation. Know it in the raw. Know it as a mystery. Perfume, women and prayer—those were the three things that Mohammad loved above all others. The inexplicable data of breathed incense, touched skin, felt love and beyond them, the mystery of mysteries, the One in plurality, the Emptiness that is all, the Suchness totally present in every appearance, at every point and instant. So, breathe, breathe, breathe.[9]

Thus is the clear light of the void linked up with the vegetative nervous system, the marriage of heaven and hell. *Karuna,* 'Attention', cry the myna birds over and over again. *Prajna-parimitha* and *Karuna,* unbounded wisdom and compassion

---

[8] *Island*, p. 169.   [9] Ibid., p. 166.

result from practising all the *yogas* of increased awareness. One of the characters, Sushila Macphail says:

Eating, drinking, dying—three primary manifestations of the universal and impersonal life. Animals live that impersonal and universal life without knowing its nature. Ordinary people know its nature but don't live it and, if ever they think seriously about it, refuse to accept it. An enlightened person knows it, lives it, and accepts it completely. He eats, he drinks and in due course he dies—but he eats with a difference, drinks with a difference, dies with a difference.[10]

Awareness leads to enlightenment, and true enlightenment consists in wisdom plus compassion. Wisdom and compassion bring the millennium to the earth.

But, a pocket of saintliness cannot exist in an insane world. Col. Dipa, with a burst of machine-gun fire, scares the myna birds away.

The novel is written in a tone solemn and serious. Cynical amusement and biting satire are left to the paranoid ambassador Bahu and the schizoid journalist Will Farnaby. The ambassador contributes to the fall of Pala on the plea that sanity cannot survive in an insane world. The journalist, at last taking 'yes' for an answer, finds only 'no' prevailing. Huxley had to face a pungent criticism of his views. The West has called him a cynical salvationist, the East has ridiculed him as a salesman of salvation. The one is angry with him for discarding Christianity, the other for importing the test-tube and the syringe into the temple. Prof. Srinivasa Iyengar writes: "The same Huxley who made fun of 'soma' in *Brave New World* now accepts the *moksha*-medicine. The 'Cynical Salvationist' has become the Salesman of Salvation through mescalin! The earlier role suits him much better".

Island is the summing up of the Huxleyan theme, the culmination of a forty-year old search. To every human ailment that contributes to disharmony and suffering, every ailment he has depicted and analysed in his previous novels, he suggests a cure in *Island*. His theory is that religion, science, ethics, sociology, tradition and custom, fashion and personal taste, dream and

10 Ibid., p. 236.

desire, each pulling its own way, each stressing on its own ideals, contribute to conflict and disharmony in man, to misery and violence in the world. So, a new system is necessary, one that accepts nature in the raw, allows full scope to all human instincts, appetites and desires, and by means of an all-inclusive mind-body training helps the individual to develop into a full-blown human being. It should be a system built into the very texture of living in the country, extending its influence into every walk of life so that the salvation aimed at is not individual but general. Rampion's deification of the body, the compassion of Mrs. Chelifer and Rachel Quarles, the anthropological approach of Dr. Miller, the Jeffersonian democracy of Propter, and the transcendental mysticism of Bruno Rontini, plus his own latest find mescalin the *moksha*-medicine, all go together to make the utopia. From *Crome Yellow* to *Island* can be traced the journey from sterility to fruitfulness and transcendence.

Myra Viveash lives on a spiritual death-bed because of her lover's death, but Sushila Macphail leads a benign life, "a Mary with swords in her heart". John Bidlake and Eustace Barnak wail in terror at impending death, but Lakshmi, with no pangs of regret or fear, discards the body with a smile on her lips. Spandrell and Mark Staithes, even Brian Foxe, stultified by their parental jailers, cramped by their own egos and perversions, run themselves to ruin. But Tom Krishna and Mary Sarojini run about 'holy, healthy and whole'. John Bidlake, Spandrell and even Rivers speak of God the cosmic joker, the practical joker. But Ranga says: "God has nothing to do with it, and the joke isn't cosmic, it's strictly man-made. These things aren't like gravity or the second law of thermodynamics; they don't *have* to happen. They happen only if people are stupid enough to let them happen". Spandrell and Rivers speak of predestination of temperament and events, but Sushila speaks of self-determination and destiny-control. Time and craving, craving and time, laments Propter. Bernard Shaw complains that a single life-time of three score and ten is not enough to become wise. But, at least twenty per cent of the Palanese are able to take short cuts to education, condense the experience of an eternity into a moment, an experience similar to that of some drowning men who are said to have seen the whole of their past life unfolding before them in a few seconds. Thus Huxley sums up his ideas, suggests the cures, and gives the structure of a utopian society which has renounced applied physics and chemistry, and has taken to "the road of applied biology, the road of fertility control and the limited production and selective industrialization which fertility control makes possible, the road that leads towards happiness from the inside out, through health, through awareness, through a change in one's attitude towards the world; not towards the mirage of happiness from the outside in, through toys and pills and non-stop distractions".

One may disagree with Huxley, but his sincerity cannot be doubted. Whether one agrees with Huxley's conclusions or not, one cannot but admit the need for a comprehensive psycho-physical training for all individuals in a society, a training different from Pavlovian brain-washing or the scientist-dictator's genetic conditioning. Huxley has indulged in his writings, neither in schoolboy smut nor in irresponsible cynical amusement, but in a positive search for harmony of being.

But, in spite of its profundity of thought, solemnity of tone, dignity of utterance, narrative ease and moving characterization, still *Island* leaves one aesthetically unsatisfied. Mass communi-cation, mind-manipulation, brain-washing, hypnotic suggestion and sleep-teaching which he satirizes in *Brave New World,* Huxley makes full use of in *Island.* Soma he holds up to ridicule, but mescalin he recommends with solemn reverence. Pavlovian conditioning he has condemned earlier, but now he uses Pavlov "for a good purpose". Of course, life rests on right acceptance and rejection, but still it looks ironical that both in Brave New World and in Pala, certain areas of knowledge are kept out of bounds, science is muzzled and a holiday from some facts is veritably enjoyed. One is made to wonder whether the Original Sin really bothers mankind. Is knowledge evil, and ignorance bliss? Everything ultimately seems to have boiled down to the question of ends and means—Pavlov and hypnopaedia for a good purpose. But the essential error that Huxley commits lies in the fact that he tries to instal mystical appliances on a conveyor belt and mass-produce spiritually-developed individuals, in a sort of a state enterprise. Therein arises the need for a *moksha-*medicine. Nature, in its own way, has created its alphas, betas and epsilons. All cannot rise to realize their essence, some are destined to remain as apes. Self-realization must come from within, it cannot be induced from without. Mescalin may increase suggestibility but not sensitivity. The doors of perception may be cleansed, but the view selected for contemplation and the grooves of thought depend on the individual. Of course, Huxley himself says that mescalin is not necessary always and for all, but still, in his eagerness to evolve a system of national regeneration, he pursues an irrational path; or, perhaps, in his excursions into the twin worlds of science and spirituality, the rational mystic he is, he is just voicing forth a pleasing utopian possibility.

Still, *Island* remains Huxley's masterpiece, a summing up of his ideas. Huxley is an institution by himself, a shocking eye-opener to many a complacent Babbitt, and a frank realist who fearlessly analyses the human predicament in a mechano-morphic world, and seeks the path to salvation. He is a giant inheritor of the Two Cultures, the heir to both Huxley and Arnold. With the incisive intellect of a scientist, the imaginative sympathy of a literary artist, enriched by encyclopaedic knowledge, with a genuinely liberal outlook, he studies the human situation and suggests the means of inducing serene unity into man's multiple amphibiousness. He realizes that:

Only in the knowledge of his own Essence,
Has any man ceased to be many monkeys.

This is the conclusion he arrives at after a forty-year old search, and, to realize the essence, he says, nothing short of everything will really do: "Patriotism is not enough. But neither is anything else. Science is not enough, religion is not enough, art is not enough, politics and economics are not enough, nor is love, nor is duty, nor is action however disinterested, nor, however sublime, is contemplation. Nothing short of everything will really do".

If *Island* gives the summing up of the Huxleyan theme, if it presents his ideal utopia, why does he, at the end, bring about its fall with a burst of machine-gun fire? Does it not look either childishly flippant or cynically pessimistic? The answer to this, perhaps, lies in the philosophy of eternal recurrence propounded by the seventeenth-century Italian scholar Vico Nietzsche and Spengler advocated similar theories which fascinated writers like Yeats, Joyce and Huxley. Vico believed that, when a human society reached a certain stage in civilization, it would fall off into primitiveness, and then a new civilization would begin to develop. This is in the very nature of life and evolution. In *Ape and Essence,* Bernard and Loola are shown to be escaping from savagery into civilization. In *Island* is shown civilization retracing the path to primitivism with machine-gun fire. But that is life, and "ripeness is all".

Huxley's suggestions may not be accepted but his sincerity cannot be questioned. His conclusions are based on a perennial philosophy which he has evolved out of the essence of all great religions. Himself a participant in a schizoid world where apes hold the leash for men to follow, with intellectual honesty he endeavours to find out how not to be a Hamlet.

6

HOW NOT TO BE A HAMLET

What you need, Denis, is a fixed income,
a plump young wife and congenial work.

ANNE in *Crome Yellow*

IN the previous chapters has been given a thematic analysis, presentation of character, and the general trend of thought in Huxley's novels. The novels have been written over a period of forty years, but still they bear close affinity and present a saga of human progress from self-division to serenity. A sympathetic study will reveal that, through all these novels, there runs a continuous stream of closely related cogent thought, that there is a sense of direction and purpose in the writing of them, and that they are not mere undergraduatish exercises in debunking.

In this chapter is traced the evolution of Huxley's Life-theory and the path he has discovered for mankind's emergence into serenity of thought and being. In an essentially materialistic world, the big blustering fools gaily carry the day, while the quiet, refined and sensitive individuals silently suffer from a self-consuming intellect. Fulke Greville asks: "Passion and reason, self-division's cause?" Reason tells Hamlet of the futility of all action, passion drives him to it. As a result he makes a mess of his own life and the lives of those around him. Huxley, in *Eyeless in Gaza,* analyses the Hamlet-nature:

Take Hamlet. Hamlet inhabited a world whose best psychologist was Polonius. If he had known as little as Polonius, he would have been happy. But he knew too much; and in this consists his tragedy. Read his parable of the musical instruments. Polonius and the others assumed as axiomatic that man was a penny whistle with only half a dozen stops. Hamlet knew that, potentially at least, he was a whole symphony orchestra. Mad, Ophelia lets the cat out of the bag. "We know what we are, but know not what we may be". Polonius knows very clearly what he and other people *are*, within the ruling conventions. Hamlet knows this, but also what they may be—outside the local system of masks and humours.

*   *   *

Polonius is much more obviously and definitely a person than the prince. Indeed, Hamlet's personality is so indefinite that critics have devoted thousands of pages to the discussion of what it really was. In fact, of course, Hamlet didn't have a personality—knew altogether too much to have one. He was conscious of his total experience, atom by atom and instant by instant, and accepted no guiding principle which would make him choose one set of patterned atoms to represent his personality rather than another. To himself and to others he was just a succession of more or less incongruous states. Hence that perplexity at Elsinore and among the Shakespearean critics ever since. Honour, Religion, Prejudice, Love—all the conventional props that shore up ordinary personality have been, in this case, gnawed through. Hamlet is his own termite, and from a tower has eaten himself down to a heap of sawdust.[1]

Being one's own termite is an existential malady in a mechanomorphic world. In the clash between idealism and actuality, "man the multiple-amphibian", Huxley says, "lives in a chronic state of mild or acute civil war", seeking a means of escape from the inner chaos. Disillusioned with organized religion, he runs in search of substitutes. And the substitutes for religion are many, from Gumbril's pneumatic trousers to Mark Staithes's armed rebellions, from Shearwater's study of the kidneys to Burlap's worship of the spirit. Huxley's essay *Substitutes for Religion* discusses political creeds, ritual, art, sex, business, dogmas, superstition and priest surrogates, individuals cling to as the "genuine article".[2] The eminent philosopher, Dr. Radhakrishnan, in his lecture *Substitutes for Religion,* discusses substitutes of a different order which individuals with intellection and insight might choose—naturalistic atheism (which includes neo-paganism

[1] *Eyeless in Gaza,* pp. 146-48.
[2] Aldous Huxley, *Proper Studies,* pp. 210-29.

and intellectualism), agnosticism, scepticism, humanism, pragmatism and modernism.[3] Huxley's essay is a jesting Pilate's satirical attack on perverse attitudes, but his novels present an artist's superb portrayal of the changing moods and temperaments of post-war Europe. Here, the artist Huxley's analysis remarkably coincides with the philosopher Radhakrishnan's—Gumbril and his tribe are neo-pagans, Cardan, with all his hedonism, is an agnostic, Philip an intellectual sceptic, Miller a humanist, Propter a pragmatist, and Huxley himself a modernist in that he is, to use one of his own phrases, a transcendental pragmatist.

Huxley, in a foreword, referring to the "all too numerous books" he has written, states that "the composition of them was a form of self-exploration and self-education".[4] His novels reveal this process at work, an intellectual and an artist making a ruthless but honest exposure of the ape and the essence in the human, and tracing a genuine pilgrimage from self-division to harmony of being. Denis, Gumbril, Calamy, Philip, Anthony Beavis, all carry within them traces of Huxley himself, and Will Farnaby's final conversion in *Island* suggests the conversion of a jesting Pilate to mysticism.

In Huxley's first novel *Crome Yellow*, Anne the pagan advises the adolescent hero: "What you need, Denis, is a fixed income, a plump young wife and congenial work". It looks rather curious that, in the Huxley crowd, it is only among the men that there are Hamlets. The women seem to have no cosmological worries. They are all, without exception, life-worshippers—the pagan Anne, the bored Myra, the vampire Lucy, the emancipated intellectual Elinor or even the benign Mrs. Chelifer and Rachel Quarles. Perhaps the essential feminity in women can never be tainted even by a mechanistic civilization. They all display a lack of abstract interests, they stand solid on the earth feeling and commiserating by instinct and intuition. They offer all their being and what all they ask for is a full-hearted response. Even the benignity of Mrs. Chelifer, Rachel Quarles and Janet Bidlake is a natural feminine compassion rather than any specious religious ideal.

Anne's advice is realistic, earthy, sagacious and essentially

---

[3] Radhakrishnan, *An Idealist View of Life*, Chapter II.
[4] Foreword to *Stories, Essays and Poems of Aldous Huxley*, (Everyman's), p. vii.

feminine in tone. This is the pagan good-timer's panacea for all ills—material well-being, physiological satisfaction and some psychologically absorbing avocation. Anne's prescription sounds sensible to most people, and it serves as a solid base for Huxley's philosophy of life. The purport of the pagan good-timer's slogan is "to hell with Hamlet and metaphysical worries". They worship the intellect, they suppress the grumbling inner voices—"we build factories and bandstands on them", says Gumbril in *Antic Hay*—and they run in a crazy search for happiness. The inner voices may be suppressed but cannot be killed. The factory wheels will have to stop one day and the bandstands fall silent. Huxley speaks through two of his characters: peace and happiness do not come to those who pursue them: they come as "by-products in the process of making something else". Huxley's farewell to good-timers is hinted at in *Those Barren Leaves*, in Calamy's renunciation and Mrs. Aldington, the pagan-queen's "weeping over her whole life, weeping at the approach of death".

Being misfits in this blustering world of good-timers, some may cloister themselves in an intellectual Wittenberg, and seek an escape from reality as truth-searchers and higher-lifers, Lypiatt's loud pursuit of art and Shearwater's worship of the kidneys, Lord Edward's experiments on asymmetric tadpoles and his brother's theistic mathematics, even Calamy's reclusion "to get at the bottom of the cosmos", are all attempts to escape from the responsibilities of life. But escape is possible only so long as life does not draw the escapist back into its vortex. Anthony Beavis, Philip's successor, comments that the contemplative life "can be made a kind of high-brow substitute for Marlene Dietrich".

These good-timers, truth-searchers and higher-lifers, not having the innate strength to face the quirks of circumstance, shrink in animal terror when they face life's realities. Some of them complain of divine injustice. Some talk of God the practical joker, the cosmic joker. Some of them wail in terror of death and the unknown beyond. The seeming meaninglessness of life terrifies them. Even a sensible woman like Elinor is shocked into superstition and fear at the tragic death of her little son Philip. Huxley concludes that the so-called 'life of reason' of the neo-pagans cannot subdue the gnawing termite within and enable man to face life in its entirety.

Rejecting the intellect, Huxley then turns to the instincts and intuitions as the genuine media for a vital understanding of life. D. H. Lawrence is his preceptor in this creed which he names 'Life-worship'. Lawrence says that "we can go wrong in our minds, but what our blood feels and believes and says is always true".[5] According to Lawrence, the ascetics who reject the body as obscene, the intellectuals who live in the world of pure abstractions, the theoreticians who talk of institutions without knowing what an individual is, all deal with non-human truths. The only relevant truth is the human truth that can be gleaned through the flesh and the blood, the instinct and the intuition, through touch, taste, sight, smell and feeling. Lawrence and his wife Frieda make their appearance as Rampion and Mary in Huxley's *Point Counter Point*. Rampion says:

> A man's a creature on a tight-rope, walking delicately, equilibrated, with mind and consciousness and spirit at one end of the balancing pole and body and instinct and all that's unconscious and earthy and mysterious at the other. Balanced. Which is damnably difficult. And the only absolute he can ever really know is the absolute of perfect balance. The absoluteness of perfect relativity. Which is a paradox and nonsense intellectually. But so is all real, genuine, living truth—just nonsense according to logic. And logic is just nonsense in the light of living truth. You can choose which you like, logic or life.[6]

Lawrence and Frieda, Rampion and Mary are extraordinary individuals with deep insight and understanding of life. They are harmonious beings whatever might be the tone and tenor of their language. They alone can feel the truth of their doctrine and live up to it. But it is a dangerous doctrine to ordinary people. Firstly, to some like Spandrell, it sounds as a "gospel of animalism". Secondly, it might be rationalized to suit individual convenience, and distorted so as to justify promiscuity. (*Point Counter Point* presents variations, distortions and parodies on the Rampion-theme). Thirdly, Lawrence's philosophy has no consolations to offer to old age. Worship of the body makes no sense to the decrepit and the dying. Fourthly, Lawrence's rejection of things spiritual is as fatuous as the ascetic's rejection of the

5 D. H. Lawrence's letter to Earnest Collings, dated 17th Jan., 1913.
6 *Point Counter Point*, pp. 560-61.

body. Is Lawrence too an escapist? Huxley's farewell to Lawrence is sounded in *Eyeless in Gaza*, in Anthony's comments on Lawrence's *The Man Who Died*:

> For Lawrence, the animal purpose had seemed sufficient and satisfactory. The cock, crowing, fighting, mating—anonymously; and man anonymous like the cock. Better such mindless anonymity, he had insisted, than the squalid relationships of human beings advanced halfway to consciousness, still only partially civilized.
>
> But Lawrence had never looked through a microscope, never seen biological energy in its basic undifferentiated state. He hadn't wanted to look, had disapproved on principle of microscopes, fearing what they might reveal; and had been right to fear. Those depths beneath depths of namelessness, crawling irrepressibly—they would have horrified him. He had insisted that the raw material should be worked up—but worked only to a certain pitch and no further; that the primal crawling energy should be used for the relatively higher purposes of animal existence, but for no existence beyond the animal.[7]

Farewell to one after the other—to the so-called life of reason of the good-timers, to the ivory tower of the fugitive truth-searchers and higher-lifers, now farewell to the life of instinct and intuition of the life-worshippers. None of these satisfies Huxley, as each tries to squeeze man down its "particular drain-pipe of weltanschauung", and none shows the path to inner harmony. Huxley expresses his doubt through Philip Quarles, whether the human being is "congenitally incapable of living wholly and harmoniously".

Huxley then falls to rethinking, and his thoughts incline towards the mystic. Man, he says, is not "a detachable, autonomous, unitary soul boxed up in a corporeal prison-tomb".[8] He is a multiple-amphibian. What we call personality is a myth. Like Blake, Lawrence and Proust, Huxley believes that the human being is a "succession of psychological states", and "the individual is important only as the place where these states occur". Into

---

[7] *Eyeless in Gaza*, p. 360.
[8] Aldous Huxley, *Literature and Science*, p. 79.

this welter of psychological atomism, Huxley, through Miller in *Eyeless in Gaza,* brings in a sense of order, a simplification, by presenting man as a triphibian[9] with, to use the hackneyed words, body, psyche and spirit. Another of Huxley's characters, Propter, in *After Many a Summer,* speaking of good and evil, refers to these three facets of human personality or, to be precise, three levels of consciousness, the animal, the human and the spiritual levels. Still another of Huxley's characters, John Rivers in *The Genius and the Goddess,* carries the theme further. He says:

> At one end of the spectrum it's pure spirit, it's the Clear Light of the Void; and at the other end it's instinct, it's health, it's the perfect functioning of an organism that's infallible so long as we don't interfere with it; and somewhere between the two extremes is what St. Paul called 'Christ'—the divine made human. Spiritual grace, animal grace, human grace—three aspects of the same underlying mystery; ideally all of us should be open to all of them.[10]

So, the cure for Hamletism is through the trinity of human personality being blessed with the trinity of grace. But attaining the trinity of grace is not so easy as it sounds, because our existential patterns are such that an almost natural antipathy exists within this trinity. To replace this antipathy with sympathy, one has to transcend all the fantasy of the mind. The animal only feels. Man can not only feel but also think and rationalize. But, his thinking and rationalization, Huxley says, are influenced, among other things, by two major factors, language and memory. Our languages, being inadequate to express precisely our thoughts, feelings and emotions, limit our capacity for rational thought and understanding. The ancients in Shaw's *Back to Methuselah* feel the same inadequacy. "What do you read, my lord?" Shakespeare's Hamlet answers "words, words, words".

Another factor which contributes to disharmony is memory. Anthony Beavis complains of the ghosts of memories haunting him. John Rivers, in *The Genius and the Goddess,* says:

> God isn't the son of Memory; He's the son of Immediate

---

[9] Literally means using the three elements land, air and water.
[10] *The Genius and the Goddess,* p. 99.

Experience. You can't worship a spirit in spirit, unless you do it now. Wallowing in the past may be good literature. As wisdom, it's hopeless. Time Regained is Paradise Lost, and Time Lost is Paradise Regained. Let the dead bury their dead. If you want to live at every moment as it presents itself, you've got to die to every other moment.

Living here and now is intense living and intense awareness of life. The Buddhists say that life is a series of becomings and extinctions.

Through Miller, Huxley suggests a kind of mind-body training coupled with an altruistic approach to life. Miller says that self-knowledge is a preliminary to self-change. So, he suggests, first of all, what Huxley describes as "a non-theological praxis of meditation", coupled with training in use of the self, beginning with physical control and through it control of the mind. This is a preliminary stage in, what Huxley calls, awareness of life. Secondly, Miller suggests an anthropological approach to life— treating men as men, because friendliness begets friendliness. Thirdly, to ensure universal peace and happiness, one should work for constructive peace.

Huxley's pacifism is misconstrued by some critics. Quoting from Propter in *After Many a Summer,* Dr. Ghose says "what revolution is to the cause of Marxism, pacifism is to Huxley's mysticism, a strategy".[11] But pacifism, with Huxley, is not a strategy but a creed. In his essay *What Are You Going To Do?,* Huxley states:

The philosophy of Constructive Pacifism proceeds from a consideration of what is to a statement of what ought to be— from empirical fact to idea. The facts upon which the doctrine is based are these. First, all men are capable of love for their fellows. Second, the limitations imposed upon this love are of such a nature that it is always possible for the individual, if he so desires, to transcend them. Third, love and goodness are infectious. So are hatred and evil.

The Constructive Pacifist formulates his belief in some such words as these. The spirit is one and all men are potentially at one in the spirit. Any thought or act which denies the

11 Sisir Kumar Ghose, *Aldous Huxley—A Cynical Salvationist,* p. 63.

fundamental unity of mankind is wrong and, in a certain sense, false; any thought or act which affirms it is right and true. It is in the power of every individual to choose whether he shall deny or affirm the unity of mankind in an ultimate spiritual reality.[12]

The Constructive Pacifist is not a coward but a brave man prepared to live up to his ideals, prepared to face ridicule, contempt, even physical violence and death.

Propter, a pragmatist, in *After Many a Summer,* takes up Miller's humanistic theories and combines them with his own political and social system of Jeffersonian democracy. Then, in *Time Must Have a Stop,* Bruno Rontini, like Miller and Propter an anti-fascist, preaches transcendental awareness as the path to inner harmony. Bruno's mystical doctrines coincide with Buddhistic thought. The Buddha says that spiritual perfection is attained not by suppression of senses and sensations but by cultivation of the mind. *Prajna* (insight) and *Dhyana* (meditation) together lead man to perfection through the four psychic stages of joy and quietness, inner peace and elation, objectivity and non-attachment, and finally serenity and transcendence. True awareness, by eliminating egoism, will bring the mind and the mental processes into harmony with all beings.

Thus, progressing by stages, Huxley finally arrives at a Lifetheory by a synthesis of the various theories he has advanced earlier through his characters—Rampion's life-worship, Miller's humanism, Propter's pragmatism and Bruno's transcendental mysticism. This Life-theory is given a succinct expression in his last novel *Island.*

Huxley, now, in one of his own phrases, a transcendental pragmatist, takes into account, in evolving his theory, all factors which condition human life and thinking. These factors can be considered under two broad heads—ecological and psychosomatic. Under the former, Huxley deals with political, economic and sociological factors, and under the latter, the needs of the mind-body at its three levels of consciousness—the animal, the human and the spiritual.

Huxley's politics are Kropotkinesque and co-operative. He advocates a welfare state on the patterns of Jeffersonian demo-

12 Aldous Huxley, *Stories, Essays and Poems* (Everyman's), p. 404.

cracy which respects the individual, guarantees the three basic freedoms, and believes in decentralization of power by employing stream-lined co-operative techniques. Then, his economics are Henry Georgian and decentralist. He believes: "Electricity minus heavy industry plus birth-control equals democracy and plenty. Electricity plus heavy industry minus birth-control equals totalitarianism and war". So, 'small farms plus electricity' is his slogan. Sociologically, Huxley believes in a new pattern of social relations through, what he calls, 'Mutual Adoption Clubs', which are voluntary associations of individuals, and which offer "a change of moral and psychological air" whenever one feels the desire for an escape from the stifling parental or familiar atmosphere. Anthropologists call such clubs 'extended families'. Huxley describes this club as "a big, open, unpredestined, inclusive family, where all the seven ages of man and a dozen different skills and talents are represented, and in which children have experience of all the important and significant things that human beings do and suffer—working, playing, loving, getting old, being sick, dying". . . .[13]

Thus Huxley, first of all, suggests an environment which minimizes the areas of friction and maximizes individual pleasure of participation in life. Then he turns to psycho-somatic factors, and says that, to become fully human, "nothing short of everything will really do". One has to draw sustenance from every available branch of human knowledge including "that ultimate science, the science that sooner or later we shall all have to be examined in— thanatology". One of the most important of the psycho-somatic factors is sex which is closely connected with the body, the intellect and also the emotions. It has also its impact on social relations. Whether the soul is an excrescence of the living body or the body a cynical comment on the soul, both co-exist and need careful looking after. So, Huxley advises sex education to all girls and boys at about the age of fifteen and a half. He rejects the religious, romantic and realistic notions of love, and pleads for enlightened, voluntary and genuine relationships based on mutual affection and respect, and kept within the discipline of accepted codes of conduct. Promiscuity, he says, is mortifying, whereas genuine love is enlivening. Then, with the sociological aspects in view, he advises birth-control, and even artificial

[13] *Island*, p. 92.

insemination for improving the race. On one side he views sex
with the emotionalism of Lawrence, on the other with the dry
matter-of-factness of a cold calculating intellectual.

Then he shoots into a third dimension, mysticism, and turns
to *Tantrik* Buddhism which has transformed the sexual act into
a mystical practice—*Maithuna* or the *yoga* of love. The *Tantrik*
Buddhists practise one mode of birth-control known as *Coitus
Reservatus.* This technique of love-making makes possible
"awareness of one's sensations and awareness of the not-sensation
in every sensation". Huxley says that sexuality in children is not
confined to the genitals. That 'paradise', he says, gets lost as the
child grows up. *Maithuna* aims at regaining that paradise.

This *maithuna* is taught at school, in Huxley's Island-utopia,
to all children between fifteen and fifteen and a half. Thus,
Huxley's views on sex are a strange conglomeration of
emotionalism, rationalism and mysticism, aiming to reconcile
the physiological and sociological needs with the psychological.

Huxley has, by now, provided for all that pagan Anne has
recommended for happiness; but Anne's prescription caters only
for animal grace and human grace, whereas spiritual grace also
is essential for harmony of being. Most people, Huxley says in
Ends and Means, live, most of the time, on the sub-personal level
identifying themselves slavishly with the prevailing popular modes
of thought and feeling. From this sub-personal, one should rise to
the personal, that is, from slavishness to self-possession. From
the personal level, the ascendance is to the super-personal.

This super-personal level is reached only during the mystical
experience. There is, however, a state of being, rarely attained,
but described by the greatest mystical writers of East and West
in which it is possible for a man to have a kind of double
consciousness—to be both a full-grown person, having a
complete knowledge of, and control over, his sensations,
emotions and thoughts, and also, and at the same time, a more
than personal being, in continuous intuitive relation with the
impersonal principle of reality.[14]

To attain this state, the human being should, first of all, become
human, be able to see, understand and sympathize with all

14 *Ends and Means,* p. 326.

beings. So, an all-inclusive mind-body training is necessary to help individuals transcend their ego and be free from inhibitions. Such a training should be given from infancy. Huxley suggests that, through physical contact and hypnotic suggestion, favourable impressions of love, sympathy and friendliness towards all beings, can be created in infant minds. Then, education of children, he says, should be of a bridge-building type combining scientific study with meditation, a conceptualized analytical study with a pure unconceptualized aesthetic or spiritual experience. In *Ends and Means,* Huxley says:

> Under the present dispensation, the educational system is designed to produce the greatest possible number of intelligent fools. We inspire children with the wish to be intelligent about the phenomena of the external world and about abstract ideas and logical relations; at the same time we teach them techniques by which this wish can be gratified. Meanwhile, however, we make very little effort to inspire them with the wish to be intelligent about themselves and, on the rare occasions when we do make this effort, we provide them with no devices for training the inward-turning intelligence to perform its task efficiently.[15]

But such a training, if given, will be a preparation for the higher levels of transcendental meditation. Huxley believes that the divine is immanent and man is self-transcendent. Transcendence over our egos, passions and perversions is possible through a conscious practice of intense awareness of all processes, physical and psychological, awareness of life, of the nearness of death and of death itself.

> Awareness of everything, of the universal and impersonal life that lives itself through each of us—that's the art of living, and that's what one has to go on practising through death and may be beyond.[16]

The Zen Buddhists say:

> Look into your own being and seek it not through others. Your

15 *Ends and Means,* p. 323.   16 *Island,* p. 239.

own mind is above all forms; it is free and quiet and sufficient; it eternally stamps itself in your six senses and four elements. In its light all is absorbed. Hush the dualism of subject and object, forget both, transcend the intellect, sever yourself from the understanding, and directly penetrate deep into the identity of the Buddha-mind; outside of this there are no realities.[17]

True awareness helps us to realize who, in fact, we are, not what we think we are. It leads to the unitive knowledge of One in all and All in one. "Thou art That, and so am I, That is me. And That's also him". This is the blessed experience of Not-two, the Hindu *Advaitha* and the Buddhist *Nirvana,* a *Nirvana* coeval with life. Wisdom implies *karuna* and liberation from craving and time. The liberated individual can live in that super-personal world of Suchness of Mind, of the Clear Light of the Void. This is enlightenment which gives the bliss of serenity.

We can gauge by now Huxley's progress from the paganism of *Antic Hay* to this transcendental mysticism expounded in *Island.* He has cast off his earlier theories of cosmic jokers and predestination of temperaments and events, and says that unitive knowledge leads to self-determination and destiny-control. His theories of atomistic psychology he has discarded, and he veers to the views of the Gestalt psychologists and speaks of a mind-body training. He realizes that even Helen's 'here and now' theory is symptomatic of escapism and, in *Island,* he says: "What one has to learn is how to remember and yet be free of the past. How to be there with the dead and yet still be here, on the spot, with the living".[18]

This is non-attachment. In *Ends and Means,* Huxley says that awareness is an essential condition of non-attachment. Unawareness is one of the main sources of attachment or evil. He says:

The ideal man is the non-attached man. Non-attached to his bodily sensations and lusts. Non-attached to his craving for power and possessions. Non-attached to the objects of these various desires. Non-attached to his anger and hatred; non-attached to his exclusive loves. Non-attached to wealth, fame,

---

[17] D. T. Suzuki, *Zen Buddhism,* p. 46.
[18] *Island,* p. 107.

social position. Non-attached even to science, art, speculation, philanthropy. Yes, non-attached even to these.[19]

This is the super-personal state in which the individual realizes inner unity and unity with all being. Self-division and self-termitism yield place to serenity and compassion, and man ceases to be a Hamlet.

But, the pragmatist he is, Huxley goes further and introduces a wonder-drug, 'mescalin', which he describes as 'moksha-medicine' or reality-revealer. The drug is said to release the sub-conscious from bondage to the conscious, infuse a mystical state of mind, and make possible self-transcendence and a deeper understanding of things. Through mescalin, Huxley hopes to transform religion into an activity "concerned mainly with experience and intuition —an everyday mysticism underlying and giving significance to everyday rationality, everyday tasks and duties, everyday human relationships.[20]

Mescalin, more than anything else, has brought Huxley columnfuls of ridicule. It is, as if with a post-prandial relish, critics have laid aside *Island* commenting that the scoffing jester has at last turned into a solemn mystic, the sceptic into a believer, the derider of 'soma' into a salesman of mescalin. Quoting from *Heaven and Hell* the sentence—"knowing as he does (or at least as he can know, if he so desires) what are the chemical conditions of transcendental experience, the aspiring mystic should turn for technical help to the specialists—in pharmacology, in biochemistry, in physiology and neurology, in psychology and psychiatry and parapsychology"—Dr. Ghose comments "the list is long but not complete: he forgets to mention pathology and medical jurisprudence".[21] To cull out a sentence from its sequence and ridicule a writer is unfair. The full passage reads thus:

Knowing as he does (or at least as he can know if he so desires) what are the chemical conditions of transcendental experience, the aspiring mystic should turn for technical help to the specialists—in pharmacology, in biochemistry, in physiology and neurology, in psychology and psychiatry and para-

19 *Ends and Means*, pp. 3-4.
20 Huxley's essay, *Drugs That Shape Men's Minds.*
21 Sisir Kumar Ghose, *Aldous Huxley—A Cynical Salvationist*, p. 172.

psychology. And, on their part, of course, the specialists (if any of them aspire to be genuine men of science and complete human beings) should turn, out of their respective pigeon-holes, to the artist, the sibyl, the visionary, the mystic—all those, in a word, who have had experience of the Other World and who know, in their different ways, what to do with that experience.[22]

Gerald Heard writes that "those who patronised his interest and achievement, as though they were some pathetic failure of nerve, either had never studied this subject or known with any intimacy this student who was as pertinacious as he was daring".[23] Huxley is neither a dry-minded rationalist nor a mortifying cymini-sectore. He is neither a quack nor a dialectical acrobat. He is a percipient individual, a fairly good poet, a connoisseur of music and art. The Jesting Pilate Huxley wrote in 1926, when he did not believe in the Other World or the Clear Light of the Void:

> We are, I think, fairly safe in supposing that religious mystics do not in fact unite themselves with that impossible being, a God at once almighty and personal, limited and limitless. But that does not in any way detract from the value of mysticism as a way to perfect health. No man supposes that he is entering into direct communion with the deity when he does Swedish exercises or cleans his teeth. If we make a habit of Muller and Pepsodent, we do so because they keep us fit. It is for the same reason that we should make a habit of mysticism as well as of moral virtue. Leading a virtuous and reasonable life, practising the arts of meditation and recollection, we shall unbury all our hidden talents, shall attain in spite of circumstances to the happiness of serenity and integration, shall come, in a word, to be completely and perfectly ourselves.[24]

Such a conception of mysticism is not much different, in essence, from the orthodox religious or theological point of view. Nor is it a far cry from this basic mysticism to a realization that

22 *Heaven and Hell*, p. 122.
23 *Aldous Huxley—A Memorial Volume*, p. 105.
24 *Jesting Pilate*, p. 192.

mysticism is no escapism, to an acceptance of the presence of the Otherness, and thence to a transformation of the intellectual cum mystic into a mystical materialist or a transcendental pragmatist. Now, the pragmatist Huxley says that, in this notionally conditioned world, it is not possible for all individuals to enter into the world of visionary experience. To such individuals, mescalin might be a boon.

Under a more realistic, a less exclusively verbal system of education than ours, every Angel (in Blake's sense of that word) would be permitted as a sabbatical treat, would be urged and even, if necessary, compelled to take an occasional trip through some chemical Door in the Wall into the world of transcendental experience. If it terrified him, it would be unfortunate but probably salutary. If it brought him a brief but timeless illumination, so much the better. In either case the Angel might lose a little of the confident insolence sprouting from systematic reasoning and the consciousness of having read all the books.[25]

At the same time, Huxley is very cautious in suggesting the use of mescalin. He has had first-hand experience of its effects. But he knows that others may not receive the same experience. Geoffrey Gorer, for instance, reviewing *Island,* says that when he took it he found "the distortions of vision and perception unpleasant and distasteful". "I would never willingly undertake it again", he says. Huxley writes:

I am not so foolish as to equate what happens under the influence of mescalin or of any other drug, prepared or in the future preparable, with the realisation of the end and ultimate purpose of human life: Enlightenment, the Beatific Vision. All I am suggesting is that the mescalin experience is what Catholic theologians call 'a gratuitous grace', not necessary to salvation but potentially helpful and to be accepted thankfully, if made available. To be shaken out of the ruts of ordinary perception, to be shown for a few timeless hours the outer and the inner world, not as they appear to an animal obsessed with survival or to a human being obsessed with words and notions,

[25] Aldous Huxley, *The Doors of Perception,* p. 64.

but as they are apprehended directly and unconditionally, by Mind at Large—this is an experience of inestimable value to everyone and especially to the intellectual.[26]

Huxley's arguments run as follows. The practices of the ascetics and mystics—seclusion, self-mortification, controlled breathing exercises, etc.—produce, in their bodies, certain bio-chemical changes which result in a psychic conditioning favourable to spiritual experiences. Similarly, if, by using a safe drug, the same bio-chemical changes can be produced, it is possible to infuse a mystical disposition even in ordinary individuals. Of course, he says, the experience received may, at times, be infernally distressing, but even these may do a lot of good to the individual.

But no spiritualist, Christian, Hindu, Buddhist or Moslem, would agree with Huxley. Drugs and divinity do not go together. The question is: Is it possible to determine whether a chemically infused spiritual experience is a genuine mystical vision or a drug-induced daydream? Whether bio-chemical changes produce the necessary psychic disposition for mystical experience, or, a genuine mystical experience results in certain bio-chemical changes, is a matter for research if such a research were possible. All spiritualists, for instance, admit that as an individual progresses towards spiritual enlightenment his eyes acquire a magnetic charm, and his body gets swathed in a strange halo, *tejas* or splendour. The bio-chemical changes may as well be the effects rather than the causes.

But one cannot help feeling that, in this world of expanding knowledge, when researches in parapsychology are bringing eastern mysticism close to western hearts, when psychedelics as a class are being segregated from dopes and intoxicants, and when consciousness-changing methods are being explored by eclectic teams of researchers, it might be possible one day to know the bio-chemical and psychic nature of mystical experience. Then, perhaps, mescalin might prove to be, as Gerald Heard remarks, "the most liberating of all our present discoveries".

But mescalin or no mescalin, Huxley's conversion to Eastern mysticism itself is not appreciated by some. A. E. Dyson writes: "Instead of the Nothing of Mrs. Viveash's boredom, we have the Nothingness of Mr. Propter's God; a very dubious exchange we

[26] Huxley, *The Doors of Perception,* pp. 59-60.

might think, in that Mrs. Viveash is at least conscious that her
Nothing is an emptiness, whereas Mr. Propter thinks that his
Nothing is everything there is".[27] Mr. Salter, of the University
of Exeter, rightly points out Mr. Dyson's error in not realizing
that Huxley's nothingness is to be associated with Buddhism.[28]
Nothingness, *Sunyata* or Void, whether Hindu, Buddhist or even
Existentialist, does not imply contentlessness or emptiness.
Nothingness can be read as 'No-thingness', meaning that which
cannot be described or comprehended in any known terms as
something. The Mahayana Buddhists assert that " 'Void' is not
an object of intellection but of *Prajna* (wisdom), that is to be
understood intuitively".[29] This concept of Nothingness or Void is
intended to help one transcend the notions of duality which treat
the Absolute and the world of reality as contrasting entities. That
the Nothingness is everything there is, has to be experienced and
known intuitively before we can realize the oneness of all being.

Huxley has also been accused of an obsession with sex and of
indulging in smut. Some have jeered at him saying that he is
solemnly preaching a new technique in love-making as a path
to salvation. Up to *Eyeless in Gaza,* Huxley harps on, what John
Atkins calls, "the flesh and carnal unpleasantness". Atkins says:

> There is no sexual happiness in 'Point Counter Point'. It is
> all madness, either the accepted, respectable madness of the
> idealists or the tolerated madness of the sensualists or the
> demonic madness of the psychologically unstable.[30]

He mentions the article in the *London Magazine* giving the
opinions of three well-known writers on Huxley's treatment of
sex.[31] Angus Wilson feels bored with "the pathological wallowing
in physical disgust" in *Point Counter Point* and *Eyeless in Gaza.*
Francis Wyndham feels differently, and says that Huxley
obliquely honours sensual life. John Wain wonders whether the
sex relationships described in novels like *After Many a Summer*

[27] A. E. Dyson, "Aldous Huxley and the Two Nothings", *Critical Quarterly,* Vol. 3, No. 4, 1961.
[28] *Critical Quarterly,* Vol. 4, No. 2, 1962, Correspondence.
[29] Beatrice Lane Suzuki, *Mahayana Buddhism,* p. 28.
[30] John Atkins, *Aldous Huxley—A Critical Study,* p. 88.
[31] *London Magazine,* August 1955.

have anything to do with the lives of normally poised human beings. One can easily see how varied are these opinions: pathological disgust, says Wilson; sneakish admiration, says Wyndham; abnormal or subnormal freakishness, feels John Wain.

Huxley has been, right from the beginning, worried over the dichotomies of flesh and spirit. In his essay *Fashions in Love,* published in *Do What You Will* in 1929, one year after *Point Counter Point,* Huxley rejects as unnatural the ascetic, romantic and realistic notions of sexual love, and pleads for enlightened and genuine relationships. Sexual desire, he says, should not be allowed to decay into irresponsible promiscuity nor should it be repressed as a carnal obscenity. Some restraints of an emotional and moral nature are needed to transform sexual desire into ennobling love. Then, in *The Genius and the Goddess* (1955), Huxley admits that sex is a part of nature and has to be provided for in a harmonious life. In *Island* (1962), Huxley appears to say that asceticism alone is not the path to salvation. Godliness in worldliness is possible. *Nirvana* and *Sansara* can go together. Sexual relations, as envisaged by Huxley in *Island* are beneficent from the sociological point of view, and, from the individual's point of view physically and emotionally satisfying. Disrobed of the taint of obscenity and transformed through moral and emotional discipline, sex relations will be looked upon as sacred, and such an attitude can bring in a cleaner atmosphere into societal life. Gandhiji also says that the sexual act should be considered as a sacred act, but being ascetically minded, he says that it should be indulged in only when the husband and wife want a child. But Gandhiji is a mystical humanist whereas Huxley is a mystical materialist. Huxley advocates birth-control, artificial insemination and *coitus reservatus,* and finds that Noyes and his Oneida community—though he does not agree with their ideals completely —from the sociological angle, and *Tantrik* Buddhism from the mystical angle, justify his theories. The *tantrik* considers the sexual act as a *yoga* (the yoking of empirical consciousness to transcendental consciousness). Heinrich Zimmer writes:

In the sexual act it is possible to recognise a pre-eminent rendition and profound human experience of the metaphysical mystery of the nondual entity which is made manifest as two. The embrace of the male and female principles, and their delight thereby, denote their intrinsic unity, their metaphysical identity. Regarded from the standpoint of logic in the world of space and time, the male and female are two. But in their intuition of their identity (which is the seed of love) the thought of twoness is transcended, while from the mystery of their physical union (their enactment and experience in time of their real and secret nonduality) a new being is produced— as though the corporeal imitation of the transcorporeal, nondual truth had magically touched the inexhaustible spring from which the phenomena of the cosmos arise. Through the sexual act, that is to say, creatures of the visible world actually come into touch, in experience, with the metaphysical sphere of the nondual source. The latter is not absolutely apart and unrelated. It is, rather, their own very essence, which they experience in every impulse of compassion—but supremely in that super-human realisation of compassion which is known in the enact-ment of the mystery play of the sexes.[32]

There is nothing extraordinary, fantastic or ridiculous in Huxley's life-theory. The basic principles are derived from a perennial philosophy which he has distilled from the essence of all religions. It is only his pragmatist approach which may not be acceptable to some. All religions think of spiritual enlighten-ment in terms of the individual, whereas Huxley speaks of 'general enlightenment'. He is an heir to both Julian Huxley and Arnold. He has inherited the analytical approach from the former, the pragmatist approach from the latter. And it was Arnold who wrote:

> But thou wouldst not alone
> Be saved, my father! alone
> Conquer and come to thy goal
> Leaving the rest in the wild.

Dr. Ghose, with pleasant verbal subtlety, sums up Huxley when he says:

Huxley continues to be a divided being, one who talks of unity in the language of analysis, of spirituality in terms of sex, of

[32] Heinrich Zimmer, *Philosophies of India*, p. 555.

beatitude in terms of bestiality, or, as recently, the divine in terms of drugs. One wonders which of these Huxleys is genuine and will survive: the serious or the mock serious, the satirist or the salvationist. Perhaps it is where the two come together, sometimes a little incongruously but always characteristically, that Huxley is most himself. It is, then, as a commentator of the modern scene rather than as a great or an original artist, in his role in bringing art back to a criticism of life and the search after the Real, that the essential seriousness of Aldous Huxley has to be recognised and will, no doubt, be re-assessed.[33]

The satirist is, quite often, a technician, and the salvationist a philosopher, and an individual can be both at once. A satirist without being a salvationist would be a malicious scoffer, a salvationist without being a satirist might just be a greasy sermonizer. It is good to be cynical, says Huxley's Propter, provided one knows when to stop. Huxley has not, perhaps, known when to stop at times. Himself deeply involved in the life he is portraying, himself a victim of that life, it is with a ruthless critical intelligence, but also with the honesty of an intense personal experience, he speaks. In his quest for a faith, he goes to the very essence of all religions and arrives at a pragmatist metaphysical theory which aims at evolving individuals "whole, hale and holy".

Whole, hale, holy—the three words derive from the same root. By etymology no less than in fact holiness is spiritual health, and health is wholeness, completeness, perfection. God's holiness is the same as His unity; and a man is holy to the extent to which he has become single-minded, one-pointed, perfect as our Father in heaven is perfect.[34]

Perhaps, Huxley's journey had not come to an end, and mescalin was only a wayside inn. If death had not snatched him away, one wonders which way and whither he would have led us in his quest.

[33] S. K. Ghose, *Aldous Huxley—A Cynical Salvationist*, p. 168.
[34] Aldous Huxley, "Seven Meditations", *Vedanta for the Western World*, p. 133.

7

LAWRENCE AND HUXLEY

LAWRENCE and Huxley are two of the most brilliant men of this age, the one a genius, the other a dazzling intellectual. To some the former passed for a madman, the latter for a scoffer. By essential nature they are both neo-puritans, but the one is mislabelled a libertine, the other a cynic. Both highly individualistic by temperament, they offer an interesting study in contrast. Lawrence is a pronounced introvert, Huxley, by his own admission, a moderate extrovert. Lawrence grasps things through intuitive perception, Huxley through intellectual analysis. The one speaks with all the fervour of the blood, the other with the urbanity and poise of a university wit. If Lawrence is the Rousseau of his age, Huxley is its Voltaire. If Lawrence is, as Dr. Leavis calls him, the "wild untutored phoenix", Huxley is a well-broken hawk. 'Be yourself', cries Lawrence. 'Know thyself', pleads Huxley.

They were both good friends, contemporaries, though Lawrence, nine years older, died thirty-three years earlier. They had genuine affection for each other. Huxley jots down in his diary under the date of 27 December 1927:

> He is one of the few people I feel real respect and admiration for. Of most other eminent people I have met I feel that at any rate I belong to the same species as they do. But this man has something different and superior in kind, not degree.[1]

And here is what Lawrence has to say about Huxley:

> But, as I say, there's more than one self to everybody, and the Aldous that writes those novels is only one little Aldous amongst others—probably much nicer—that don't write novels —I mean it's only one of his little selves that writes the book

[1] Huxley's introduction to *Letters of D. H. Lawrence*, p. xxx.

and makes the child die, it's not *all* himself. No, I don't like his books: even if I admire a sort of desperate courage of repulsion and repudiation in them. But again, I feel only half a man writes the books—a sort of precocious adolescent. There is surely much more of a man in the actual Aldous.[2]

Lawrence's father was a Nottingham miner, a handsome and impetuous person. His mother, a little puritanical, came from a family bordering on the middle-classes. Lawrence inherited the impetuosity of his father and the puritan spirit of his mother. He is a passionate being, taking a phoenix-eye-view of things, rejecting with pungent scorn all empirical knowledge, and trying to squeeze in the whole universe into an intuitively conceived pattern of his own. The one clue to the universe, he says, is "the individual soul within the individual being"; all that science has to say about the origin of the universe and man is worse than the tale that tells us "the cart conceived and gave birth to the horse". His theory is:

When the living individual dies, then is the realm of death established. Then you get Matter and Elements and atoms and forces and sun and moon and earth and stars and so forth. In short, the outer universe, the Cosmos. The Cosmos is nothing but the aggregate of the dead bodies and dead energies of bygone individuals. The dead bodies decompose as we know into earth, air and water, heat and radiant energy and free electricity and innumerable other scientific facts. The dead souls likewise decompose—or else they don't decompose. But if they decompose, then it is not into any elements of Matter and physical energy. They decompose into some psychic reality, and into some potential will.[3]

So, man, according to him, is the centre of the universe. The primal consciousness in man is pre-mental, the mind is only "the last flower, the cul de sac". He propounds a new doctrine, and speaks of four nerve centres which, distributed along the spinal cord, determine the nature of our consciousness. The most

[2] D. H. Lawrence, Letter to Lady Ottoline Morrel, dated 5 Feb., 1929.
[3] D. H. Lawrence, *Fantasia of the Unconscious*, p. 120.

important is the solar plexus, a sympathetic centre, at which the individual realizes "I am I, the clue to the whole". The second is the lumbar ganglion, a volitional centre, at which is realized the duality of things: "I know that I am I, in distinction from the whole universe which is not as I am". Then, in the upper region, above the diaphragm is again a sympathetic centre, the cardiac plexus, at which the child goes forth seeking to understand the mystery of things, to get a revelation of the unknown. Then finally is the volitional centre, the thoracic ganglion, the centre of mental activity, of curiosity, of the desire to discover, to invent, to know. And education, Lawrence says, should aim at a full and harmonious development of these primary modes of consciousness, because we want effectual human beings, not just conscious ones. "The final aim is not *to know,* but *to be".*

This doctrine of the plexuses and planes, vividly presented in two of his books, *Psychoanalysis and the Unconscious* and *Fantasia of the Unconscious,* is a superb rationalization of, what he calls, his data of living experience and sure intuition. It is a deduction drawn through emotional perception not from any empirical study. A bigoted anti-intellectual, he rejects as puerile the objective science of rational knowledge. In a letter to Earnest Collings, he writes:

My great religion is a belief in the blood, the flesh, as being wiser than the intellect. We can go wrong in our minds. But what our blood feels and believes and says, is always true. The intellect is only a bit and a bridle. What do I care about knowledge. All I want to answer to my blood, direct, without fribbling interventions of mind, or moral, or what-not. I conceive a man's body as a kind of flame, like a candle flame for ever upright and yet flowing: and the intellect is just the light that is shed on to the things around. And I am not so much concerned with the things around—which is really mind—but with the mystery of the flame for ever flowing, coming God knows how from out of practically nowhere, and being *itself,* whatever there is around it, that it lights up. We have got so ridiculously mindful, that we never know that we ourselves are anything—we think there are only the objects we shine upon. And there the poor flame goes on burning ignored, to produce this light. And instead of chasing the mystery in the fugitive half-lighted things outside us, we ought to look at ourselves and say 'My God, I am myself.[4]

Huxley defines this religion of Lawrence as Life-worship contrasting it with that of ascetics like Pascal whom he calls death-worshippers. The life-worshipper's creed is presented by Huxley in his *Do What You Will* (1929). The life-worshipper's aim is to live intensely, on all the facets of his being, balancing "excess of self-consciousness and intelligence by an excess of intuition, of instinctive and visceral living". Huxley himself has turned, at one stage, to Lawrence for inspiration. Life-worship has had great fascination for him, and he presents Lawrence as Kingham in his book *Two or Three Graces* and as Rampion in *Point Counter Point*. The life-worshipper gives an important place to sexual life whereas the death-worshipper rejects it as obscene and bestial. Huxley and Lawrence, both have been fascinated and tormented by sex. Both have worried themselves over the paradox of man who is an animal as well as an angel. But, whereas Lawrence, with his doctrine of intense living and intuitive perception, has sanctified sexual life, Huxley, during the 1920's, viewed sex with intellectual disgust. Then, his Calamy, in *Those Barren Leaves,* considers indulgence in sexual pleasures a hindrance to spiritual life. But, later on Huxley has come to realize that, in spite of all its vulgar earthiness, sex has to be provided for in a harmonious life. He is drawn to Lawrence and his wife Frieda, exceptional beings who are able to live the life they have been preaching. Philip Quarles (Huxley's self-portrait) in *Point Counter Point* says that Rampion and Mary live in a more satisfactory way than anyone he knows. Lawrence says:

And God the Father, the Inscrutable, the Unknowable, we know in the Flesh, in woman. She is the door for our in-going and our out-coming. In her we go back to the Father: but like the witnesses of the Transfiguration, blind and unconscious.[5]

And he speaks of "mystic suave loins of darkness" and "mindless communion of the blood". His theory is that, alone,

[4] D. H. Lawrence, Letter to Earnest Collings, dated 17 Jan., 1913.
[5] D. H. Lawrence, Foreword to *Sons and Lovers,* also in a letter to Edward Garnett.

woman is nothing and man is 'manque', but together they are the "wings of the morning". Exulting in a strange romantic emotionalism, Lawrence says:

> Man is a column of blood: Woman is a valley of blood. It was the primeval oneness of mankind, the opposite of the oneness of the spirit.[6]

He advocates a new conception of life, of the fusion of the old primeval "blood-and-vertebrate consciousness with the white man's mental-spiritual consciousness, the sinking of both beings into a new being".[7]

Like mescalin in the case of Huxley, Lawrence's philosophy of sex exposed him to ridicule and vituperative attacks. He has been called a prurient sensualist, his doctrine a gospel of animalism, or, as Bertrand Russel says, a cult of insanity. The censors have dubbed some of his writings pornographic and banned their circulation. The vehemence of his passion is attributed to coarse sensuality, the audacity of his utterance to crude uncultured egoism. Some of Lawrence's own friends like Middleton Murry have condemned his views, and at best pitied him. Perhaps, had Lawrence possessed a little of the university-educated middle-class sophistry and euphemistic subtlety, he would have been acclaimed with popular gusto. As it is, Huxley's classic introduction to Lawrence's letters, and Dr. Leavis's brilliant critical appraisals have helped much towards a correct understanding of Lawrence as a man and as an artist. Dr. Leavis says "he is still the great writer of our phase of civilisation". Lawrence, as an individual, belongs to a class by himself. He is different in kind. By essential nature he is a puritan, sensing the very nature of things through sure intuitive perception, and, from his visionary heights, expounding life in broad swift strokes of genius. Those who can neither rise to his heights nor align themselves to his channels of thought, find it hard to accept him. Lawrence writes to Lady Ottoline Morrel: "God forbid I shall be taken as urging loose sex activity. There is a brief time for sex, and a long time where sex is out of place."[8]

[6] D. H. Lawrence, *The Plumed Serpent*, p. 446.
[7] Ibid., p. 444.
[8] *Letters of D. H. Lawrence*, p. 773, letter dated 28 December, 1928.

One year before the publication of *Sons and Lovers,* as early as in 1912, Lawrence wrote to Mrs. Hopkin:

Let every man find, keep on trying till he finds, the woman who can take him and whose love he can take, then who will grumble about men or about women. But the thing must be two-sided. At any rate, and whatever happens, I do love and I am loved. I have given and I have taken—and that is eternal. Oh, if only people could marry properly; I believe in marriage.[9]

Those who call Lawrence a crude sensualist, "rotten and rotting others", have not either studied him properly or understood him. Huxley writes that Lawrence's "special and characteristic gift was an extraordinary sensitiveness to what Wordsworth called 'unknown modes of being' ". In *Point Counter Point,* Huxley depicts Lawrence-Rampion as an extremely sensitive being who could smell people's souls. Even Middleton Murry admits that "Lawrence had a mysterious gift of 'sensing' the hidden and unconscious reality of his fellow beings. Lawrence's methods of approach and his interpretation of life may seem unacceptable, but his conclusions, sympathetically considered, do not seem to be far removed from those of religion or psychology or, in some cases, even science. For instance, what Lawrence calls the solar plexus, lumbar ganglion, etc., have a physiological basis and find their counterparts in the autonomic nervous system in the human body. Secondly, his theories of the different levels or layers of consciousness based on the plexuses and planes broadly correspond to what is said in the Hindu *Tantrik* system of *yoga* One can be sure that Lawrence has not borrowed these ideas either from Buddhism or Hinduism. He firmly believes that "Buddha worship is decadent and foul", and "it is ridiculous to turn to the East for inspiration". Moreover, if he had borrowed, he would surely have acknowledged his indebtedness to them because the one dominant quality in him which even his most outspoken critics admit is his "terrifying honesty". Here is what the *Tantra* says on the spiritual centres distributed along the spinal cord:

The devotee imagines the divine power (Śakti) as being asleep

9 Ibid., p. 49.

within him, withdrawn from operation in his gross physique, coiled away like a sleeping serpent (kuṇḍalinī) at the root of the spine, in the deep place known as the mūlādhāra, "the root (mūla) base (ādhāra)". The sādhaka then pronounces mantrā to arouse her, while controlling carefully his inhalations, breathing deeply first through one nostril then the other (prāṇayāma), to clear the way for her through the spiritual channel (suṣumna) that is supposed to run through the interior of the spine. He is then to think of her as aroused. She lifts her head and begins to move up the suṣumna, touching in her passage a number of centers or "lotuses" (cakras, padmas), which are regarded as the seats of the elements of the body. The mūlādhāra is the seat of "earth"; it is pictured as a crimson lotus of four petals. The next center above, called svādhiṣṭhāna (śakti's own abode), is at the level of the genitals and is the seat of the element "water"; it is pictured as a vermillion lotus of six petals. The next, at the level of the navel, is known as maṇipura, "the city (pura) of the lustrous gem (maṇi)", so called because it is the seat of the element "fire". It is pictured as a blue-black lotus of ten petals. According to the psychology of this system of lotuses: mūlādhāra, svādhiṣṭhāna, and maṇipura are the centers from which the lives of most people are governed, while the superior centers represent higher modes of experience. The fourth, at the level of the heart, is the lotus in which the first realization of the divinity of the world is experienced. Here, it is said, the God reaches down to touch his devotee. Or again, here the sages hear the sound (śabda) of Brahman. . . . Because this is heard in the lotus of the heart, that center is called anāhata; it is pictured as a ruddy lotus of twelve petals, and is the seat of the element "air".

"Ether", the fifth and ultimate element, is centered in the chakra of a smoky purple hue and of sixteen petals at the level of the throat. This is the Viśuddha Chakra, "the completely purified". Beyond, at the point between the eyebrows, is the Lotus of Command (ājñā), white as the moon, possessing two petals, shining with the glory of perfected meditation, wherein the mind, beyond the zones veiled by the five elements and thus completely free of the limitations of the senses, beholds immediately the seed-form of the Vēdas. This is the seat of the Form of Forms, where the devotee beholds the Lord—as in the Christian heaven. Beyond is the center beyond duality, Sahasrāra, the varicoloured lotus of a thousand petals at the crown of the head. Here Śakti—who is to be thought of as having ascended through all the lotuses of the suṣumna, waking each lotus to full blossom in passing—is joined to Śiva in a union that is simultaneously the fulfilment and dissolution of the worlds of sound, form and contemplation.[10]

Lawrence's solar plexus, cardiac plexus and thoracic ganglion, as centres of awakening consciousness, are similar to the manipura, anāhata and viśuddha chakras in the *yogic* system. Whereas Lawrence stops with the thoracic ganglion, with a sanctification of the corporeal life, the Hindu *yoga* moves higher up through two more centres of transcendental consciousness, centres which facilitate the "contemplative attitude of luminous intuition". But this transcendental sphere, Lawrence deliberately rejects as non-human. But for this rejection, Lawrence sounds almost like a *Tantrist* himself. The *Tantrist* believes that the whole macrocosm abides bodily within himself, the microcosm, and he names it "God". Lawrence says that each individual is his own Holy Ghost. Huxley, significantly, makes his Rampion say "God's not apart, not above not outside". But, whereas the *Tantrist* seeks to awaken his spiritual consciousness, Lawrence rests contented with a mystical materialism which rejects both religion and science. He says:

If we want to talk about God, well, we can please ourselves. God has been talked about quite a lot, and He doesn't seem to mind. Why we should take it so personally is a problem. Likewise if we wish to have a tea party with the atom, let us: or with the wriggling little unit of energy, or the other or the Libido, or the Elan Vital, or any other Cause. Only don't let us have sex for tea.[11]

When Lawrence says that man and woman are like the bow and arrow, the bow without the arrow is as nothing, and the arrow without the bow only a short-range dart, ineffectual, and

10 Heinrich Zimmer, *Philosophies of India,* pp. 584-85.
11 D. H. Lawrence, *Fantasia of the Unconscious,* p. 3.

that together, in absolute union, not as mere instruments of passion one to the other, they transcend the barrier between themselves and the great unknown around them, he is mystical in utterance and comes quite close to the *Tantrik* beliefs which Huxley himself has finally accepted. Thus, we find that Lawrence, through intuitive vision, arrives at conclusions similar to those arrived at by mystics through meditation and by Huxley through reason. Perhaps, Cardan (*Those Barren Leaves*) is right when he says that there are eighty-four thousand paths to salvation!

Just as *Island* sums up Huxley's views, Lawrence's last story *The Man Who Died* (1930) gives us his ultimate conception of love, love that leads to a true union of souls, and to a union with that other world, outside self. Prof. A. C. Ward calls it Lawrence's ultimate masterpiece. He says:

> But that lovely last-named fable is a perfect thing, a final reconciliation of the elements that had warred within him, a discovery of atonement on the threshold of death, a vision of apocalyptic harmony between Osiris and Christ.[12]

After all, Huxley also seeks this reconciliation of Osiris and Christ. But, unlike Huxley, Lawrence wishes to be guided by the wisdom of the blood alone, and he rejects all empirical knowledge and reason; and his rejection is often ill-tempered. Huxley writes that when Lawrence refuses to accept what science says, it is not because he cannot understand things scientific, but he does not want to understand them. He is a man with exceptional insight, but, at times, refuses, almost perversely, to see things. Frieda, in a moment of annoyance writes:

> Lawrence always wants to treat women like the chicken we had the other day, take its guts out and pluck its feathers sitting over a pail—I am just wildly arguing with Lawrence, and he is so stupid, I think, in *seeing* things, that cannot be seen with eyes, or touched or smelt or heard.[13]

Huxley, with all his admiration for Lawrence has neither completely accepted him nor rejected him at any time. He writes

[12] A. C. Ward, *Twentieth Century Literature,* p. 60.
[13] Frieda's Letter to Garnett, Autumn, 1912.

that Lawrence's doctrine is apt to be misunderstood, distorted and exploited for personal convenience by a variety of individuals. It will also be misconstrued as a cult of animalism. Lawrence speaks with emotional fervour from his phoenixian heights in a strangely virile language whose tone and tenor are apt to be misunderstood by ordinary people. "He seems to hack his meaning out of the words, as his forbears had hacked coal from the pits", says Prof. Ifor Evans.

Lawrence and Huxley move on parallel tracks in their conclusions on life as well as art. Whereas Lawrence says that the wisdom of the blood is a sure guide to happiness, Huxley says that for harmonious living, wisdom of the blood alone is not enough; a comprehensive mind-body conditioning is necessary, and one has to take the help of every available branch of human knowledge including the science and art of death. "Nothing short of everything will really do". Whereas Lawrence believes that a millennium can never dawn on this earth, Huxley hopes it can.

They are both brilliantly clear-headed, endowed with supreme intelligence and insight. Both are dissatisfied with the world around them, a world that has gone pervert clinging to all kinds of substitute ideologies mistaking them for the "genuine article". Both of them, idealists in their own way, live in their particular ivory towers looking at the world around, more as sensitive spectators rather than as positive participants. Both are afraid of personal contacts being shy and individualistic by nature. Juliette Huxley says that Huxley is a kind of "amphibious creature, rejecting emotional contacts with skilful evasion using his intellectual equipment as a shield". "It's as though he only felt safe among ideas".[14] Lawrence himself confesses: "for my part people don't mean much to me, especially casuals: them I'd rather be without".[15] Both of them used their art as a means of self-education. Lawrence says: "But one sheds one's sicknesses in books—repeats and presents again one's emotions, to be master of them".[16] Huxley says that the composition of his books has been a "form of self-exploration and self-education".[17] If

14 *Aldous Huxley—A Memorial Volume*, pp. 42-43.
15 D. H. Lawrence, Letter to Hon. Dorothy Brett dated 9 Feb., 1927.
16 Ibid., Letter to A. W. McLeod dated 27 October 1913.
17 Huxley's foreword to *Everyman's Selections*.

Lawrence's motto is "Art for my sake", Huxley's is at least not Art for Art's sake. Both are novelists of ideas, who have extended the bounds of fiction. Huxley believes in "musicalization of fiction", in presenting a comprehensive view of life in all its diversity and multiplicity. And Lawrence, in his characteristic way says:

Only in the novel are *all* things given full play, or at least, they may be given full play, when we realise that life itself, and not inert safety, is the reason for living. For out of the full play of all things emerges the only thing that is anything, the wholeness of a man, the wholeness of a woman, man alive and live woman.[18]

True to their natures, where as Huxley adopts, what Prof. Isaacs calls, the stream of thought technique, Lawrence is carried away in a stream of passion. Huxley is seeped in "intellectualism and conscious emotionalism", Lawrence relies on spontaneity of feeling and utterance. He writes:

The novels and poems come unwatched out of one's pen. And then the absolute need which one has for some sort of satisfactory mental attitude towards oneself and things in general makes one try to abstract some definite conclusions from one's experience as a writer and as a man. The novels and poems are pure passionate experience. These "polyanalytics" are inferences made afterwards, from the experience.[19]

Both are world-betterers at heart, and both have been dubbed as failed Messaiahs. Perhaps, the words of Prof. Scott James on Lawrence equally apply to both:

He was a romanticist whom circumstances compelled to behave like a realist. He was a Christian, driven into the camp of anti-Christians; a moralist doomed to have his books condemned for immorality; an ordinary man who got trapped in a corner as a rebel and was forced to sustain the character.[20]

[18] D. H. Lawrence, *Phoenix,* p. 538.
[19] D. H. Lawrence, Foreword to *Fantasia of the Unconscious,* p. 5.
[20] R. A. Scott James, *Fifty Years of English Literature,* p. 126.

10

They are both products of a certain phase of European civilization, and both have tried to revitalize that civilization using their art as the instrument, and both have influenced a generation of writers to pursue new modes of thought and technique.

8

THE HUXLEYAN NOVEL

"**B**UT then I never pretended to be a congenital novelist", confesses Huxley as Philip Quarles in *Point Counter Point.* Philip is described in the novel by another character Molly as a 'zoologist of fiction', 'learnedly elfish', 'a scientific Puck', etc. And these are the epithets by which Huxley himself has been described by critics some time or other. G. H. Mair calls Huxley "a literary pathologist dissecting his human specimens";[1] Richard Church writes that "there is something clinical, lethal about his work"[2] and puts him in the Gastric Ulcer School.[3] Walter Allen says that Huxley is an essayist in fiction;[4] and, according to G. S. Fraser, his novels, especially the later ones, read more like "fragments from a philosophical debate".[5] Prof. Isaacs links him up with Herman Broch and says that both Huxley and Broch "represent the novelist as polymath, as "Polyhistor".[6] Peter Westland finds Huxley enmeshed in science, especially in biology, and "groping towards a mysticism from which he as often shrinks".[7] John McCormic declares that what Huxley displays is only the "pseudo-brilliance of a precocious school-boy".[8] Even D. H. Lawrence, a good friend, calls Huxley the novelist a "precocious adolescent".[9]

---

[1] G. H. Mair, *Modern English Literature*, p. 222.
[2] Richard Church, *British Authors*, p. 123.
[3] Richard Church, *The Growth of the English Novel*, p. 61.
[4] Walter Allen, *Tradition and Dream*, p. 67. Referring to the melo-dramatic in Huxley's novels, Allen writes: "The horrors are merely the illustrations of a number of intellectual propositions; they provide the action among the essays as it were".
[5] G. S. Fraser, *The Modern Writer and His World*, p. 76.
[6] J. Isaacs, *An Assessment of Twentieth-Century Literature*, p. 121.
[7] Peter Westland, *Contemporary Literature*, p. 60.
[8] John McCormic, *Catastrophe and Imagination*, p. 286.
[9] D. H. Lawrence, Letter to Lady Ottoline Morrell, dated 5 Feb. 1929.

And it is no wonder because the Huxleyan novel is a puckishly impudent piece of literary art. Huxley the intellectual is far in advance of his age, and his novels contain "more truth than fact", and truth is, quite often, most annoying. Moreover, Huxley's perception is incisive and comprehensive, his presentation graphic with the boldness and sureness of touch of an expressionist painter. But his approach and angle of vision are oblique. There is a tinge of the cartoonist in him when he presents transparent close-ups of people and events revealing the shocking fluidity of, what Prof. Isaacs calls "the submerged icebergs of the unconscious". In his treatment, there is a slight distortion which, while facilitating the presentation of a compelling point of view, betrays the permeating presence of the artist right through. It is this distortion that gives to the Huxleyan novel the twin qualities of literary impishness on one side, and an undertone of solemn self-revelation on the other. What makes his writings unpalatable to many is this incongruous combination of a bantering tone with saintly solemnity, a combination which goes better with painting and sculpture than with the literary art. Huxley's visual talents are those of a painter—perhaps his defective eye-sight is partly responsible—but his medium of expression is that of a writer. And words have a certain coarseness and bluntness of expression as they do not possess the tonal softness and the decorous suggestibility of colours. It is significant that in Huxley's novels are widely interspersed either thematic suggestions for a picture or a precise verbal analysis of some painting.

Prof. Isaacs mentions how when in the post-impressionist exhibition of 1910, Van Gogh, Gaugin, Cézanne and Picasso's paintings were first exhibited, "visitors roared with laughter, the donkeys brayed". Then, Arnold Bennet wrote:

I have permitted myself to suspect that, supposing some writer were to come along and do in words what these men have done in paint, I might conceivably be disgusted with nearly the whole of modern fiction, and I might have to begin again. This awkward experience will in all probability not happen to me, but it might happen to a writer younger than me; at any rate, it is a fine thought".[10]

10 J. Isaacs, *An Assessment of Twentieth-Century Literature*, p. 26.

If a painter were to come along and re-create in colours some of the passages in Huxley's novels, thus rid of their verbal harshness, the intensity and depth of his feeling, the picturesqueness of his conception, and the true spirit of his thought could perhaps be grasped with sympathy.

II

It was Dostoevsky, Picasso and Freud who opened up a new track for artistic creation. They turned the artist's attention from the dial-plate to the inner machinery at work. They added new material to art, and this new material consists, as V. S. Pritchett says, not so much in new sights as in new seeing. Then came the World War I and it changed the whole complexion of things. It brought in its wake general despair and disillusion, a slow collapse of all accepted values. Disgusted with all that had been inherited, desiring something new and meaningful, the younger generation of artists in the nineteen-twenties made a fresh approach to understand life through exploring the secret springs of human thought and feeling. In the literary field, poetry, drama and fiction, all joined this adventure, and the novel, being the most amoebic of literary forms, was able to take for its theme everything under the firmament. Flouting literary conventions, armed with Freudian psycho-analysis and the techniques of the sister arts, the novelist dared to give to his portrayals the visual appeal of the post-impressionistic painting and the dangerous abandon of the Russian ballet. The ideal of Art for Art's sake and the ethics of artistic objectivity were rejected as fatuous, and the novelist turned to make a ruthless analysis of every aspect of life. But, behind all his apparent harshness, one can easily sense the undertones of an anguished awareness and a yearning for a purposeful life, undertones which lend the savour of the novelist's personality to the work.

Miriam Allott calls these novelists exclusive artists who are analysts of individual feelings and emotions. Huxley is an exclusive artist, a sensitive and critical interpreter of men and matters. He has chosen the novel for a vivid portrayal of contemporary life. But his is not mere 'Kodak fiction'. He delves deep into the mysteries of the human mind, and dramatizes the inner motivations and impulses, and the drama has the poignancy of personal experience and the allure of self-revelation. It is not just with sympathy but with a strange empathy too, he looks at life and "spins the web from his own inwards".

But the exclusive writer treads a dangerous knife-edge. Himself a victim of the life he is portraying, he is always in the danger of presenting a victim's squint-eyed view of things. So, the exclusive writer must needs primarily be an artist intellectually honest and thoroughly clear-headed. Huxley's terrifying honesty and brilliant clear-headedness are accepted even by his bitterest critics. However irritating they may find his portrayals, they all admit the sincerity of his attitudes and efforts.

III

Like any other art form, the novel too has its own ethics. In its early beginnings, Richardson laid down its motto: "Instruction, madam, is the pill; amusement is the gilding". Later, other writers like Hardy with his commentaries on the Tragic Spirit, and Meredith on the Comic Spirit, used the novel to present an interpretation of the human situation and a philosophy of life. Still others, like Swift, Thackeray, Samuel Butler, forged the novel into a powerful weapon to present not so much a criticism of life as a caustic ridicule of folly. And the modern exclusive writers have propounded their own codes. With James Joyce, writing is an act of faith, art a religion to be used in the service of humanity. With Virginia Woolf, art is the unifying principle of life, with Lawrence it is "a thought adventure", with Huxley it is a means of "self-exploration and self-education". All these writers have released the novel from the tyranny of a rigid frame-work, and their centre of interest has been the changing flux of the atomistic human mind. Their technique is to catch the meaningful moment from the fleeting crowds of fluid impressions, project it into prominence so as to evoke a new conception of life and a new understanding of things. They have raised the novel to the level of the epic, only their heroes are not mythical but mundane, be it Leopold Bloom, Miss La Trobe or Anthony

Beavis. Though they are themselves on the drift along with a rudderless humanity, yet they transcend the vulgar levels of moralistic predilections, squeeze themselves out of the narrow drain-pipes of a pre-formed *weltanschauung,* and look for the meaning and the goal of human life. They are all puritans at heart, moralists by temperament. Huxley is no exception, and artistic creation, to him, is a means of personal and general enlightenment.

IV

Huxley's novels are novels of ideas. The novel of ideas suffers from certain inherent drawbacks. First of all, its characters must be men and women with ideas to express, and so its arena is limited. Secondly, it entails a certain bandying of ideas, which may assume the form of discussion and debate rather than pleasing dialogue. Thirdly, the ideas themselves cannot always be amusingly Wodehousean, but may pertain to subjects solemn and serious, at times even heavy and abstruse. Hence there is the danger of the traditional novel-structure, as an edifice of character and action, crumbling, and the narrative sliding into an essay or a pedagogic monologue. That's why, Huxley's Philip Quarles says that "the real, the congenital novelists don't write such books", and Huxley, by his own admission, is no congenital novelist.[11]

But neither James Joyce, Virginia Woolf nor D. H. Lawrence is a congenital novelist. Absence of the traditional story content can throw the novel-structure apart only if unity and coherence are not given to it through some other means. Joyce's verbal music, Mrs. Woolf's poetic sensibility, Lawrence's emotional flights, coupled with the coherence of their personal attitudes, lend unity to their work, thought and technique being superbly moulded into a well-knit pattern. But Huxley is different. He is himself on a search for unity and has no coherence of personal attitude. His novels present not only the crisis of the humanity but also his own personal crisis. The composition of them, he confesses, has been a process of self-exploration and self-education. In the translation of experience into verbal thought,

[11] *Point Counter Point,* p. 410.

whereas Joyce and Mrs. Woolf carry the reader on a placid stream of consciousness, Huxley draws him on along a stream of deliberate, discursive, analytical thought. Unity and coherence are super-imposed on his theme by the point of view from which he presents his 'story'. The 'rudderless consciousness' of the humanity he portrays serves as a matrix for the patterns he weaves.

V

V. S. Pritchett says that "the effect of psychological intuitions and discoveries upon our novel is to make it reminiscent, auto-biographical, plotless". But, in Huxley, this absence of plot-story combination is compensated by a sure sense of architecture in piecing together various strands of subtle thoughts, moods and situations.

For instance, in *Crome Yellow* and *Antic Hay*, Huxley employs the simple device of assembling a group of individuals in a house-party or in some social or literary coterie, a device employed by T. L. Peacock in his novel *Headlong Hall*. The reader's interest is sustained by sparkling wit and satire and the jesting Pilate's love of caricature. *Those Barren Leaves*, with its plot laid in a Mediterranean setting, runs on lines similar to those employed by Norman Douglas in *South Wind*. These are mainly conversation pieces, ideas and not action having the prime place, and the little action that there is, is only to import a change of scene for technical convenience, or, at times, to illustrate or throw into relief some chosen aspect of human character or motivation.

Finnegan's Wake is said to have been written for "the ideal reader suffering from an ideal insomnia", but Huxley's novels are written to shake the reader into wakefulness, throw him into teasing thought, at times to annoy him by touching a raw spot or even, though unintentionally, make him jealous with their astounding cleverness. Jocelyn Brooke aptly remarks that, like his own creation Knockespotch, Huxley too has delivered us "form the dreary tyranny of the realistic novel".[12] He has also

---

[12] Jocelyn Brooke, *Writers and Their Work*, No. 55, p. 6.

released us from the dreamy tyranny of the stream-of-conscious-ness novel.

This device of getting together a few persons with diverse attitudes and setting in motion cross-currents of ideas, is followed in *After Many a Summer* and *Time Must Have a Stop* also. *The Genius and the Goddess* follows the same device of meeting under a roof, but a slightly different pattern. One Christmas eve, a host narrates to his guest, over a few glasses of whisky, a brief chapter from his life. A little baby-boy, a grandson, the host's daughter and son-in-law are the only other people who enter for a moment, just a casual interruption giving occasion to a digression or an off-the-tangent remark on life in general. The whole narrative reads like a monologue but for a few words of the guest here and there by way of an interested listener's what-happened-nexts. It is a compact, well-narrated reminiscence. The device is simple but cleverly used. The Katy-Maartens-Rivers episode could have been a sufficient theme for a long erotic novel. But Huxley changes the whole complexion of the tale by making a sober old man narrate it in a reminiscent mood, and with all his digressions, chance remarks and wryness of tone, creates in the reader's mind a chastening impression of the comi-tragedy of human existence. As the 'story' is being narrated, the host and the guest recede into the background, the characters in the episode assume a live role and the drama is restaged. It is the conclusion, by way of an anti-climax, that brings us back to the Christmas eve and the whisky glass, as the host bids farewell to the guest with the words: "This is a Christian country and it's the Saviour's birthday. Practically everybody you see will be drunk". Well, the host and the guest too are, the reader too, with the reminiscence though not with whisky.

It is with *Point Counter Point* that Huxley has made his major contribution to fictional techniques. The title is primarily based on the conception that the music of the human mind is not a single melody but a counter-point, a succession of harmonies and discords. Huxley's aim is musicalization of fiction. He writes:

The musicalization of fiction. Not in the symbolist way, by subordinating sense to sound. But on a large scale, in the construction. Meditate on Beethoven. The changes of moods, the abrupt transitions. More interesting still, the modulations, not merely from one key to another, but from mood to mood. A theme is stated, then developed, pushed out of shape, imperceptibly deformed, until, though still recognizably the same, it has become quite different. In sets of variations the process is carried a step further. Those incredible Diabelli variations, for example. The whole range of thought and feeling, yet all in organic relation to a ridiculous little waltz tune. Get this into a novel. How? The abrupt transitions are easy enough. All you need is a sufficiency of characters and parallel, contrapuntal plots. While Jones is murdering a wife, Smith is wheeling the perambulator in the park. You alternate the themes. More interesting, the modulations and variations are also more difficult. A novelist modulates by reduplicating situations and characters. He shows several people falling in love, or dying, or praying in different ways—dissimilars solving the same problem. Or, vice versa, similar people confronted with dissimilar problems. In this way you can modulate through all the aspects of your theme, you can write variations in any number of moods. Another way: The novelist can assume the god-like creative privilege and simply elect to consider the events of the story in their various aspects—emotional, scientific, economic, religious, metaphysical, etc. He will modulate from one to the other—as from the aesthetic to the physico-chemical aspect of things, from the religious to the physiological or financial. But perhaps this is a too tyrannical imposition of the author's will. Some people would think so. But need the author be so retiring? I think we're a bit too squeamish about these personal appearances nowadays.[13]

Huxley has followed this technique in some form or other in every novel, even in *Crome Yellow*. He employs it in full in *Point Counter Point* to present a bewildering picture of a whole society, and the artistry with which he manipulates the theme, makes the novel, as Prof. Bullough says, a technical triumph. Prof. Bullough writes:

The relationships of the characters in their several over-lapping groups are shown in well-handled series of parallel or contrasting episodes. Sometimes the situations are connected by the

13 *Point Counter Point*, pp. 408-9.

appearance of the same person in different surroundings; sometimes the link is by simple association of ideas; or a reference to a person introduces a section showing how he is behaving at the moment; and there is frequent parallelism of theme, when we see how different personalities are thinking politically, or making love, or facing death. The whole work attains thus a continuity and solidity unique in Huxley's writings; and he has truly attained his object at least as successfully, within his own limits, as did Proust and Joyce and Virginia Woolf, to all of whom he owes something.[14]

But there is something that Huxley does not owe to anyone, and that is the orchestral conception of the theme. His method is announced in the novel itself, in Tolley's orchestra in the Tantamount House:

Young Tolley conducted with his usual inimitable grace, bending in swan-like undulations from the loins, and tracing luscious arabesques on the air with his waving arms, as though he were dancing to the music. A dozen anonymous fiddlers and 'cellists scraped at his bidding. And the great Pongileoni glueily kissed his flute. He blew across the mouth hole and a cylindrical air column vibrated; Bach's meditations filled the Roman quadrangle. In the opening largo John Sebastian had, with the help of Pongileoni's snout and the air column, made a statement: There are grand things in the world, noble things; there are men born kingly; there are real conquerors, intrinsic lords of the earth. But of an earth that is, oh! complex and multitudinous, he had gone on to reflect in the fugal allegro. You seem to have found the truth; clear, definite, unmistakable, it is announced by the violins; you have it, you triumphantly hold it. But it slips out of your grasp to present itself in a new aspect among the 'cellos and yet again in terms of Pongileoni's vibrating air column. The parts live their separate lives; they touch, their paths cross, they combine for a moment to create a seemingly final and perfected harmony, only to break apart again. Each is always alone and separate and individual. 'I am I', asserts the violin; 'the world revolves round me'. 'Round

14 Geoffery Bullough, "Aspects of Aldous Huxley", *English Studies*, Vol. 30.

me', calls the 'cello, 'Round me', the flute insists. And all are equally right and equally wrong; and none of them will listen to the others.[15]

In the novel, Rampion blows the tune, and new aspects, variations and parodies are played by the other characters; and there is a crowd of them, each portrayed with tender care and clever evocative touches. The tunes are many and the movements diverse. Sex and spirituality, politics and religion, science, literature and art, life and death, every theme is played out, and some of the instruments fall back with broken strings. And the novel ends on a dissonant note with a harmonica play by Burlap and Beatrice in the old-fashioned bath-tub.

Technically the novel is most satisfying. Parallel and contra-puntal themes are pieced together with subtle artistry, the one sliding into the other, and together are made to give a jarring but colourful picture of a disjunct humanity.

Eyeless in Gaza strikes a new note with its shuffling of time-elements. In Chapter III, Huxley gives us the principle behind the technique: "somewhere in the mind a lunatic shuffled a pack of snapshots and dealt them out at random, shuffled once more and dealt them out in a different order, again and again, indefinitely. There was no chronology. The idiot remembered no distinction between before and after".

Huxley shuffles the time-elements in a masterly fashion. The story is told in four layers of time, to be finically exact, five. Right on the surface is the year 1934 with the protagonist Anthony Beavis recording in his diary reflections and reveries which draw their sustenance from the events between August 30, 1933 and February 23, 1935. At the bottom is the period from November 6, 1902 to January 1904 presenting Anthony's childhood experiences. Above is the period from June 16, 1912 to July 24, 1914 Anthony's initiation into amour and his infernal role in wrecking a friend's life. Above this, is the period from December 8, 1926 to April 14, 1928 covering the sad story of Mary Amberley, his preceptress in amour, and her daughter Helen. In between are thrown two days of the year 1931 by way of a casual link. The topmost layer traces Anthony's progress from detached intellectualism and irresponsible sensuality to

15 *Point Counter Point*, pp. 31-32.

THE HUXLEYAN NOVEL 157

constructive humanism. Stray chunks from the other layers of time cleverly shuffled and dealt out at random, serve to throw light on Anthony's complex personal charade.

Huxley has forerunners in this technique. William Faulkner adopts a similar method in his novel *The Sound and the Fury* (1929) in which he presents the truly idiot universe of a moron Benjy Compson. The sequence of the four layers of time the novel deals with, is April 7, 1928, June 2, 1910, April 6, 1928 and April 8, 1928. The first three layers present the three important characters in the novel—the idiot Benjy, his brother Quentin, his degenerate father Jason. The fourth chapter is a sort of a commentary on the tragedy of the three crippled minds.

Christopher Isherwood also follows a similar technique in *The Memorial* (1932). There are about ten major characters, post-war specimens, their thinking all warped and distorted by the war. The novel is in four sections, the first one leads to the climax presenting the characters as they were in 1928. Then in a flashback, the second shows as they were in 1920, the third as in 1925, and the fourth section leads us on to 1929, a follow-up of the climax, and shows that time has brought to them no resipiscence but only stagnation, decay and drift.

In both Faulkner and Isherwood there is a ruthless precision in characterization, and the novels are remarkable pieces. But, compared with *The Sound and the Fury* and *The Memorial, Eyeless in Gaza* is a more complex and subtly worked novel. In the shuffling of chronologies, both Faulkner and Isherwood have followed the common cinematic method of flashback. Huxley's method is not so simple as that. Huxley says that our thought processes look as if somewhere in the mind, a lunatic has shuffled a pack of snapshots—layers of consciousness—and dealt them out at random. Out might come August 30, 1933 or April 2, 1903. Hence there is no regular sequence, as in Faulkner and Isherwood, in the arrangement of the different layers of time. The novel looks, at first sight, a haphazard gathering of reflections and reminiscences. It is a novel of 620 pages 12 m., fifty-four chapters, fifty-one of which deal with a single day or at the most two. Of the three remaining chapters, one covers a period of six months, another a full season autumn, and the third a month. There are over a dozen characters with Anthony Beavis as the central figure. This vast body of material, Huxley has marshalled with exceptional skill and gives almost a full life-sketch of at least five of these characters by cleverly touching upon a few climactic situations in their life. But, what appears at first sight a haphazard dealing out of reminiscences, reveries, moods and situations, is not so haphazard at all. There is a method behind all this madness. The main stream of the novel runs between April 4, 1934 and February 25, 1935. In between the chapters dealing with this period are sandwiched the other layers of time jumbled up. And one can find a subtle relationship between one chapter and the next, or rather the one slides into the other. It is not just a forgotten past suddenly bubbling up to the surface, but from one psychic moment, through some association of ideas, the mind seems to skip on to some other moment.

For instance, the first chapter is dated August 30, 1933, and presents Anthony Beavis with Helen Amberley at a Mediterranean resort. He had a deep liking for her, but, afraid of entanglements, indulged in "false pretences" of detached sensuality. This phrase "false pretences", at the end of the chapter, draws the reader to the next one beginning with Anthony's exclamation: "I know what I ought to do but continue to do what I ought not to do". Then the third chapter takes the reader back to August 30; this chapter ends with the scene of Anthony lying beside Helen softly stroking her naked body, counting each stroke—"thirty-two, thirty-three, thirty-four".... The next chapter too begins with a count—"thirty-two, thirty-three . . . ."; it was Anthony on November 6, 1902, then a boy of eleven, counting the advertisement boards of beef essence out of a train window, while on the way to his mother's funeral. Thus with a delicate linking up of thought processes, Huxley leads us on from one chapter to another, and by the time we are a quarter-way through the novel, we are conscious of the patterning of five different stories, those of Anthony's father, Mary Amberley, Helen, Brian Foxe and Mark Staithes, with Anthony as the flourishing thread weaving them all together into an intricate carpet design.

It is with technical fastidiousness, not with acrobatic zeal, that Huxley has followed this time-pattern. Time is a tyrant both in life and literature. And the most thrilling moments are those in which the vulgar time-sense is transcended in the ecstasies of heightened awareness. E. M. Forster says that there are two aspects to our daily life—"the life in time and the life by values;

the story is a narration of the life in time, and a good novel includes the life by values as well". He writes:

> The story is neither moral nor is it favourable to the understanding of the novel in its other aspects. If we want to do that we must come out of the cave.

We shall not come out of it yet, but observe already how that other life—the life by value—presses against the novel from all sides, how it is ready to fill and indeed distort it, offering it people, plots, fantasies, views of the universe, anything except this constant 'and then ... and then', which is the sole contribution of our present inquiry. The life in time is so obviously base and inferior that the question naturally occurs: cannot the novelist abolish it from his work, even as the mystic asserts he has abolished it from his experience, and install its radiant alternative alone?[16]

Forster says that the time-sequence cannot be destroyed, and "the novel that would express values only becomes unintelligible and therefore valueless". Forster is right because, however much chronological sequence may be jumbled up, there is always a central precision that runs through any good narrative, be it that of Dostoevsky, James Joyce, Gertrude Stein, Virginia Woolf or Aldous Huxley. The living present alone is the diving board for the mind to take its leap. Both memory and anticipation condition the present, and what an individual is can best be understood if one can rove through climactic moments of intense experience in his past. Such moments, 'epiphanies', Miriam Allott calls them, occur in a dimension outside the normal time, the fourth dimension, as Proust calls it. The exclusive writer projects into prominence such moments to present a kind of psychodrama in which life by values transcends the life by the clock. But the clock is there as the solid basis, the feather-bed in which the dream-world is experienced, or, as in *Those Barren Leaves,* it may be the surface of the warm Tyrrhenian sea floating on which Francis Chelifer surveys his past till a swinging boat-hook knocks him out, and time stands still till he regains consciousness.

Island and *Brave New World* are similar in pattern, the one a utopia, the other 'a dystopia', "a eugenic paradise" as Prof.

16 E. M. Forster, *Aspects of the Novel,* p. 41.

Bullough calls it. In both the novels, a visitor from outside enters the territory, goes around, acquaints himself with the new way of life. In *Island* he is converted, in *Brave New World* he makes his exit through suicide.

From the structural point of view, *Island* is most unsatisfying. The mystic has taken over from the artist, and solemnity has softened the satire and comedy. The visitor, Will Farnaby, a journalist by profession, a typical specimen of a perverted civilization, enters the territory with a fractured leg. While the bone is on the mend, he reads 'What's What' on the island, and after he recovers he is coached in the new way of life by every one from a little girl in her early teens to a ripe old man. Then he falls in love with an angelic woman, and their love-scene looks like that of a quakeress petting a wounded puppy and teaching it good manners. Even the ending of the novel is unsatisfying. It looks as if a fine house of cards is built, and then with childish flippancy, with a flick of the hand, the whole thing is shattered. Col. Dipa, with one burst of machine-gun fire, brings the utopia to an end. But thereby hangs another tale with Vico and his doctrine of recurrent catastrophe.

But, the novel grips our interest as it offers a summing up of Huxley's views, indicates the end of a quest, and gives positive suggestions instead of an agonized search and the tentative inferences presented in the previous novels. It is a comprehensive work, with almost every aspect of human life discussed—politics, religion, theology, science, economics, sociology and sex, literature, painting, sculpture, music and dance; not to speak of psychology, psychotherapy and even thanatology. The softness of tone, sincerity of conviction, lucidity of thought and, above all, the surprisingly new way of looking at things that Huxley exhibits, make the novel transcend all the inherent weaknesses of structure.

Brave New World is a perfect work, well-planned and well-executed. Satire, comedy and farce mingled with a wry pity give us a shocking picture of a scientifically planned state which has personified abstractions and depersonified human beings. It is a regular novel with more of dialogue and action, less of discussion and debate, and without epistolary or autobiographical intrusions. The savage, brought up by a mother, acquainted with Shakespeare, and unconditioned in a genetic laboratory, serves to pinpoint the inhumanity of the Procrustean state. The linking up of the savage reservation with the state capital, and the discomfiture of Tomakin, the director of hatcheries, by a revelation of his fatherhood, are cleverly manoeuvred episodes. There is succinctness in structure, and cogency of expression. If the novel suffers in artistic value, it is because of its theme but not technique.

Ape and Essence is written in the form of a film-script with a preface stuck on. Huxley must have deliberately chosen this form to tone down the horror of the tale. It is a fantasy on what the world may be like after a thermo-nuclear war. We are given a horrifying and repulsive picture of a degenerate humanity seeped in superstition, fear and devil-worship. In the preface, the script is shown to have been written by a misanthrope by name Tallis, and sent to a Hollywood studio for acceptance. It is rejected by the studio and even by the truck carrying it to the incinerator. Thus, in the preface itself, Huxley seems to suggest that the fantasy is to be taken as the creation of a cynical crank and can be rejected by the reader too.

The script reveals Huxley's thorough acquaintance with the intricacies and the needs of a scenario. After all, Huxley is no stranger to the film world and its techniques. During the Battle of Britain days, he was engaged by the Metro Goldwyn Mayers to write the script for their film version of *Pride and Prejudice*. In *Ape and Essence,* Huxley makes a clever use of the cinematic techniques. He keeps a narrator unseen in the background to serve both as an interpreter as well as a commentator on the main theme. The script begins with the direction that, after the usual titles and credits, the narrator comments on the human-ape and a baboon civilization. Then enters a baboon-beauty holding Faraday on the leash. It is a perverted world where apes hold the leash for men to follow. Then the camera moves across, the time of action shifts to a hundred years later, and a large schooner appears sailing past. The narrator announces that it is the ship carrying an expedition from New Zealand for a rediscovery of North America, a century after the Third World War and the end of the baboon civilization. Then a cut-back to the past shows the baboons at work on nuclear and bacteriological weapons, and then another scene presents baboon-marshals whipping the Einsteins on the leash to press the button releasing atomic warheads. The button is at last pressed, the missiles take some time to hobnob with the targets, and so the baboons fall to

11

breakfast. Then the camera switches over to another breakfast table, the deck of the schooner with the expedition members at their breakfast, and the narrator says these are the survivors of that Judgement, and the rediscovery begins. This is a dramatic use of flash-backs, close-ups, fade-ins and fade-aways, linking up two points of time a century apart. Then the scene shifts to and fro between the schooner and the civilization ashore, and one of the members of the expedition is taken prisoner, and his experiences in the New World are presented. It is only the preface which has given the air of a novel to the book, otherwise it has all the tempo and tension of a drama. Huxley has planned the whole thing with such scrupulous attention even to the minutest details in both the theme and the technique, that Prof. Collins calls him "a labourer in Hell".[17] But Prof. Isaacs pays a high compliment to the novel in a passing reference:

The greater the chaos, it has been said, the greater the order which results from subduing it. A thousand paths must be used to approach it: allegory and analogy, the philosophy of history, the personally conducted tour through it, the neat, tidy packeted sample of chaos, or the help of the cinema with its flux and montage, its power of darting, its devices of narration, its controlled ecstasies of chase and climax, its camera angles and simultaneity, its wedding of music and motion. There is something of it in 'The Waves', and in 'Tea with Mrs. Goodman', in the agricultural show in 'Madam Bovary' or the simultaneities in Perez de Ayala's 'Tiger Juan', or Dos Passos's 'Manhattan Transfer', or 'Wuthering Heights' even. There is something of it in the brackets of time in Virginia Woolf's, something even in that blinding flash in Mr. Aldous Huxley's 'Ape and Essence': " 'Saturation bombing', what a deliciously juicy phrase", something in the devastating bracket in Ernest Hemingway's new book which pins down half the agony of man.[18]

The ending of the novel too is symbolic. While running away from the devil-worshippers, Dr. Poole and his American sweetheart Loola are shown to have come to a grave which happens to

17 A. C. Collins, English Literature of the Twentieth Century, p. 242.
18 J. Isaacs, An Assessment of Twentieth Century Literature, pp. 131-32.

be that of the supposed script-writer Tallis himself. They read the epitaph which tells that Tallis has preferred death to life on this earth. Then Loola opens a knapsack and hands over to Dr. Poole a boiled egg which he cracks on the headstone, and while peeling scatters the fragments of the shell over the grave. That's the end. Tallis is rejected by the studio, the garbage van, the incinerator, now he is rejected by the two lovers, his own creations, which is symbolic of lust for life rejecting the cynical love of death. And all these rejections together suggest that the novel has to be taken not too seriously but only as a cautionary tale.

VI

In this context, a reference can be made to Huxley's techniques in bringing his novels to a finish. He seems to specialize in anti-climax. From a climactic situation or from a state of high emotional tension, he suddenly brings us down into the vulgar quotidian streams of existence. It is a come-back which leaves us with a jolt, and gives us, at times, an impression of flippancy, heartlessness and even misanthropy. But, second thoughts reveal to us that there is a power and a purpose behind his methods.

For instance, *Point Counter Point* ends with Spandrell getting himself shot dead by the British Freemen. Rampion and Mary stand looking dazed. On the floor lies Spandrell's body with a bullet-hole in the temple. Through the open door behind comes the celestial melody of Beethoven's music. Suddenly the music stops, there is only the scratching of the needle on the disc. A line of asterisks, and then Burlap and Beatrice are shown romping in the old-fashioned bath, like two little children. "The whole bathroom was drenched with their splashings. Of such is the Kingdom of Heaven". With these words the novel ends. The ending, at first, looks disconcertingly frivolous, but slowly its full significance dawns on us. On one side stands the life-worshipper Rampion, a broken-fiddle by now. On the other side lies the death-worshipper Spandrell's body in solid affirmation of his rejection of Rampion's 'gospel of animalism' and acceptance of "the blissful convalescence in heaven". And to the scratching of the gramophone needle on the disc, are Burlap and Beatrice playing a beastly parody of the Rampion-theme. Is this the worship of the body? Is Spandrell right in choosing death? Has Huxley rejected Lawrence even in *Point Counter Point?*

There is another implied suggestion also. It is the cognitive man alone who suffers. The fool and the animal have no cosmological worries. For gullible fools like Beatrice and hypocrites like Burlap who fly into the world of religion and art for fun, fashion and profit, and retain untainted their pure animalhood, exulting in the tactual thrills of the body—for such is the earth a kingdom of heaven!

After Many a Summer ends on a surprisingly realistic but jarring note. The millionaire Joe Stoyte, Dr. Obispo and Virginia Maunciple stand in the underground cellar of the Gonister castle. They have just seen the disgusting spectacle of the earl and his paramour transformed into horrid ape-like creatures by Time— two centuries of animal existence. The earl and the woman suddenly vanish into the darkness of their dungeon, and the visitors hear only "a stertorous growling in the dark and little cries". Then the novel ends with these words:

> Mr. Stoyte broke the silence. 'How long do you figure it would take before a person went like that'? he said in a slow hesitating voice. 'I mean, it wouldn't happen at once . . . there'd be a long time while a person . . . well, you know; while he wouldn't change any. And once you get over the first shock—well, they look like they were having a pretty good time. I mean in their own way, of course. Don't you think so, Obispo'? he insisted.
> Dr. Obispo went on looking at him in silence; then threw back his head and started to laugh again.[19]

The theme is the animal fear of death and the consequent frantic clinging to life and the yearning for longevity. Considering the biological processes of evolution and the formation of new life-forms, there is a possibility that physiological longevity may result in man ultimately growing back into the ancestral ape. Moreover, longevity by itself without corresponding psychological re-conditioning may become a curse and not a boon. But life is

[19] *After Many a Summer,* p. 245.

such that even if every other kind of fear is overcome the fear of death haunts every human being and makes life miserable, at least to some people. Fear of death, "of falling into the hands of the living god", of the Last Judgement, makes Joe Stoyte prefer to live even as a filthy ape. "Well, they look like they were having a pretty good time", he remarks. We may not burst out in cynical hilarity as Dr. Obispo does, but we cannot help a wry chuckle at this vulgarly human clinging to life.

The Genius and the Goddess ends on a note of light satire. After taking the reader through an absorbing psychodrama, it brings him back, all on a sudden, into the consciousness of the work-a-day world. The novel ends with the host bidding goodnight to the guest advising him to drive carefully: "This is a Christian country and it's the Saviour's birthday. Practically everybody you see will be drunk". Well, the host and the guest too have had their drinks. That's the way of the world—solemn occasions celebrated in gay hilarity.

Of all the novels, the way *Brave New World* ends, makes a poignant impact on the reader's mind. The savage feels polluted by his contact with the civilized Londoners. One evening, in a fury of penitence, he whips himself and the woman Lenina. The Brave New Worlders mistake it for a thrilling whipping-stunt. The next evening, swarms of helicopters bring visitors hoping for another display. The savage is not to be seen. Someone pushes open the doors of the light-house, and under the crown of the arch are dangling a pair of feet. The novel ends with the words: "Slowly, very slowly, like two unhurried compass needles, the feet turned towards the right; north, north-east, east, south-east, south, south-south-west; then paused, and, after a few seconds, turned as unhurriedly back towards the left. South-south-west, south, south-east, east". . . . 'This is the highest stunt of all, look at me, all of you', the dangling feet appear to say swinging around looking at everybody. The reader is left wondering as to its effect on the Brave New Worlders. One feels that even the conditioned human beings must have been de-conditioned a bit. This is the tragedy of a sensitive individual in a world of automatons.

Finally, however unsatisfying aesthetically is the ending of *Island,* technically it is vested with fine symbolism. Col. Dipa, with one burst of machine-gun fire, conquers the island. Robert Macphail is shot dead. At a distance, Will Farnaby and Sushila

Macphail stand staring into the darkness. Armoured cars are returning home in triumph. As they sweep round a corner, the head-lights of one car after another light up the statues of the Tathagata throwing into sharp focus the serene unruffled glory of the face.

This is highly symbolic. Violence and greed may seem to prevail, but the unbounded wisdom and compassion of which the Tathagata Buddha is the living symbol remain as valid as ever. In that dark moment of the triumph of evil, as the armoured cars rumble past, Will Farnaby and Sushila find the Tathagata shine all the brighter. It is also significant that, whereas in most of his novels, Huxley, at the end, brings the reader suddenly back into the realities of a sordid daily existence, it is only in *Eyeless in Gaza* and *Island* that he affirms the persistence of Eternal Absolutes behind all the vulgar surface realities of life. This denotes a change in the man and in his attitudes, a transformation of the jesting Pilate into a solemn seeker.

VII

A structural analysis of Huxley's novels naturally leads to a discussion of some of his narrative techniques. These are linked up with his doctrine of 'musicalization of fiction'. This is a doctrine which has been propounded by Andre Gide: "What I should like to do is something like the art of fugue writing. And I can't see why what is possible in music should be impossible in literature".[20] E. M. Forster says, "in music fiction is likely to find its nearest parallel".[21] In *Point Counter Point,* Huxley says that what a novelist has to have is "a sufficiency of characters and parallel contrapuntal plots. While Jones is murdering a wife, Smith is wheeling the perambulator in the park. You alternate the themes". Through this modulation from one theme to another, and from one aspect to another, he succeeds in giving a strange dissonant antiphony of life. Though he has explained this technique in *Point Counter Point,* he has used it even in his earlier novels.

[20] Andre Gide, *Les Faux Monnayeurs,* Part II, Chapter III, p. 210.
[21] E. M. Forster, *Aspects of the Novel,* p. 155.

Here is an incident from *Antic Hay*: Gumbril, Myra and their
party on a night jaunt stand near a coffee stall in Hyde Park.
One side stands this Bohemian group of a well-to-do leisurely
class. A little away, a small group of cab drivers and tramps
stand round a carter and his sobbing wife. Huxley skips from
one group to the other:

" 'The cop, 'e gave evidence against me'. 'Limping in all four
feet', 'e says. 'It wasn't', I says and the police court vet,
'e bore me out. 'The 'orse 'as been very well treated', 'e says.
But 'e's old, 'e's very old'. 'I know 'e's old', I says. But where
am I goin' to find the price for a young one"

"X^2-Y^2", Shearwater was saying, "$= (X + Y) \times (X—Y)$
and the equation holds good whatever the values of X and Y.
It's the same with your love business, Mrs. Viveash. The relation
is still fundamentally the same, whatever the value of the
unknown personal qualities concerned. Little individualities
and peculiarities—after all, what do they matter"?

"What indeed"? said Coleman. "Ticks, mere ticks. Sheep
ticks, horse ticks, bed bugs, tape worms, taint worms, liver
flukes". . . .

" 'The 'orse must be destroyed', says the beak. "e's too old
for work'. 'But I'm not', I says. I can't get a old age pension
at thirty-two, can I? 'ow am I to earn my living if you take
away what I earns my living by' "?

Mrs. Viveash smiled agonisingly. 'Here's a man who thinks
personal peculiarities are trivial and unimportant', she said.
'You're not even interested in people, then'?

'I don't know what you can do', 'e says. 'I'm only 'ere to
administer the law'. 'Seems a queer sort of law', I says. 'What
law is it'?

Shearwater scratched his head. Under his formidable black
moustache he smiled at last his ingenuous, childish smile.
"No", he said. "No, I suppose I'm not. No". He laughed, quite
delighted, it seemed, by this discovery about himself.

" 'What law is it'? 'e says. 'The croolty to Animals Law.
That's what it is', 'e says".

The smile of mockery and suffering appeared and faded.
"One of these days", said Mrs. Viveash, "you may find them

more absorbing than you do now".[22]

This is not just a simple modulation or even an abrupt transition from one theme to another. Huxley goes a step further and adopts the cinematic technique of simultaneity, of quick darting to and from one theme to the other, and together the two themes give a coherent picture of a forlorn humanity. On one side is the moneyed leisurely group vainly trying to kill time somehow. On the other are the husband and wife baffled by the laws of life, "the Croolty to Animals Law" being cruel to them. It is a powerful rounded portrayal of apathy, frustration, bewilderment, cynical despair, yet buried underneath, a touching sympathy that ultimately goes to the rescue of the unfortunate couple.

There is another example, a perplexing cacophony from *Brave New World*. 'I am I', says each character, and each blares his or her own tune. There are four parallel themes running. One is the controller explaining the historical background of the Brave New World. The second is Lenina and her friend discussing love affairs. The third is an assistant pre-destinator and a colleague conversing about nice girls. The fourth is children having hypnopaedic teaching at school. At first, short passages from each theme are given in rotation. Then abruptly a sentence from each is reeled off in quick succession:

"You're hopeless, Lenina, I give you up".

"The Russian technique for infecting water supplies was particularly ingenious".

Back turned to back, Fanny and Lenina continued their changing in silence.

"The Nine Years' War, the great Economic Collapse. There was a choice between World Control and destruction. Between stability and" . . . .

"Fanny Crowne's a nice girl too", said the Assistant Predestinator.

In the nurseries, the Elementary Class Consciousness lesson was over, the voices were adapting future demand to future industrial supply. "I do love flying", they whispered, "I do love flying, I do love having new clothes, I do love" . . . .

"Liberalism, of course, was dead of anthrax, but all the

[22] *Antic Hay*, pp. 64-65.

same you couldn't do things by force".

"Not nearly so pneumatic as Lenina. Oh, not nearly".

"But old clothes are beastly", continued the untiring whisper. "We always throw away old clothes. Ending is better than mending, ending is better than mending, ending is better". . . .

"Government's an affair of sitting, not hitting. You rule with the brains and the buttocks, never with the fists. For example, there was the conscription of consumption".

"There, I'm ready", said Lenina; but Fanny remained speechless and averted. "Let's make peace, Fanny darling".

"Every man, woman and child compelled to consume so much a year. In the interests of industry. The sole result". . . .

"Ending is better than mending. The more stitches the less riches; the more stitches" . . . .

"One of these days", said Fanny, with dismal emphasis, "you'll get into trouble".[23]

In the cinema, such a technique starting with a montage first, and then to a mad darting from one scene to the other will dazzle the eye with the changing focuses; and then, what sounds, at first, a comic prattle of each individual character, gradually coheres into a meaningful picture. The political and social background, the hypnopaedic teaching of children, the casual sensualities of the grown-ups are all touched upon in one merry-go-round. This is a highly effective handling of simultaneous moments of time.

Another device which Huxley indulges in with an almost impish obstinacy, is the intercalation of autobiographical memoirs, diaries, epistles, extracts from monographs and What's-What-pamphlets, or, sometimes, a scene or two from a play presented as being witnessed by the protagonists in the novel. The epistolary method of narration is, after all, a stale device used for an effective analysis of sentiment by many writers right from our fictional ancestor Richardson. It is only in *Point Counter Point,* we find a few letters shown to have been written by one of the characters Lucy Tantamount. Otherwise, Huxley does not evince any special interest in this method. Inset short stories, scenic extracts from plays—as, for instance, the history of Crome in *Crome Yellow,* a few scenes from a play witnessed by the main characters as in *Antic Hay* and *Island,* or a 'feelie' seen in

[23] *Brave New World,* pp. 39-40.

Brave New World—though rather out of the ordinary in fiction, serve to break up the monotony of a flat narrative, and also add to our understanding by throwing into relief one or more facets of the main theme.

But, Huxley has a special partiality for autobiographical memoirs, diaries and personal note-books. Chelifer's fragments from an autobiography in *Those Barren Leaves,* Philip Quarles' note-book in *Point Counter Point,* Anthony Beavis's diary in *Eyeless in Gaza,* not to speak of Bruno Rontini's scribblings and Sebastian Barnak's memoirs in *Time Must Have a Stop,* and the Hauberk papers in *After Many a Summer,* are some of the examples. But none of these interpolations has any special narrative qualities of its class. Each one of them fits into the body of the novel without, in any way, injuring either the unity and coherence or the structure and the texture. The chapter-headings like 'Fragments from the Autobiography of Chelifer' or 'Philip Quarles's Note-book' or 'Anthony Beavis's Diary' do not, in any way, either contribute to or enhance our understanding of the theme, and, even without the captions, the matter merges in full harmony into the main body of the novel. Huxley seems to have given these chapter-headings only in open defiance of the conservative structural traditions of the novel. Elsewhere he has said that talent can import sincerity into a piece of writing,[24] and here, he perhaps wants to show that talent can also import unity and coherence even among entirely disjunct chunks of matter.

Chelifer's words—"Arms outstretched like a living cross I floated face upwards on that blue and tepid sea"—have nothing of the solemn prosaicness of a dreary autobiography, and are a sufficient invitation to the reader to partake of a reverie. All the fragments from Chelifer's autobiography read like portions from a stream-of-consciousness novel. Swinging between the present and the past, between the warm Tyrrhenian sea and Gog's Court, Chelifer exults in a sentimental brooding over life's little ironies. Huxley links up, with clever artifice, the reminiscence with the running present. The first section of the novel, 'An evening at Mrs. Aldwinkle's", intraduces to the reader all the major characters in full attire. Now the second section shows them out on the sea in a patino as seen through the eye of Chelifer. The reader is invited to compare notes. It is a clever device, each one

[24] Huxley, *Music at Night,* See the essay "Vulgarity in Literature."

of the characters including the brooder Chelifer himself, shown in a new perspective. Then, a swinging boat-hook knocks out Chelifer, and he wakes up into a new world. Now swings the reverie between the tyranny of an erotic hostess at the Malaspina Palace and his slavery in the editorial office in Fetter Lane in London. The whole piece presents an individual's attitude to life in its full flux, and is a moving picture of a human jelly-fish destined by his very nature to be a life-long victim. It is a brilliant portrayal of human awkwardness, and fits very well into the main scheme of the novel. 'Fragments from Chelifer's Autobiography' —there is nothing fragmented about the whole piece, nor is the caption at all necessary, unless the reader is expected to constantly and consciously remember—God knows what for—that he is reading Chelifer's reflections only as re-created by the novelist.

With 'Philip Quarles's Note-book', Huxley has brought in another device, that of a novelist within a novel. This is a favourite trick of his, though given justificatory comment only in *Point Counter Point*. Denis in *Crome Yellow,* Miss Thriplow in *Those Barren Leaves,* Philip himself in *Point Counter Point,* the narrator in *The Genius and the Goddess,* are all novelists, and many of his other characters are men of letters. After all, the exclusive novelist is a conscious deliberate artist, and, as Prof. Isaacs says "is himself not only a part of the novel, but often the most important part":

The classic example among modern novels is Andre Gide's 'The Counterfeiters' (Les Faux Monnayeurs) published in 1925. It is a novel about a novelist who is writing a novel. While he is writing this novel, the novelist (that is, the one in the novel), keeps a diary recording the progress of his task. To complicate matters still further, Andre Gide himself kept a real diary while he was writing his novel about a novelist who keeps a diary while he is writing a novel. In the wake of this book, Aldous Huxley in 1928 wrote his 'Point Counter Point', whose very title reveals an attitude towards the structure of fiction. He uses the same device. Several of the chapters are headed "From Philip Quarles' Note-book". It is a five-fold complication. There is the novelist commenting in his note-book on the nature of fiction. There is the title of the book, 'Point Counter Point', labelling the structure and the method. There is the

motto from Fulke Greville underlining the idea of counterpoint:
. . . . In the foreground of the novel there is the story
itself, but even the deployment of that is an object lesson in
the discontinuity of time, and finally the characters, who are
presented with diabolical clarity, are themselves vehicles, in
accordance with Mr. Huxley's theory, of the ideas which form
the counterpoint of the book. It is a "novel of ideas".[25]

In the late fifties, Lawrence Durrell has enlarged upon this
device in his *Alexandria Quartet*. The novelist within the novel
helps the reader in understanding what kind of novel is being
written, and what approaches and attitudes condition the
novelist's own perception of things. Huxley writes:

Put a novelist into the novel. He justifies aesthetic generalisa-
tions, which may be interesting—at least to me. He also
justifies experiment.   Specimens of his work may illustrate
other possible or impossible ways of telling a story. And if
you have him telling parts of the same story as you are, you
can make a variation on the theme. But why draw the line
at one novelist inside your novel? Why not a second inside his?
And a third inside the novel of the second? And so on to
infinity, like those advertisements of Quaker Oats where there's
a quaker holding a box of oats, on which is a picture of another
quaker holding another box of oats, on which, etc., etc.   At
about the tenth remove you might have a novelist telling your
story in algebraic symbols or in terms of variations in blood-
pressure, pulse, secretion of ductless glands and reaction
times.[26]

Huxley has not progressed right upto this tenth remove, but
remains a little behind "enmeshed in biology". In *Literature and
Science,* he says that modern scientific knowledge confronts the
writer with a challenge. The traditional raw material of art
compounded of myth and romance has to be harmonized with
"the new findings and hypotheses now pouring in upon him from
the sciences of his own day". Darkling we listen,

[25] J. Isaacs, *An Assessment of Twentieth Century Literature*, pp. 117-18.
[26] *Point Counter Point*, p. 409.

While thou art pouring forth thy soul abroad
In such an ecstasy

says the romantic poet. And science tells us that the ecstasy is just a proclamation to the other cock-nightingales that he had "staked out a territory and is prepared to defend it against all comers". Huxley writes:

To the twentieth-century man of letters this new information about a tradition-hallowed piece of poetic raw material is itself a piece of potentially poetical raw material. To ignore it is an act of literary cowardice. The new facts about nightingales are a challenge from which it would be pusillanimous to shrink. And what a challenge! The words of the tribe and of the Text Book must be purified into a many-meaninged language capable of expressing simultaneously the truth about nightingales, as they exist in their world of caterpillars, endocrine glands and territorial possessiveness, and the truth about the human beings who listen to the nightingale's song. It is a strangely complex truth about creatures who can think of the immortal bird in strictly ornithological terms and who at the same time are overcome (in spite of ornithology, in spite of the ineradicable dirtiness of their ears) by the magical beauty of that plaintive anthem as it fades 'past the near meadows, over the still stream'.[27]

Well, this is how Huxley attempts the harmonization in his novels. Chelifer, dozing on the 'translucent mattress' of the sea, gets a crack on the temple from a swinging boat-hook.

I was conscious of swallowing a vast quantity of brine, of breathing water into my lungs and violently choking. Then for a time I knew nothing; the blow must momentarily have stunned me. I became more or less conscious again, to find myself just coming to the surface, my face half in, half out of water. I was coughing and gasping—coughing to get rid of the water that was in my lungs, gasping for air. Both processes, I now perceive, achieved exactly the contrary of what they were intended to achieve. For I coughed up all the stationary

[27] Aldous Huxley, *Literature and Science*, pp. 98-99.

air that was in my lungs and my mouth being under water, I drew in fresh gulps of brine. Meanwhile my blood, loaded with carbonic acid gas, kept rushing to my lungs in the hope of exchanging the deadly stuff for oxygen. In vain; there was no oxygen to exchange it for.[28]

And here is what Huxley has to say about adolescence and love:

How hard it is, without those still non-existent words, to discuss even so simple and obvious a case as Ruth's! The best one can do is to flounder about in metaphors. A saturated solution of feelings, which can be crystallised either from outside or the inside. Words and events that fall into the psycho-physical soup and make it clot into action-producing lumps of emotion and sentiment. Then come the glandular changes, and the appearance of those charming little zoological specimens which the child carried around with so much pride and embarrassment. The thrill-solution is enriched by a new kind of sensibility that radiates from the nipples, through the skin and the nerve-ends, into the soul, the sub-conscious, the super-conscious, the spirit. And these new psychoerectile elements of personality impart a kind of motion to the thrill-solution, cause it to flow in a specific direction—towards the still unmapped, undifferentiated region of love. Into this flowing stream of love-oriented feeling, chance drops a variety of crystallising agents —words, events, other people's example, private phantasies and memories, all the innumerable devices used by the Fates to mould an individual human destiny.[29]

Call this eccentricity or originality—after all, both sail close together. Huxley wants a new language capable of giving comprehensive expression to the psycho-physical soup in which the human being wriggles. He says:

What we need is another set of words. Words that can express the natural togetherness of things. Muco-spiritual, for example, or dermatocharity. Or why not mastonoetic? Why not visoerosophy? But, translated, of course, out of the indecent obscurity of a learned language into something you could use

28 *Those Barren Leaves*, p. 134.
29 *The Genius and the Goddess*, pp. 53-54.

in everyday speech or even in lyrical poetry.[30]

But, it is this viscerosophy that has exposed Huxley to charges of cynical amusement, schoolboyish smuttiness, misanthropy.

VIII

These narrative techniques, Huxley has employed with telling effect in character portrayal. Felicity of expression, an uncanny precision in thought, a sparkling sense of humour and an infallible eye for folly and hypocrisy have enabled Huxley to give his readers powerful word-pictures of his characters, vivid in profile as well as in depth. Huxley displays the vicious punch of Swift as also the sly obliqueness of Lytton Strachey, when he exposes his characters in all their awkwardness of attitude. The only reverent portraits he has are those of Helen in *The Genius and the Goddess* and a few of the Palanese in *Island*. Here is a typical profile—the old man Falx in *Those Barren Leaves*— Strachean in execution:

> Mr. Falx, indeed, invited admiration and respect. With his white beard, his long curly white hair, his large dark liquid eyes, his smooth broad forehead and aquiline nose, he had the air of a minor prophet; a denouncer, a mouthpiece of the Lord, a caller to salvation, a threatener of wrath to come. Having been born in the middle of the nineteenth century and having passed the years of his early manhood in the profession which, between three and seven, every male child desires to embrace —that of the engine driver—he had become not exactly a prophet, but a labour leader.[31]

Sometimes he revels in evocative splashes of colour as with Mrs. Aldwinkle on the patino in *Those Barren Leaves* or Lucy Tantamount in *Point Counter Point*:

[30] Ibid., p. 52.
[31] *Those Barren Leaves*, p. 30.

Lucy, as usual, was the French tricolor; blue round the eyes, a scarlet mouth and the rest dead white against a background of shiny metal-black hair. I made some sort of a joke. She laughed, opening her mouth—and her tongue and gums were so much paler than the paint on her lips that they seemed (it gave me a queer creepy shock of astonished horror) quite bloodless and white by contrast. And then, without transition, I was standing in front of those sacred crocodiles in the palace gardens at Jaipur, and the Indian guide was throwing them bits of meat, and the inside of the animals' mouths was almost white, as though the mouths were lined with a slightly glace cream-coloured kid.[32]

He pays scrupulous attention even to the minutest details in appearance and temperament including the exact age of each character. The only exceptions among over a hundred characters of his are Francis Chelifer and Philip Quarles in whose case only their approximate age can be guessed from circumstantial evidence in the narrative. His portraits have all the suggestiveness of a genuine cartoon without the malicious flippancy of caricature. In his schizophrenic world, he shows that his men alone have cosmological worries. His women are all earthy and mundane. They don't bother themselves about God and heaven or the millennium. All their dreams and desires are for someone to love and to be loved by. Response is what they crave for. Whether it is Mrs. Bidlake, Rachel Quarles or Mrs. Chelifer running after lame-ducks, or Myra Viveash, Lucy Tantamount or Helen Amberley seeking someone to thrill their whole being, they are out to give and receive sympathy, understanding and love within the narrow circle of their personal lives. It is only his men who are worried about themselves and the universe. They dream of achievement, they desire transcendence. Torn between divided loyalties, between passion and prejudice, love and lust, aspirations and actualities, they wander about in disarray.

But perhaps, Huxley is right in this conception of the feminine nature. Woman finds self-fulfilment when she plays her role as a mother and as a wife. But, man is, after all, the drone who, after playing husband and father, finds himself untethered and roves at large between the heavens and the earth.

32 *Point Counter Point,* p. 407.

It looks rather odd that Huxley, with all his incisiveness, has not been able to tell a simple love-story. It is only the 'asymmetric tadpoles' he prefers. In *Those Barren Leaves,* he tries to present two charming creatures, Irene and Hovenden, but what he succeeds in giving us is a picture of adolescent calf-love of a teen-aged girl, induced by an erotic aunt, falling in love with the nearest available male of suitable age. In *Island* is the story of Sushila Macphail and Will Farnaby, and here too Huxley fails to give touching expression to their feelings of love, and their courting scenes are merely teaching sessions, the lady-love sermonizing to her lover. In *The Genius and the Goddess,* Huxley presents a charming woman, Helen Rivers, but he disposes her off in about forty lines, giving the rest of the novel to a jarring tale of clandestine love. After all, Huxley has given tender expression to Denis's feelings for Anne, Gumbril's for Emily, Chelifer's for Barbara, Ranga's for Radha, and why couldn't he do the same with his women? Is he out of his depths when he comes to deal with the feminine kind? Or, himself a divided being seeking inner harmony, does he possess a natural partiality for divided beings? Or, is it a self-confession that he makes through Philip Quarles who confesses to his wife Emily that he cannot tell a simple love-story?

Perhaps, to be fair to Huxley, this aspect of his theme has to be considered from another angle. Huxley finds contemporary Europe rocked by political and social upheavals by way of wars and revolutions. Faith in religion and traditional beliefs has been shaken to its roots. Einstein and Freud have stripped life of all its decorous vesture, and have exposed it in all its nakedness. The result is a sceptical matter-of-factness in human attitudes, Lucy Tantamount's bantering ridicule of her father's prudery is typical of the changed temperament. Reckless gaiety at one extreme and cynical disillusion at the other, are the symptoms of the new malady that afflicts the human race, and Huxley, himself a victim, seeks a cure for it. This is a fast-spreading malaise, and needs a quick cure. Or else, Huxley feels, it will take humanity back to apery. His theme is the conflict between the ape and the essence, and the way to reconcile the two and re-create man in his wholeness. Hence his theme is this malady, and his characters are all afflicted beings seeking "the route to hope and health".

Besides, humanity, at the animal level, identifies itself with

12

the physiological body, and, at the saintly level, it achieves transcendence. Only at the human level, it is tormented by the dichotomy of the flesh and the spirit. And hence, it is only the cognitive individuals who suffer, men and women sensitive and self-consuming, emancipated intellectually as well as economically, and having enough leisure to be bothered about life and its purpose.

This choice of characters naturally leads us on to the charge of bourgeois partiality levelled against Huxley. Both Philip Henderson and Dr. Ghose accuse Huxley of an intense dislike for the poor. Henderson says that Huxley deals with "artists and individuals who have no social significance at all". Dr. Ghose says: "His aversion for the poor is chronic. He looks at them from the outside, often does not look at all".

Every world-betterer may sound bourgeois just as any sourpuss world-leveller may appear to be a champion of the proletariat. Huxley's aversion for poverty, squalor and dirt is an aesthetic aversion for a social disease that has got to be eradicated, not, as Dr. Ghose seems to suggest, to be tolerated as a historical necessity. Moreover, Huxley's characters are men with ideas to express, the .01 per cent of the human race. They are the intellectuals, the people who really matter in any society. They are the originators of fashion and taste, the creators of ideas. They are university educated, economically well-to-do, and uncrippled by the stultifying effects of poverty. But, Huxley says, they are not happy. Material and intellectual well-being have not given them happiness. Though free from the usual crippling circumstances of life, still they suffer from an inner anguish. Huxley's aim is to trace from its origins this existential malady. He has chosen his characters deliberately, fully aware that "congenital novelists do not choose such characters".

This choice of characters has brought in the criticism that the Huxleyan novel is a puppet stage, that the characters are not individuals but types, that they all echo their master's voice, think and talk like Huxley himself, that some of them look like cases from a psychological textbook, Walter Allen writes:

> Then the characters become caricatures, lath-and-paper dummies with gramophones in their bellies, existing as it were in a perpetual brains-trust session, indulging more and more

in what are in fact detachable essays. Moreover, they are repeated from novel to novel: the heartless vamp, the would-be-diabolist, the seeker of sensation for sensation's sake, the research worker who is a child at everything outside the narrow field of his research, the earnest young man who confuses litera-ture with life, the artist-without-talent who bawls of his own genius, the introverted writer who, faced with the meaningless-ness of life, is in search of meaning. And the caricatures are drawn from literature and from life indiscriminately.[33]

Huxley's characters are individuals not types. They are not stuffed dummies rigged up for Huxley's bayonet-charging. They are drawn from life, touched with a stroke of exaggeration here and a distortion there, but they never lapse into caricature. In Forster's terminology, they are not flat characters but round. If Mrs. Woolf's genius lay in parenthesis, Huxley's lies in his off-the-tangents. Through seemingly chance digressions and off-the-tangent remarks, he makes his characters reveal the several facets of their own character, not just one loose screw in their mental structure. They are individuals not dull types, may be live cranks but certainly not dead dummies.

Myra Viveash might be wriggling in a spiritual mire, but her comments on art and music, her sympathy for the cab-driver and his wife, her affectionate regard for Gumbril senior, and her absorbing interest in birds, would reveal her to be a charmingly versatile woman though with a tragic protuberance on the emotional plane. So too are all his characters rounded portraits not flat profiles—the talkers Scogan and Cardan, or John Bidlake and Sidney Quarles, even Illidge and Everard Webley, not to speak of Mark Staithes and Will Farnaby. It is a huge crowd, from the educated, refined and hypersensitive upper-middle-classes. Flouting all conservative literary and fictional traditions, tempering satire and irony with wryness of tone, Huxley awakens his readers to the tragedy of spiritual emptiness in a mechano-morphic world. He goads them into serious thought, touches their raw spots, and even angers them, sometimes with Shavian shock-therapy or with Drydenesque side-thrusts or with Strachean leg-pulling but never with Swiftsian malice.

He is a versatile and prolific writer who has published over

[33] Walter Allen, *Tradition and Dream*, p. 66.

forty-five books—novels, short stories and poems, essays, monographs and travelogues. His novels are illustrative of his attitude, analysis and understanding of the life around him. Satire and irony, he finds to be more potent weapons than sermonization. His novels might be, at times, bantering in tone, but his essays and monographs reveal the essential sincerity and seriousness of his attitudes. He is a conscious, deliberate artist fully aware of the power of the written word. A man of varied interests, astoundingly knowledgeable—the Encyclopaedia Britannica is reputed to have been his constant travelling companion—it is a learned language that he writes. He betrays a liking for the rarer word, the more scholarly expression, and takes pleasure in squeezing words into new expressive grammatical forms to suit his needs. Jocelyn Brooke writes that, at times, "his style suffers from over-facility, a lack of tautness, and an increasing use of certain rather irritating mannerisms". This is rather too harsh a judgement. Huxley has written many books with almost the same theme recurring in his monographs as well as in his novels. It is but natural and perhaps inevitable too, that certain expressions and mannerisms get used over and over again. For instance, *Eyeless in Gaza* reads as if filled with long passages from *Ends and Means.*

Whatever might be the defects of style and technique, Huxley's novels make a stimulating reading, and offer spicy food for thought. He is the fore-runner of the modern Angry Young Men, the only difference being whereas the Angry Young Men do not know what they are angry about, Huxley does.

9

CONCLUSION

I N one of his short-stories, Huxley describes a character, Dick
Greenow, as "intellectually a Voltairean, emotionally a
Bunyanite". This is a description which aptly applies to Huxley
himself. Huxley might be, at times, annoying with biting satire,
but his is always the soothing touch of "an urbane, civilised and
honourably serious mind".[1] In *Jesting Pilate,* amidst all the jesting,
referring to the human beings, "immortal souls, first cousins of
the angels, own brothers of Buddha, Mozart and Sir Isaac
Newton", Huxley asks: "Why are we here, men and women,
eighteen hundred million of us, on this remarkable and perhaps
unique planet? To what end?"

He has always been a seeker, whether as a jesting Pilate or
as a salvationist. Art, to him, has been a means of self-exploration
and self-education. "Art", he says, "is not the discovery of
Reality—whatever Reality may be, and no human being can
possibly know. It is the organisation of chaotic appearance into
an orderly and human universe".[2] Geoffrey Gorer writes:

Aldous Huxley has taken well-being (in his phrase Good-
being)—the physical and psychological health of every member
of the society—as his supreme value; and has tried to devise
a society in which individual well-being is maximised. To the
best of my knowledge, this is a completely novel approach in
utopia-building. For all Huxley's predecessors, health and
happiness have been seen as the quasi-automatic result of
removing oppression, or superstition, or injustice, or poverty,
and not as primary aims. Nor has much thought been given
to the content of this automatically derived health and
happiness. It is tacitly (and quite inaccurately) assumed that

[1] G. S. Fraser, *The Modern Writer and His World,* p. 78.
[2] *Jesting Pilate,* p. 91.

everybody knows what health and happiness are; and they are really defined negatively, by the absence of the evils which the utopian plan removes.[3]

Many writers, contemporaries of Huxley as well as predecessors and successors, popularized their own ideas of a utopian society. H. G. Wells, for instance, as a prophet and as a revolutionary, seemed to his younger contemporaries to typify the intellectual climate of the time. But Huxley, a prophet and a revolutionary like Wells himself, is as Anthony Burgess calls him, the greatest anti-Wellsian. Jocelyn Brooke writes:

Huxley seemed unquestionably the most stimulating and exciting writer of the day: his style in itself was a novelty— highly wrought yet extremely readable, deriving from unfamiliar models, and providing a refreshing contrast to that of such older writers as Galsworthy, Bennet and Wells himself. Mr. Huxley was gay, 'sophisticated', and (for those days) agreeably shocking; but more important, for his young readers, has the impact of an alert, penetrating, widely-ranging intelligence. By comparison, most other contemporary writers seemed stuffy, unenlightened, old-fashioned.[4]

Angus Wilson, John Wain, Kingsley Amis acknowledge Huxley's influence on their writings. Wilson calls him the God of his adolescence. During the 1920's, Lawrence, Huxley and Virginia Woolf influenced the younger generation much more than Joyce or Wyndham Lewis. With all his realistic attitudes towards life, Joyce shows sympathy and love towards his fellow-men, but Wyndham Lewis is bitterly anti-human. Whereas Lewis is, at times, almost crude in his satirical attacks, Huxley is urbane and polished. Huxley is nearer to Evelyn Waugh in techniques, but Evelyn Waugh is a snob and his arena is the world of fashion, and Huxley's is the world of the intellect. Like Huxley, Angus Wilson too tackles the problem of the humanist faced with the conflict between the ape and the essence in man, but in the development of their attitudes, while Wilson moves towards an escapist avoidance of commitment, Huxley, with firm conviction,

[3] Geoffrey Gorer, "There is a Happy Land....", *Encounter,* July 1962.
[4] Jocelyn Brooke, *Writers and Their Work,* No. 55, p. 6.

moves towards a rational mysticism.

In a period of acute social and emotional crisis, as in the post-war world, the general mood of the sensitive humanity is, to use Kierkegaard's word 'angst'. Kierkegaard is the father of the existentialist philosophy. Most writers of the post-war period, especially the younger generation, have accepted the existentialist analysis of life (though not its conclusions), particularly the belief that awareness of a secret inner anxiety is intrinsic to the human condition itself. Huxley too portrays this latent anxiety in humanity, the separateness of subject and object, the difficulty of choice and commitment, the consequent nausea. But, if at all Huxley is an existentialist, he is more with Kierkegaard and Jaspers than with Sartre. He reacts against the morbid introspection of the existentialists, and cuts his way through to an affirmation of the god-head in man.

He might sound at times flippant, at other times bitterly cynical. But there is an essential sympathy in his attitudes to life in general. His target is, what Noel Coward calls, "the massed illiteracy" of the new socially dominant classes in the society. Like Noel Coward, and like one of his own characters Chelifer, Huxley too is a "reversed sentimentalist". He may sound revolutionary in tone, caustic in attack, but he is a tender sentimentalist at heart. Miss Anita Loos gives an interesting anecdote about Huxley:

Incredible as it may appear, there were times in our relationship when I was able to feel a little superior to Aldous. He once came to me to say that, staunchly as he had remained apart from the movie industry, he now felt tempted to try for a job in it. The Battle of Britain was on in full force, his income was curtailed by it, and his obligations increased. Did I think he might possibly make good in one of the studios? I laughed at his ridiculous humility and told Aldous nothing could be easier than to find him a job. I was working at M.G.M. at the time and, on investigating the new projects coming up, found one which seemed ideal—a movie version of *Pride and Prejudice,* which was ready for dialogue. When I informed the producer that the great writer was available, he set up an appointment with Aldous for the very next day.

Very soon after their interview my phone rang; Aldous was calling, with Maria on the extension, and their mood was that

184   ALDOUS HUXLEY—A STUDY OF HIS NOVELS

of gloomy resignation.

"I'm sorry", Aldous said, "but I can't take that movie job".
I wanted to know why not.

"Because it pays twenty-five hundred dollars a week", he
answered in deep distress. "I simply cannot accept all that
money to work in a pleasant studio while my family and friends
are starving and being bombed in England".

"But Aldous", I asked, "why can't you accept that twenty-
five hundred and send the larger part of it to England"?

There was a long silence at the other end of the line, and
then Maria spoke up.

"Anita", she said, "what would we ever do without you"?

"The trouble with Aldous", I told her, "is that he's a genius
who just once in a while isn't very smart".[5]

Huxley is "undoubtedly the most stimulating and exciting
writer of the day". There is nothing of the poseur about him,
there is only the sincerity of a genuine artist. John Atkins says:
"Huxley stands convicted, and the rest of us can go our way,
comfortable in blinkers, and secure in the good books of our
Borstal Gods".[6]

If not with unreserved admiration, at least with a connoisseur's
sympathy, his writings are to be judged. Time has revealed, and
will reveal, the accuracy of his anticipation, the genuineness of
his fears, many of which have come to be true. According to
Anthony Burgess, Huxley has helped, more than any other writer,
to equip the contemporary novel with a brain. Paul West says
that "his diatribes were life-enhancing". It is an indisputable fact
that Huxley has left his impress on contemporary literature and
thinking. One cannot but, in conclusion, recall Huxley's own
words in his preface to the *Collected Essays*:

Sometimes, it seems to me, I have succeeded fairly well in doing
what, in one field or another, I had set out to do. Sometimes,
alas, I know that I have not succeeded. But "please do not
shoot the pianist; he is doing his best". Doing his best, *selon
ses quelques doigts perclus,* to make his cottage upright say as
much as the great orchestra of the novel, doing his best to

[5] *Aldous Huxley—A Memorial Volume,* pp. 94-95.
[6] John Atkins, *Aldous Huxley,* p. 234.

"give all things full play". For the writer at least, and perhaps also for the reader, it is better to have tried and failed to achieve perfection than never to have tried at all.[7]

[7] Aldous Huxley, *Collected Essays,* preface, p. ix.

INDEX

ALDOUS HUXLEY held a unique position as a writer, and was a powerful influence on the minds of his contemporaries for over four decades from the nineteen-twenties to the sixties. His books are both enlightening and entertaining. He was a great novelist, a brilliant essayist, and a discerning critic of art, literature, and music.

This book by Dr Bhaskara Ramamurty is perhaps the first full-length study dealing, in detail, with both the thematic and technical aspects of Huxley's novels. Dr Ramamurty analyses the themes of the novels, and making apt references to the other prose writings of Huxley, traces the modern Pilgrim's Progress as presented in the novels, Huxley's analysis of the ape and essence in man, and the recipe he suggests to help the ape realize the essence.

Dr Ramamurty writes with force and precision. He is in sympathy with Huxley, sometimes, one feels, too much in sympathy. Yet, this is a brilliant study, and the chapters on Huxley's philosophy and fictional techniques make excellent reading.